DATE DUE			

GAYLORD

Iraq's Dysfunctional Democracy

Iraq's Dysfunctional Democracy

David Ghanim

 PRAEGER

AN IMPRINT OF ABC-CLIO, LLC
Santa Barbara, California • Denver, Colorado • Oxford, England

Library of Congress Cataloging-in-Publication Data

Ghanim, David.
  Iraq's dysfunctional democracy / David Ghanim.
    p. cm.
  Includes bibliographical references and index.
  ISBN 978–0–313–39801–8 (hard copy : alk. paper) — ISBN 978–0–313–39802–5 (ebook)
1. Iraq—Politics and government—2003– 2. Democracy—Iraq. I. Title.
JQ1849.A91G43   2011
320.9567—dc22   2011017325

ISBN: 978–0–313–39801–8
EISBN: 978–0–313–39802–5

15 14 13 12 11   1 2 3 4 5

This book is also available on the World Wide Web as an eBook.
Visit www.abc-clio.com for details.

Praeger
An Imprint of ABC-CLIO, LLC

ABC-CLIO, LLC
130 Cremona Drive, P.O. Box 1911
Santa Barbara, California 93116-1911

This book is printed on acid-free paper ∞

Manufactured in the United States of America

Contents

Preface   vii

Introduction   ix

1.   A U.S. Legacy   1

2.   The Politics of Victimization   19

3.   Dwindling Minorities, Debased Women   33

4.   De-Ba'thification and Politics of Exclusion   53

5.   Uprooting the Ba'th and Sectarianism   71

6.   Deficient Justice   89

7.   Sectarian Execution   105

8.   Elections and Illusive Democracy   117

9.   Confessionalism and Legitimacy   135

10. Externalization of Legitimacy   147

11. Federalism and Politics of Separatism   161

12. Nationalism and Territories   181

13. Armaments, Oil, and Corruption   197

14. Republic of Corruption   213

Conclusion   231

Selected Bibliography   237

Index   245

Preface

No country has ever dominated international politics and media like Iraq. This international attention to the case of Iraq has generated a flood of publications covering the country. However, only a few publications have focused on the internal Iraqi experience per se. This book departs from mainstream literature on Iraq and focuses instead on domestic affairs in the country. An Iraqi perspective on what has happened since the regime change is highly needed. This book discusses the political development in Iraq since 2003, and the term "new Iraq," which has been used in discourses describing the new experience. An approach that focuses on Iraq's internal situation does not diminish international interest in the country. On the contrary, developments in Iraq have serious implications on various aspects of international politics and academic debate.

Whether or not most Americans approve, Iraq has become a U.S. legacy. For this reason, having a good and inspiring legacy in Iraq is in the best interests of the United States. Unfortunately, the American adventure in Iraq is primarily an exercise in hastily decided policies that lack careful thinking. Worse, the U.S. administration has adopted a rather simplified approach to understanding the Iraqi situation. While many people blame American political leaders for their failure to grasp the realities of Iraqi society, Iraqi history clearly demonstrates that this failure of apprehension extends to the Iraqis themselves. This is hardly surprising given Iraq's long history of suppressing academic and intellectual freedom, the supremacy of partisan and identity politics, as well as the authoritarian order dominating social existence.

The United States has failed to find weapons of mass destruction or connections to terrorism in Iraq. Far more important, it has failed to establish democracy in that country. Merely replacing one authoritarian ruler with several ethnic and sectarian autocrats has severely disappointed the Iraqis, who have suffered enormously from authoritarian rule. The failure to establish democracy in Iraq also has serious implications for the Middle East, a region stubbornly resistant to democratic change. Although this failure works to the advantage of the many authoritarian rulers who dominate the region, it comes at the expense of the region's current and future generations.

While the U.S. administration should perhaps have taken the objective of establishing democracy in Iraq more seriously and dealt with it patiently, Iraq, and the Middle East for that matter, missed a unique opportunity to improve the societies of that region. The Iraq War has involved huge human and financial costs on the part of the United States and other countries that the Iraqis need to acknowledge and appreciate. Regardless of what we think of the war, it has provided a unique opportunity for Iraqi society to break its decades-long cycle of violence and revenge. Iraq's obvious failure to seize this historic moment may be the biggest mistake in the country's history.

In this book, I adopt a critical approach to the new developments in Iraq, focusing on the Iraqis' share of the responsibility for this miserable outcome. Contrary to conventional belief, a critical approach can be clothed in optimism; silence or indifference is clothed in pessimism. I remain optimistic that if we insist on applying constructive criticism, Iraq will one day become a new and better country. This book, therefore, is dedicated to the people of Iraq, acknowledging their suffering and encouraging them to create a prosperous future. While their suffering is their own making, their destiny is also in their own hands.

The greatest gratitude goes to my commissioning editor at Praeger Publishers, Valentina Tursini, for believing in this project and for her support and feedback on improving this work.

Introduction

Iraq has long been the main focus of international politics and media. It is unsurprising that there are many published works on the country. However, most of these works focus on the Iraq War in 2003 and the American occupation. Unfortunately, this comes at the expense of a more "internal" approach and analysis of the Iraqi experience per se. This project departs from the mainstream approach on Iraq and tries to fill a gap in the literature concerning this country. The purpose of this text is to study the situation in Iraq since 2003 and to investigate the credibility of the term "new Iraq," which has been used in discourses describing the new experience in the country. This book highlights how the old and the new interact, and how change and continuity interplay in this experience. The major concern of this treatise is to find out if the new experience in the country truly represents a serious interruption from the violent past of Iraq or just a new name to an old and well-established game. It intends to scrutinize the many contradictions of the new experience, if not the very myth of new Iraq.

This text focuses on the dysfunctionality of democracy in Iraq as well as the centrality of violence, rationalized and justified by claims of victimhood, to Iraqi society and politics, and explores the various modalities of a broader context of violence: victimization, revenge, de-Ba'thification, lustration, incomplete and sectarian application of justice, separatist federalism, divisive and destabilizing constitution, illusionary democracy, deceptive legitimacy, and pernicious corruption. This text adopts a critical approach to the so-called new Iraq. Yet critical approaches are always clothed in optimism, and therefore this work remains optimistic that Iraq will eventually find its way to a genuine democracy, tolerance and prosperity.

The major objectives of this book are:

- To argue that building a new democratic and tolerant Iraq cannot be grounded on the destructive politics of victimization;
- To question identity politics, and to argue that confessionalism and consensual power-sharing political arrangement can only lead to illusionary democracy and deceptive legitimacy; and
- To discuss a broader context of violence in Iraq that includes: victimization politics, flawed justice, uprooting Ba'thism, ethno-sectarian elections, a divisive and destabilizing constitution, ethnic and separatist federalism, insidious corruption, and the oppression of women and minorities.

This work suggests serious implications for U.S. foreign policies, particularly the objective of spreading democracy by force and the creation of a new democratic Middle East.

The book consists of fourteen chapters in addition to an introduction and a conclusion.

Chapter 1, "A U.S. Legacy," discusses Iraq as a U.S. legacy and the unique opportunity presented by the Iraq War for Iraq, the Middle East, and U.S. foreign policy. It also argues how the myth of "new Iraq" could end up as a façade for a continuation of an old and violent politics that dominated the modern history of the country. Chapter 2, "The Politics of Victimization," explores how a cycle of victimization, where victims and victimizers are merely changing places, tends to lock society in a perpetual situation of violence. It looks into the role that the politics of victimization plays in exasperating societal violence and creating new victims in the new Iraq.

Chapter 3, "Dwindling Minorities, Debased Women," outlines the deteriorating situation and status of women and minorities, which is a paradox in the so-called new democratic Iraq. Chapter 4, "De-Ba'thification and Politics of Exclusion," investigates the process of de-Ba'thifying Iraqi society and the accompanying outcome of diminishing scarce human resources. Chapter 5, "Uprooting the Ba'th and Sectarianism," explains how the process of de-Ba'thification is feeding sectarianism and vengeance in society.

Chapter 6, "Deficient Justice," delineates the expectations for justice after a long history of injustice in Iraq and discusses the flawed trial of the leaders of the old regime. Chapter 7, "Sectarian Execution," focuses on the implications of reinstating capital punishment and the sectarian approach adopted in terminating the life of the deposed dictator for justice in Iraq and the Middle East.

Chapter 8, "Elections and Illusive Democracy," sketches the several elections that were held in Iraq since 2003, and discusses the gap between elections and democracy. Chapter 9, "Confessionalism and Legitimacy," highlights the failure of consociation and power-sharing political arrangement in building democracy in Iraq. Chapter 10, "Externalization of Legitimacy," argues that the absence of an in-built democratic legitimacy will leave undemocratic leaders with only external, yet deceptive, sources of legitimacy to maintain.

Chapter 11, "Federalism and Politics of Separatism," considers the controversial and divisive constitution that has recently been adopted in Iraq, which is in a sense a victors' constitution. It also probes whether ethnic federalism that has been adopted can lead to established democracy in the country. Chapter 12, "Nationalism and Territories," looks into the issue of the so-called disputed territories and the expansionist drive to incorporate these territories in the semi-independent Kurdish entity, which is in line with the adoption of extremist regional nationalism.

Chapter 13, "Armaments, Oil, and Corruption," highlights the pernicious corruption that is associated with the militarization of society and the arms deals as well as the high and lucrative corruption connected with oil deals and oil smuggling. Chapter 14, "Republic of Corruption," examines how corruption is becoming the untouchable and how the politicized rhetoric of antigraft results in even more corruption. The concluding chapter outlines some of the implications of Iraq becoming a U.S. legacy for American foreign policy and the prospects of democracy in the Middle East. It discusses some of the challenges the Iraqi society needs to address if it sincerely aspires to become a truly new Iraq of a peaceful, tolerant, and democratic society that would benefit all Iraqi citizens.

1

A U.S. Legacy

WAR AND OPPORTUNITY

The increasing militarization and external expansionism of Saddam Hussein's dictatorial regime led to a long and costly war with Iran followed by the invasion of Kuwait in 1990. International coalition forces succeeded in liberating the Kuwaitis from the foolish adventure of Saddam, but failed to liberate the Iraqis, as there was no UN mandate to go to Baghdad and topple the Iraqi regime. Nevertheless, twelve years later, the Iraq War did achieve what should have been carried out previously. One might argue that late is better than never, but this view is very misleading. The circumstances under which these two wars unfolded were quite different, and this has had serious consequences.

There are at least four differences to consider when dealing with the case of Iraq. The first is that in the period between the two wars, Iraqis endured an extremely difficult and humiliating situation due to more than a decade of stringent economic sanctions. The full material and psychological impact of these sanctions has not been fully considered, and it may require substantial future research and studies to find out. However, Iraqi society has undoubtedly been deeply affected. Second, the whole of the Middle East has also changed, in the sense that it has become more conservative, particularly with the rise of political Islam. Identity politics has become even more dominant, and destructive conflict with the West more pronounced, culminating in the spread of global terrorism. Under these circumstances, the Iraq War and forceful regime change was tolerated less, if not a source of antagonism.

Third, the latest war has led to the bizarre situation of Iran being a major player in Iraq. Many people argue that Iran was the real winner and beneficiary of the war. In contrast to the early 1990s where Iran was still suffering from the impact of a long and damaging war with Iraq, the country is now following a more aggressive policy of conflict, building nuclear armaments and forcefully expanding in the Middle East, including into Iraq. However, this external adventurism masks an increasingly fragile and less legitimate internal political process in the country, not unlike Iraq under the old regime. The strong involvement of Iran in the political process in Iraq, with the support of the ruling Shiite religious parties, complicated the expected outcome of regime change in Iraq. The U.S. administration allowed this outcome to materialize, particularly when they started to feel that the entire process of regime change in Iraq had become a costly burden. Nonetheless, this is in contrast, ironically, with the declared objective of ending extremism and authoritarianism, and establishing democracy in Iraq and also in the region.

Fourth, international support for the Iraq War was only a fraction of the support that was secured in the previous war. Back then the international backing was overwhelming and could have easily tolerated an extension of that war to topple the Iraqi regime itself. The irony of the argument that there was no UN mandate for the task, is that in 2003, the regime was toppled not only without any mandate from the United Nations but also against the will of the international community and in the face of widespread condemnation and opposition to the war. This opposition to the war also complicated the American adventure in Iraq and greatly affected, whether directly or indirectly, the outcome of the conflict. Lacking international support and legitimacy, the U.S. administration was forced to rush the transfer of authority and sovereignty to the Iraqis. As a result of rushing, opportunist Iraqi politicians stepped into the political process, claiming to represent the Iraqi people when they were actually interested in serving their own personal interests. Deprived of the backing and contribution of the United Nations and the international community, the U.S. administration was entirely dependent on these Iraqi politicians, their perception of the history of the country, and their vision for the future of Iraq.

Thus politics in the so-called new Iraq came to focus on sectarian and ethnic identity politics, ethnic separatism, the Islamization of society, revenge policies of uprooting political opponents, and the debasement of women and minorities. Some of these policies benefited from the full and effective support of the U.S. administration. Because of this juncture, the original vision for the future of Iraq has been distorted, and the opportunity of what success in the Iraq War could have represented for ordinary Iraqis seems to be—or rather has been allowed to be—lost forever.

All of these factors have complicated the regime change in Iraq and can largely explain how this project became a debacle, and increasingly unattainable. However, the official motivations given for the Iraq War were weapons of mass destruction, connections to al Qaeda and terrorism, and ending the brutal rule of Saddam Hussein, thereby spreading democracy to first Iraq and then the rest of the Middle East. The first two motives proved to be false, yet it could still be argued that with Saddam in power they could have become a reality at any juncture in the future. However, when the first two reasons proved to be unfounded, the third motive could have had the potential to make sense of this war. This, however, does not imply that democracy is a direct objective of the Iraq War, or any war for that matter. Democracy and war are a contradictory combination; democracy can be a only by-product of war. A successful realization of democracy in Iraq could have put the Iraq War in a new and helpful perspective. However, the U.S. administration, for various reasons, took a rather ambiguous route to proving the only remaining factor that could have offered legitimacy for the war.

One of the most naïve assumptions associated with the war is that if the previous ruler of Iraq is a dictator, then those who oppose him within the country are perceived to be democrats by implication. Otherwise, how else can you explain a project that aims to depose a dictator yet empowers several others at the same time; and how do you explain entrusting a process as complex as applying democracy in a region as authoritarian as the Middle East to undemocratic elites? Indeed, the same elites entrusted with establishing democracy in Iraq proved to be the main obstacle to attaining that objective. Thus the Iraq War, while removing one big obstacle from establishing democracy—the rule of Saddam Hussein—immediately created several new problems by empowering ethnic and sectarian authoritarian leaders. It appears that the Iraq War is more about reshuffling governance within the dominant authoritarian order than establishing democracy in Iraq. If the old Iraq was about violent authoritarian politics, so is the new Iraq. Identity politics is as violent and destructive as the old politics.

Faced with the antagonism of the international community and the absence of UN backing, the Americans swiftly entered into a partnership with opposition of the old dictator and justified this as a partnership with the Iraqi people. Yet the assumption about the convergence of interests between ordinary people and the elites has proved to be wrong. In reality, these elites were mainly interested in advancing their own interests, which had been curtailed by the highly monopolized control of wealth and power under the old regime. Thus this was a simplified approach of personalizing authoritarianism. While it is true that the old regime was highly personalized, in the form of the ruthless ruler Saddam Hussein, we tend to forget that authoritarianism is based on structure and culture, rather than just one ruler. It was extremely naïve to expect the removal of Saddam to work as a panacea for all Iraq's problems. Removing a dictator from power while keeping intact the very same authoritarian structure and culture that continue to produce dictators, is unfathomable. If we are aware of structural problems in society, entrusting undemocratic leaders to solve them or to deal with the legacy of authoritarianism is yet another grave mistake. After all, these leaders are the product of this very same authoritarian background.

Thus an unholy partnership between the U.S. administration and Iraqi ethnic and sectarian elites has developed before and in the aftermath of regime change. The end result of this alliance is the suffocation of real changes that would facilitate establishing democracy in the country. When the entire case of Iraq was personalized in the personal rule of the previous dictator, dismantling the entire state apparatus that was under the direct control of the deposed ruler became a logical conclusion to this newly developed partnership. This new development has become an inevitable outcome to meet the various interests and ambitions of the newly empowered Iraqi elites. A highly centralized state has been weakened, rather than democratized, to the advantage of ethnic and sectarian local powers—yet are still highly centralized from within. Weakening and democratizing the state are two essentially contradictory processes.

The Iraqi army has been dissolved to allow for the empowerment of local militias that are under the direct control of the country's new rulers. Despite the rhetoric about democracy and elections, the legislative assembly is still controlled behind closed doors by leaders of the political parties. Consociation and power-sharing political arrangement ensured that central administrative power was distributed in a mutual concession deal, while dividing the wealth of Iraq between these new leaders and their cronies. Because of this unholy deal, controlled corruption goes unchecked and the country has been transformed from a republic of fear under the old ruler into a republic of corruption under his replacement.

The weakening of the Iraqi state is undeniable. Munson elaborates: "The diffusion of Iraq's state powers that occurred with the collapse of the old regime proved difficult to reverse. Furthermore, many political bosses had no desire to return these powers to the central government. As a result, the official political process has yet to solve many delicate issues and has failed to produce a government capable of rebuilding trust and effecting reconciliation."[1] As a result of the collapse or deliberate weakening of the Iraqi state, rule of law, which is a foundation to democracy, has worsened in Iraq. The U.S. policies of tolerating looting, organized crime, and the ascendancy of violent militias have resulted in increased violence, which has especially affected women and minorities. Additionally, U.S. policies of strong involvement in the institutionalization of uprooting the Ba'thists has fed a cycle of violence, victimization, revenge politics, and exclusionary political process, conditions found under the old regime.

Replacing direct and highly centralized dictatorship with indirect authoritarianism manifested in advancing identity politics in Iraq is a dangerous route to take in a country with a long history of suffering and injustice. This identity politics is not only violent and destructive; it is also the very antithesis of democracy and even of politics per se. It has resulted in the rise of ethnic separatism and religious fundamentalism. It is not surprising that women and minorities have paid a heavy price under the supposedly new and democratic Iraq. Nadje al-Ali and Pratt explain: "In the current context of occupation, the United States has exploited the issue of women's liberation to justify its military intervention. The consequence is that Iraqi women are experiencing a tremendous backlash."[2] They continue: "Women's rights have been sacrificed at the expense of sectarian and ethnic political agendas, which in turn have fuelled the violence engulfing most of Iraq and prevented independent actors from making a stand. It is essential to emphasize that the deterioration in women's rights following the fall of the B'ath regime was not inevitable but rather the result of particular political decisions."[3]

However, the Iraq War is not only about Iraq, but also about the entire Middle East, which currently serves as a dangerous incubator for violence and terrorism. In initiating the Iraq War, Iraq was originally considered only a first step in a long process of helping to create a new and democratic Middle East. In this respect, the problems that Americans have encountered in Iraq, in addition to the problems caused by their policies, seem compounded. The contradictions and the debacle of the U.S. experimentation in democratizing Iraq have

wide regional implications. The intricacies of the Iraqi reality, however, have tempted Americans to de-emphasize democracy for the
benefit of security, encouraging exit from Iraq at the lowest cost possible. The difficulty of democratizing Iraq reinforces considerations
of security and the accommodation of autocratic rulers, an old and
well-established yet unhelpful American policy in the region.

The difficulty of democratization in the Middle East, on the other
hand, also reinforces the often debated argument on the exceptionalism
of this region in an increasingly democratizing global world. The key
question, however, is not why the United States has abandoned its
vision of democratizing the region. Rather, it is why Middle Easterners
themselves are not bothered by this democratic deficit and their inflexible resistance to change and the global trend of democratization. The
failure of democracy in Iraq will alter the vision of a new Iraq into the
reality of an old Iraq keeping in line with the rest of the Middle East.
The old Iraq and the old Middle East each score a point in the struggle
between new visions and obstinate resistance. Nevertheless, a depressing and authoritarian victory will certainly suffocate the dreams and
ambitions of the current and future generations in this region.

There is no question that the U.S. administration has sincere and
good intentions to see Iraq become a democratic country. Living in a
global world, the vision of a democratic Iraq, or a democratic Middle
East for that matter, is in harmony not only with U.S. interests but also
with those of the international community. Nevertheless, reality matters
more than hopes and goals. In that sense, the original vision and the
reality are drifting apart, rapidly. One cannot continue to discuss the
new democratic Iraq while adopting policies that reestablish authoritarian order and perpetuate vicious cycles of revenge, violence, and exclusion. It is astonishing how the U.S. administration tolerates this huge
gap between projected vision and unfolding reality. The reasons for this
situation go beyond simple naïveté. Perhaps the explanation lies in the
orientalist assumptions about the Other, or neo-orientalist assumptions
where cultural differences are highly essentialized and elevated. In that
sense, what is valid for "us," as these assumptions go, is not necessarily
valid for "them." Perhaps it is this kind of argument that has made it
easier for Americans to simplify a complex reality and to make a deal
with politicians who are an integral part of the chronic problems of Iraq.

However, this sort of argument makes it easier to jump to unwarranted conclusions, such as "we did our best, yet Iraqi society stubbornly resisted change." This argument is not necessarily wrong;
Iraqi society insists on reproducing old politics rather than seizing a

unique opportunity to build a peaceful and democratic society. The failure to democratize is no doubt a grim problem that Iraq, and indeed the whole Middle East, needs to critically address without blaming the outside world for this failure.

The idea that "we did our best" is not entirely true, either. In reality, what has been implemented in Iraq in the aftermath of the war has nothing to do with establishing a genuine democracy. A project as big and complex as that stipulates consistency, strategic patience, and long-term commitment; these are the very qualities that the American project in Iraq is lacking. Instead, this project has taken a shortcut, and shortcuts are not always useful; indeed, they are often counterproductive. Shortcuts blur visions and make it easier to make mistakes. Lacking international backing, the U.S. administration took the shortcut of empowering authoritarian ethno-sectarian leaders to put an Iraqi face on regime change and naïvely believing that this might provide a solution to the original legitimacy deficit of the Iraq war. Not only did this empowerment fail to achieve the missed legitimacy, particularly when local leaders fail to deliver to the Iraqis, but also empowering local autocrats stifles chances of establishing real democracy.

Forging partnership with an oligarchy of autocrats is one of the most solemn strategic mistakes the U.S. administration has ever made in Iraq. The Egyptian playwright Ali Salim comments that Machiavelli warned against using opponents of the old regime in the service of establishing the new rule. Regardless of how much you offer old opponents, they will still perceive this as less than what they really deserve, therefore becoming a source of trouble. Instead, Machiavelli recommended using supporters of the old regime who will be as faithful to the new regime as they were to the old one, providing them with a second chance not only in life but also in serving in bureaucracy and politics.[4] One wonders whether the U.S. administration has ever read Machiavelli, before embarking on the adventure in Iraq.

A more patient approach that focused on establishing real sustainable democracy would have surely provided the needed legitimacy and would have made the entire American adventure in Iraq a real success. In this respect, the shortcut solution of forging hasty alliances with undemocratic elites has made regime change in Iraq a useless adventure. The new U.S. administration is also adopting a shortcut solution to a problem that is considered an unwarranted legacy from the old administration. The new policy of detachment and hasty exit from Iraq is actually worsening the political situation in the country by giving autocratic elites a free hand to dictate the political process, and this is leading in the direction of reestablishing authoritarianism, away from the original vision of a democratic Iraq. This does not imply that extending the stay of the U.S. army in Iraq, which is scheduled to leave by the end of December 2011, is the solution. Serious and responsible commitment to the case of Iraq does not necessarily involve a military presence. Regardless of whether the U.S. separates from Iraq, Iraq will remain a U.S. legacy in the future. Yet this is an additional factor for why the U.S. administration should have been more careful and patient in the situation with Iraq. If one cannot escape the reality of Iraq becoming a U.S. legacy, then creating a successful and good legacy is certainly better than a disastrous one.

Nevertheless, this book is not about blaming the Americans for the failure in Iraq. In honesty, the Iraqis should be grateful for American sacrifices that helped to create a unique prospect for Iraqi society. Notwithstanding their role in this debacle, focusing attention on the American role would conveniently overlook a much needed Iraqi perspective on what has happened since 2003. After all, the Iraq War is about Iraq, or more precisely about historical opportunity for an Iraqi society that should, therefore, be up to the challenge. Seizing this opportunity that comes after long suffering and violence is in harmony with meeting the interests of the Iraqis and ensuring their prosperity. A failure to seize this opportunity would condemn this society to more decades of violence and misery. This book, therefore, is about the role that the Iraqis must play in eradicating what seems to be a perpetual cycle of disregarding the often violent lessons of history.

NEW IRAQ, OLD POLITICS

Seeing an old man sitting on bench in a park, a mean-spirited young man decided he would have some fun with this old man. So he caught a small bird and planned his trick: "I will ask the old man what I have in my hands. If he guesses correctly, I will ask him if the bird is dead or alive. If he says the bird is dead, I will release the bird and have fun; but if he says the bird is alive, I will squeeze my hands and kill the bird and still have fun." He asked the old man: "What do I have in my hands?" The old man having seen what the young man had done replied: "You have a bird." The cruel young man asked: "Old man, is the bird dead or is he alive?" To which the wise man replied: "The fate of that bird is in your hands."

This metaphorical story could describe what is now going on in Iraq. Clearly, Iraq has an ugly legacy and a troubled history; and evidently, the dramatic change in Iraq in 2003 came through external military intervention. Nevertheless, the fate of the country is in the hands of the Iraqis. They, and only they, can turn their country into a real democratic and prosperous country. Or they can continue the legacy of violence and destruction. What does the experience of more than eight years tell us? Are the Iraqis up to the difficult challenge?

The defeat of Saddam Hussein's authoritarian rule represents a turning point in Iraqi history. This change did not come easily, however. It was the result of one of the most controversial wars in modern history, a war that has encountered strong opposition for its large human and financial costs. It is the Iraqi people themselves who have suffered and paid the most for this change. However, having an opportunity to build a better society is something; seizing that opportunity is something else altogether. The citizens of post-Saddam Iraq have two choices to adopt. They can adopt the alternative that leads to a peaceful and prosperous society, or they can follow the option that leads to continued violence and misery. Which option will Iraq take up?

After the January 2009 provincial election, two Iraqis sitting in a café in downtown Baghdad discussed their country's future. One Iraqi believes it is possible to return Iraq to the old days: "Iraq is like a carpet that was torn. Now we're mending it. If we can put each thread back in place, the artistry of its design can return." To which his interlocutor replied: "It won't look the way it looked before."[5] Was the first citizen too optimistic? Is it possible to mend a society so badly torn apart by a series of tragic events? Do Iraqis want their country to be the same as before, considering that the current miseries in Iraq are deeply rooted in the modern history of the country? Was the second citizen, on the other hand, too pessimistic? Is there no hope for Iraq? Is the country lost forever? Yet maybe his response actually reveals a type of optimism, in the sense that although Iraqi society will never be the same, this change could lead to an even better society. However, it remains to be seen whether Iraqis can create a better society, an even more beautiful carpet; whether Iraqis can learn from their mistakes, immunize themselves from the tragic past, and create a more equitable and stable society.

April 2003 is a remarkable time in the history of Iraq. It will long be considered the dividing historical line between the old and the new Iraq. However, this view will make sense only if indeed the old Iraq and the new Iraq are two different experiences. To be sure, nobody expects a total division between the two periods. Clearly, the new Iraq will be an interaction between the old and the new and an interplay of continuity and change. The question is:, which part—the old Iraq or the new Iraq—has the most influence in the new experience? Does the bitter experience of the old Iraq lead to peace and prosperity, or does the new Iraq reinforce violence and intolerance? Is the current experience merely an introduction of new players to the very same and familiar old game of Iraqi politics, of Middle Eastern politics?

In the aftermath of regime change, the use of "new Iraq" to describe present condition has forcefully entered the political discourse. This term has even become a source of legitimacy for the new rulers of the country. Yet it is unclear whether the political use of the term is merely political rhetoric or language that describes more complex conditions. What does this term "new Iraq" mean with respect to the continuity of violence, sectarianism, corruption, and the oppression of women and minorities? Is the new Iraq a new national myth in Iraqi history, leading to the next act in what would seem to be an eternal Iraqi tragedy?

But then life, in a sense, is a process of accumulating myths and the eventual struggle to discredit such myths, freeing people from being controlled by such national myths. This is true for individuals as well as societies. There are many basic myths of life, but there are at least three myths that have always proved more common, yet more stubborn to challenge and dishonor: religion, nationalism, and gender. Unfortunately, these three myths continue to define and influence the new Iraqi experience. To be sure, myths are always part of history and all histories have mythical aspects; yet one still wonders whether reproducing myths make building a new society easier. Is it wise to talk about the new Iraq when it is only the players who are new, players who (intentionally or not) are taking Iraqis right back down a road that ends at the old Iraq? Why does this supposed new Iraq with its confusing rhetoric actually reestablish an old and typical Middle Eastern game of confusing rhetoric with reality?

One of the defining criteria for distinguishing between the old Iraq and new one is the ability to learn from history. Yet this is exactly where the new Iraq is failing. It is astonishing how the new Iraq reveals itself as yet another experience of violence and exclusion when there is a serious and ugly legacy of violence in the history of the country. National reconciliation, which is a key issue of absolute significance to the new Iraq, was actually reduced to just a few conferences and some empty official statements. Iraq has failed to learn not only from its own history but also from that of other countries that have similar experiences of horrible pasts.

These experiences stressed truth and reconciliation as necessary steps in turning a new chapter in history. Yet in Iraq, these terms were

reduced to rhetorical politics. However, the difficulty of achieving reconciliation is not only an Iraqi problem but rather a more general
Middle Eastern problem. After all, even 15 years of brutal civil war
in Lebanon did not end in serious reconciliation. This region appears
to be suffering from a deficiency in social capital. Nelson Mandela or
Mahatma Gandhi were not born or raised in the Middle East. The horrifying experiences of world wars and the Holocaust have led the
Western world to cultivate and invest in a culture of human rights.
One wonders why the awful experiences of violence and three wars
in Iraq failed to trigger a similar process in the so-called new Iraq.

The new ruling class in Iraq has adopted confessionalism and
power sharing, and it has presented this political arrangement as an
exercise in democracy. Yet this adoption signaled an astonishing disregard of the clear reality that this political solution has proven an utter
failure in Lebanon. If this method of ruling is perceived as democracy,
then this would seem to be the only democracy that leads to a civil
war. The question is why the new ruling elites have adopted this particular political deal when other choices do actually exist. Where is the
learning process and why does Iraq insist on repeating not only the
mistakes of the others but its own mistakes too?

The power-sharing system has been at the core of the Kurdish experience in the north of Iraq since 1991. Yet this system did not prevent
the two leading Kurdish parties from fighting each other for several
years in the 1990s. A scrutiny of the Kurdish experience would also
reveal that elections cannot guarantee the establishment of democracy
or the prevention of violence; democratic experimentation leads to
increased corruption, and only the few ruling elites actually benefit
from ethnic and sectarian politics. In a speech to hundreds of supporters in Sulaimaniya in March 2010, Talabani, the president of Iraq,
regarded the rival political faction, Gorran, as a threat to his party and
as "the enemies of the Kurds."[6] Yet the new experience in Iraq insists
on ignoring all these illustrative experiences. The absence of learning
from experiences is mostly due to the fact that there is no vision about
new Iraq beyond overthrowing the regime of Saddam and the subsequent division of the spoils between the leaders of the opposition.
An Iraqi citizen puts it this way: "It's true we have freedom, but what
do we have beyond it? Where's the law, where's the state, where's the
sense of citizenship?"[7]

In his study on Iraq, Wimmer recommends that the new experience
should be grounded on the following prerequisites: an electoral system that favors vote polling across ethnic lines; federalism on a

nonethnic basis with a strong component of fiscal decentralization; and a strong regime of minority rights and a judicial apparatus capable of enforcing the rule of law.[8] Yet the unfolding new experience of Iraq is the very antithesis of all these recommendations. What the country has experienced until now is holding sectarian and ethnic elections, imposing ethnic federalism, the absence of the rule of law accompanied by the supremacy of violent militias, and the oppression of minorities and women. A member of parliament admits: "We have failed to build a state of institutions, of law and order. Our institutions are based on ideological, sectarian and ethnic foundations. They are dangerous, they are shaky and they could collapse at any moment."[9] Indeed, it is tempting to ask: what is really new about the new Iraq?

New Iraq is grounded on the politics of victimization. While this politics is not new in Iraq, it has become highly institutionalized in the new experience. Must victims always imitate their abuser, and hence feed a vicious and perpetual cycle of violence and victimhood? How can we explain the paradox that the list of new victims in the new Iraq is rather extensive? Who is actually benefiting from the politics of victimization? Is victimization a politics from above, deliberately fed and pursued by dominant political elites for narrowly defined interests?

There is a need to highlight the centrality of victimhood to Iraqi politics, whether old or new. This is particularly true considering that this kind of politics has become the driving force that feeds and affects the new political process in the country. Victimhood has become an undercurrent that subtly defines the whole political process. Politicized victimhood has a tendency to produce a politics of exclusion, a politics of vengeance, political sectarianism, and the politics of identity. All of these are destructive politics, if not the very antithesis of politics and democracy. In this respect, can one explain the significance accorded to the policy of uprooting the Ba'thists as part of this overall theme of the politics of victimization?

Politicized victimhood is accompanied by the ascendancy of ethno-sectarian politics in the new Iraq. The empowerment of any community is no doubt a desirable outcome. The question nonetheless remains: whose interests is this empowerment serving and at whose expense? This is a legitimate question that should be raised regarding the current empowerment of the Shiites and the Kurds since 2003. Must this empowerment be at the expense of Iraq as a nation-state? Why is this empowerment producing a rather divisive and destabilizing, not to mention highly controversial, constitution? While decentralization is a must for the establishment of a democratic Iraq, the question remains as to whether ethnic federalism is the best or the right way of achieving decentralization. Does the experience of Iraq confirm federalism as a route to democracy? Taking into consideration the nature of the constitution and of the federalism that was initiated in the aftermath of the Iraq War, as well as the struggle over the so-called disputed territories, one wonders if all of these are no more than just new names in the essential continuation of the very old and violent politics that has dominated Iraq for decades.

Victimhood and ethno-sectarian politics are leading to consociations and consensual power sharing. In so doing, the political scene in the country is transformed away from the rule of one dictator, to the inclusion of almost all the political elites in the country. One way of looking at this political arrangement is to consider it as a remarkable democratic development. Yet this could be very misleading, as one can still observe authoritarian politics in the making, behind a façade of democracy. Since everyone is included in this political arrangement, one wonders what the point of holding elections is. Sectarian and ethnic elections are useless exercises, and seem to be detached from a meaningful democratic process. A national census to measure the demographical strength of every community would surely suffice. A scrutiny of the negotiations over the distribution of official posts between the political elites before and after every election in Iraq would unequivocally reveal that there is a political bazaar in the making, rather than a truly democratic process.

Sectarian and ethnic politics make elections and the formation of a government a very complicated and protracted process. Since the entire political class is preoccupied with the electoral campaign, the government becomes paralyzed for a few months before the elections; the result of the election is usually contested by most of the contenders, leading to further delay; and then the deliberations between party leaders to build coalitions and form the new government often take months. Despite the pressing need to improve governmental services to help Iraqis escape from miserable living conditions, the dominant politicians have demonstrated astounding selfishness by allowing the deliberations on the formation of the government following the March 2010 elections to drag on for more than nine months. One can easily estimate that for almost one year, out of four, the government has been lost in these compromises and haggling. Yet the remaining three years have still been characterized by pernicious corruption, inefficiency, and the politics of nepotism, patronage, and clientelism. While the interests of the political class are secured in this protracted process, this definitely comes at the expense of interests of the people.

Thus confessionalism and the rushing of elections tend in reality to reflect deceptive legitimacy and illusionary democracy. But the adoption of the electoral mechanisms, which is quite different from the adoption of democratic values, is still useful in dispelling the image of the authoritarian order that is still dominant in the Middle East. The relationship between elections and democracy in Iraq and the Middle East is highly questionable, and needs to be sincerely investigated. Elections and democracy are everywhere associated with peace and prosperity, but in this region they fail to deliver to the people. This failure to deliver, in turn, leaves the ruling political elites with no option but to seek external sources of legitimacy: religion, aggressive nationalism, and conflict with the Other. This, however, is the case of Iraq, whether old or new.

One of the rare achievements of the new experience in the country is the appearance of free press and of the freedom of expression. This is a major departure from the previous authoritarian regime that imposed a politics of fear and silence. Nevertheless, this positive development is still not founded on a solid institutionalized ground. The few positive achievements that Iraqis have won seem to be gradually eroding as authoritarian order is apparently reestablishing itself with time. What would be the point of being able to open your mouth and criticize things, when the ruling elites have deaf ears?

The Iraqi media, which flourished after the regime change, has quickly come under threat. At least 190 journalists have been killed since 2003, and not all of them by terrorist violence. The secretary of the Journalist Union declares that 354 journalists have been killed since 2003, including 6 journalists in 2010.[10] Many journalists have paid a heavy price for being critical and outspoken. Imad Abbadi, the head of the political section at the independent Diyyar satellite channel, is the latest victim in the attempt to silence the media. He was shot with a silenced gun in an assassination attempt that he barely survived in November 2009, for being outspoken critic of widespread government corruption. Sardesht Othman, a 23-year-old freelance journalist and student, was abducted and murdered in May 2010 after he wrote articles criticizing Kurdish government officials, including the president of the region.

According to 2010 report of the Journalistic Freedom Observatory (JFO), 130 Iraqi journalists were subject to assaults, harassment, detention, and prevention. Thirty-nine cases occurred in Baghdad and 36 cases in Kurdistan. Lawsuits and trials against journalists and their establishments have reached the figure of 40 cases, of which 60 percent in Iraqi Kurdistan.[11] The Kurdistan Democratic Party filed a defamation lawsuit on July 25, 2010, demanding $1 billion in compensation from an opposition newspaper for publishing a report about illegal oil trade in Iraqi Kurdistan. This is the biggest compensation demand in the history of Iraqi journalism.[12] The absurdly high amount requested for this case intends to sturdily discourage any future media criticism of the highly autocratic and corrupt governance in the Kurdish region. About 200 journalists and writers protested in Baghdad in August 2009 against increasing government harassment and lawsuits against journalists, particularly those investigating security and corruption. They were also protesting against the introduction of new rules for censoring books, and a proposal to ban certain websites.

Prime Minister Maliki told reporters in early 2009 to be more cooperative and less critical of the government.[13] Maliki's call for more cooperative journalists extended to foreign publications too. In November 2009, an Iraqi court has ordered the British newspaper the *Guardian* to pay £52,000 after ruling that it defamed the Iraqi PM Maliki. The case has been in connection with an article published in April 2009 stating that Maliki is becoming increasingly autocratic. In deciding this case, the court referred to an old Iraqi law disallowing foreigners to publish pieces that are critical to the prime minister or the president. Yet the court appeared to have overlooked the fact that the reporter in question was an Iraqi. The *Guardian* editor comments: "Freedom means little without free speech—and means even less if a head of state tries to use the law of libel to punish criticism or dissent."[14]

Suppressing freedom of expression has recently been extended to restraining the right to protest and organize public demonstration. After thousands of Iraqis took to the street in the summer of 2010 to protest a chronic lack of government services, particularly power shortages, the prime minister's office issued a secret order instructing the interior minister to refuse permits for public demonstrations, and the order has been carried out effectively. While these demonstrations are not necessarily far from the influence of partisan politics and political rivalry among Shiite elites, popular discontent with poor governmental services is genuine and widespread. A Human Rights Watch officer bitterly comments: "To take away the rights and freedoms Iraqis have been promised in exchange for all the suffering they have endured since the war is to add insult to injury. When the Iraqi officials learn that silencing the voice of the people is only a formula for strife?"[15] This is a big question, indeed. Why does new Iraq function mainly as a continuation of the old one, and why does Iraqi society lack an interest in learning from history? A human rights activist counsels: "Today, they are preventing peaceful, legal demonstrations, tomorrow, we are afraid they will do more than this."[16]

Authoritarianism is reestablishing itself in Iraq, with new faces and under a different façade. McFaul argues: "The moment when a new regime consolidates is rarely so clear, however. And only sometimes does the fall of autocracy produce democracy; as often as not, it produces a new form of dictatorship."[17] Basham concurs: "Paradoxically, a more democratic Iraq may also be a repressive one. It is one thing to adopt formal democracy but quite another to attain stable democracy."[18] Munson adds: "Because no country can go from dictatorship to democracy overnight, especially not one subject to the sort of historical legacies found in Iraq, Iraq could very easily slip back into authoritarianism or even state failure over the short term. Democracy, if reached, is a distant prospect. It will take years to build the infrastructure, institutions, and trust required to sustain a peaceful democratic mechanism for the transfer of power in Iraq."[19]

It is not in the interest of Iraq to initiate yet another myth—the myth of the new Iraq—as this is a society that is still suffering from the many destructive myths in its past. This is particularly true given that Iraq, at least until now, failed to build a truly new experience of a peaceful and prosperous society. It is true that the Iraq War represented a dramatic moment in Iraqi history, but what would be the point of overthrowing one dictator when the outcome is empowering several others? Many Iraqis have started to doubt the benefits of democracy and elections, to long for the old security provided by the old regime, or even to wish for the emergence of a strong ruler capable of restoring order. While this is a paradox, it is an understandable and justifiable condemnation of the new experience in the country. Presently, Iraq is at crossroads. If Iraq misses this unique opportunity, it would perhaps be the biggest mistake Iraqi society could have ever made in its modern history. Frankly, this could be far worse than all the atrocities committed by the ruthless rule of the deposed dictator.

The demarcating line of 2003 that is perceived to be the dividing line between old Iraq and new one appears illusionary and misleading. Yet one still hopes that Iraq will eventually succeed in discarding the old, destructive, and violent game of politics and will replace it with more tolerant and democratic politics. This, however, is possible only by adopting new rules, values, and principles. In other words, rather than dividing Iraq into old and new, what Iraq really needs is to have new lenses that can scrutinize the reality of the very same Iraq, regardless of which term is used. This book is a modest attempt in that direction.

NOTES

1. Peter J. Munson, *Iraq in Transition: The Legacy of Dictatorship and the Prospect for Democracy* (Dulles, VA: Potomac Books, 2008), 5.

2. Nadje al-Ali and Nicola Pratt, *What Kind of Liberation: Women and the Occupation of Iraq* (Berkeley: University of California Press, 2009), 167.

3. Ibid., 174.

4. Ali Salim, "Many Generals, No Generalship," *Asharq al-Awsat*, November 21, 2010.

5. Anthony Shadid, "Iraqis Stake Hopes on Election," *Washington Post*, January 30, 2009.

6. Sam Dagher, "Bloc Takes on Entrenched Kurdish Parties in Iraq," *New York Times*, March 6, 2010.

7. Anthony Shadid, "Unity Elusive as Iraq Grasps Trappings of Democracy," *New York Times*, March 5, 2010.

8. Andreas Wimmer, "Democracy and Ethno-Religious Conflict in Iraq," *Survival* 45, no. 4 (Winter 2003–2004).

9. Shadid, "Unity Elusive."

10. Osama Mahdi, "Attempts to End Violence against Iraqi Journalists Are Still Ineffective," *Elaph Electronic Newspaper*, January 4, 2011, http://www.elaph.com/Web/news/2011/1/622755.html.

11. Ibid.

12. Journalistic Freedom Observatory (JFO), "Ruling Party Demands One Billion Dollars in Defamation Lawsuit," August 2, 2010, http://www.jfoiraq.org/newsdetails.aspx?back=1&id=719&page=.

13. BBC News, "Iraqi Protest at Media Censorship," August 14, 2009, http://news.bbc.co.uk/2/hi/middle_east/8202698.stm.

14. BBC News, "Iraqi Court Fines British Paper," November 11, 2009, http://news.bbc.co.uk/2/hi/middle_east/8355644.stm.

15. Human Rights Watch (HRW), "Iraq: Stop Blocking Demonstrations," September 17, 2010, http://www.hrw.org/en/news/2010/09/17/iraq-stop-blocking-demonstrations.

16. Ibid.

17. Michael McFaul, "Tinderbox," *Hoover Digest*, no. 2, 2003, http://www.hoover.org/publications/hoover-digest/article/6184.

18. Patrick Basham, "Can Iraq Be Democratic?" *Policy Analysis*, no. 505, January 5, 2004, 1.

19. Munson, *Iraq in Transition*, 9.

2

The Politics of Victimization

VICIOUS CYCLE OF VICTIMIZATION

The violent and authoritarian regime of Saddam Hussein created many Iraqi victims. However, the regime change in 2003 has offered a historical opportunity for some former victims, particularly Shiites and Kurds, to become the new rulers of Iraq. Though the perception of victimhood probably exists among some segment of all societies and is usually linked to politics, the new Iraq is taking the politics of victimization to an unprecedented level. The dominance of the previous victims over the new government has institutionalized victimization, making it an integral part of politics and governance in addition to being the justification for claims of power, wealth, and legitimacy.

Granted, the politics of victimization is hardly new in Iraq. The old regimes have constantly played the role of victim to perceived international or regional conspiracies, extending this victimization to, and enforcing it on, the whole nation. This is done within the context of a conspirational perception of history and international politics. To a certain extent, the new regime is playing the same game of being victim to a persistent conspiracy, particularly by neighboring countries, against the new Iraq.

It is widely known that the deposed regime employed the utmost brutality and cruelty against Iraqis, particularly the Kurds and Shiites who dominate the present-day regime. Yet there is a big difference between victimization by a previous regime and the use of this victimization to legitimize the new political process. The politics of victimization is one of the most convenient methods of extracting externally derived legitimacy in undemocratic political systems. The former regime counted on confrontation with the outside world, which was motivated by a perception of being victim to a constant conspiracy against the country, to provide a source of legitimacy for its autocratic rule. However, all claims of victimization have elements of exaggeration and myth in them, including those by the present regime.

While it is true that the deposed regime undoubtedly created many victims in Iraq, the Kurdish and Shiite political elites are also responsible for this outcome. There is little justification to ground the whole political process in new Iraq on exaggerated claims of victimization when the leaders of the victimized communities helped to create their own victimization, a topic that historians and political scientists have neglected. Whereas the main focus is on the brutality of the previous regime in creating this situation of victimization, the "self-victimization" resulting from the actions of ethno-sectarian leaders is a conveniently neglected subject in Iraqi history. However, this is not intended to underestimate the cruelty of the former regime or to belittle the sufferings of various communities in Iraq.

Humphrey warns against the overauthorization of the suffering victim: "There is the danger of victims monopolising the interpretation of history based on the authenticity of their suffering, thereby holding back the next generation's own work on history."[1] Indeed, a complete and unbiased critical investigation of the history of the victimized communities in Iraq, particularly the Kurds and the Shiites, has yet to be written. A victimization approach to history is devoid of serious examination and often produces deficient and prejudiced history. A solemn and careful investigation of Iraqi history will reveal that the elites of these communities share the responsibility of the victimization of their own people. While the official version of history tends to be mythicized, so does the victim's version of history. Consequently, the truth is lost among the competing myths.

Though brutality cannot be justified under any pretext, not all claims of victimization are fully substantiated. Inquiry of how Iraqi politics has unfolded since 2003, particularly sectarian and ethnic politics, whether violently or democratically, reveals a clear connection between political development and politicization of the issue of victimhood. The Shiite and Kurdish ruling elites played a significant role in aggravating political conflicts in the new Iraq. This escalation of political conflict reached a level of unprecedented sectarian violence and infuriated ethnic politics that could easily ignite dangerous armed conflicts. In fact, Iraq did witness a brutal sectarian conflict during 2006–8, and a very tense ethnic conflict. Due to the high risks involved in identity politics that are strongly linked to claims of victimization, the new Iraq seems to be as violent and conflict-ridden as the old Iraq. The question is whether this sort of far-fetched sectarian and ethnic politics is a new phenomenon or a continuation of earlier politics exercised by the former victims who might have contributed to the original and previous situation of victimization. This is, however, no trivial question when it comes to the current political process in Iraq or to the unavoidable critical survey of Iraqi history.

Even if we leave aside the violent politics by the ruling victims in the aftermath of regime change in 2003, Iraqi history is full of incidences of violence that were either instigated or aggravated by the victims themselves. The fight between the Kurds and the Iraqi government in the early 1960s was strongly motivated by the newly enforced land reform.[2] This reform antagonized the economic and political interests of the Kurdish tribal leaders, and hence, the conflict was motivated by defending well-entrenched material interests rather than being an ethnic issue. Undoubtedly, many atrocities were committed against the Kurds, but it is also true that Kurdish politicians themselves contributed to this outcome by adopting risky policies, violence, and an unrealistically ambitious and overreaching agenda.

The same is also true for the Shiites who adopted a negative stand toward the government as early as the 1920s when they boycotted the government. Much of the Shiite hostility toward the government has been motivated by their opposition to the establishment of women's rights in Iraq. More rights to women would actually jeopardize the absolute power wielded by religious clerics in family and personal affairs. Furthermore, the sectarian approach adopted by the Shiites and their exaggerated closeness to Iran have greatly affected their relationship with the Iraqi government. During the Iraq-Iran war, both the Shiite and Kurdish politicians chose the option of becoming allies with Iran against Iraq. The militia Badr that belong to the Islamic Supreme Council of Iraq fought alongside Iranian troops. The same was the case with the Kurdish rebels in the north, leading to the tragedy of Halabja in 1988, executed by an extremely ruthless and inhumane regime. Hiltermann argues that there are serious lessons to be learned from the experience of Halabja:

> After all, while Saddam Hussein unequivocally was guilty of a crime against humanity by sending his bombers to drop their poisonous load on a Kurdish city, the Kurdish parties played a role that cannot be ignored—one that is actively being questioned by people in Halabja and beyond. It was the Kurdish

parties who chose to ally themselves with Iran during a war that
was existential for both countries, and it was they who guided
the Iranian Revolutionary Guards into Iraqi territory to throw
out Iraqi forces and liberate Halabja. However justified the war-
time alliance may have been given the Iraqi regime's extreme
brutality, the *peshmerga* made a gamble, knowing full well what
the regime was capable of doing, and would do, in reprisal
against the defenseless townspeople. If there was anything surprising about the Halabja chemical attack, it was its extraordinary scale and ferocity, not that it took place or even that it
involved gas, which the regime had been using against the Kurds
for almost a year at that point. The result was not only a civilian
catastrophe but also the utter collapse of the Kurdish national
movement, which gave up the fight and fled. The parties had
clearly overreached and they suffered the consequences.[3]

Uncontestably, leading people to disaster is an exercise of irresponsible politics, a politics that was characteristic of the former dictator
who led Iraq to three unnecessary and tragic wars. Bearing in mind
the horrible consequences of these tragedies, irresponsible actions are
actually violent politics. However, an even more explicit manifestation
of violence from the victims occurred during the revolt of 1991 that
followed the debacle of the invasion of Kuwait. It was a brutal erup-
tion where the violence displayed by the Shiites and the Kurds was
not only unmistakable but also horrific. Tripp states: "In the towns
seized by the rebels, a terrible revenge was wrought on those whom
they regarded as agents of or collaborators with the regime."[4]
   On the violent nature of the revolt in the south, Farouk-Sluglett and
Sluglett observe: "In the southern cities, the insurgents had captured
and killed local Ba'thist officials, members of the security services
and their families, venting their hatred for the regime upon them."[5]
Jabar adds: "Ba'th and government high-ranking officials were butch-
ered, in some cases mutilated. The violence was horrific."[6] Mackey
concurs: "Operating more as a mob than an organized force, they
vented their hatred against the symbols of Baghdad ... They hung
their captives from the rafters of an Islamic school, shot them in the
head before walls turned into execution chambers, or simply slit their
throats at the point of capture. The abandoned bodies collected in the
streets where enraged Shia spit their venom of the lifeless figures."[7]
   Reports on the excesses of the rebels are well documented by
Makiya. In the Shiite holy city of Najaf, "many officials were hung in

the basement of the Islamic school next to the mosque. People dragged officials in the street and shot them. They were so angry they cut them up and burned them. Others came and spat on the bodies."[8] In Basra, the rebels proclaimed the establishment of the Shiite Republic of Basra; they stormed hotels and burned bars and casinos. Surrendering or captured army personnel were executed, occasionally in "trials" presided over by clerics, who passed judgments against *kafir*, or apostate, "the enemies of God." Apostasy is a form of treason against a very basic and all-encompassing group identity and loyalty, the penalty for which, according to Islamic law, is consistently death.[9] In the city of Samawa, one Ba'thist official was crucified on the walls of the local *husainiyya*, a Shiite religious site for the commemoration of the life of Imam Hussein, grandson of the prophet Muhammad. "Then his arms, legs, and head were chopped off, and the pieces left on top of the town rubbish dump until the smell became unbearable."[10]

On the violent nature of the revolt in the north, Mackey tells what happened when the *peshmerga*, the Kurdish rebels, entered the city of Kirkuk: "Over the next hours, no one bothered to count how many servants of Baghdad were shot, beheaded, or cut to shreds with the traditional dagger struck in the cummerbund of every Kurdish man. By the time Kurdish rage has exhausted itself, piles of corpses lay in the street awaiting removal by bulldozers."[11] An eyewitness tells what happened when the Kurdish rebels controlled Kirkuk. They caught the Ba'thists, displayed them in town, and asked the people to say who did what to whom. "When the Kurdish leader of the group holding the prisoners agreed upon an execution, people would jump at the prisoner with knives before the sentence could even be carried out. People were beheaded; their bodies were cut into pieces. All was revenge and settling accounts; it was a slaughter-house."[12]

An eyewitness said that the bodies of security agents, intelligence officers, and Ba'th party men were torn to shreds in the town of Sulaimaniya. In the well-fortified central security headquarters, the eyewitness continues, "seven hundred security and party men died here and we had to walk on top of their corpses. Those who had survived the fighting were tried and executed on the spot by the people using iron saws and knives even as they screamed and sobbed."[13] Makiya articulates that in the town of Raniya a crowd dragged police and Ba'thist officials being detained in the town mosque onto the roof of the local hotel; "their names were read out. 'Shall we throw him over or not?' the men holding the Ba'thist would shout out to the crowd below. The huge crowd gathered below gave its verdict, and one by one the men were pushed off the three-story building. An angry crowd, including young women, rushed at the broken bodies and shredded what was left with knives."[14] Marr warily concurs: "As in the south, they committed atrocities on Ba'th Party and security personnel and undertook some looting, but these disorders were far fewer and more focused than in the south."[15]

Any opposition to a violent, authoritarian rule is a peaceful and democratic opposition. This is a clear misconception as proven by recent developments in Iraq. Intense and even violent rivalries among previous victims, along with their militias, are undisputable facts in Iraqi history. Bitter struggles for wealth and power have occurred in both the southern and northern parts of the country. In southern Iraq, different Shiite militias struggled over supremacy, spoils, and even oil smuggling. Similarly, in the north, the two dominant Kurdish parties engaged in "fraternal" fights over supremacy, wealth, and smuggling between 1994 and 1997. These conflicts have left thousands dead and injured, and tens of thousands have been displaced. The brutality of the previous regime against the Kurds has been replicated, but this time at the hands of Kurdish leaders themselves. Only when it was proven that either party no longer had the military means to eliminate the other did the fighting stopped. Even so, the ceasefire was only fundamentally motivated by newly emerging financial opportunities associated with the establishment of the oil-for-food program, which earmarked 13 percent of the revenues of that program to the Kurdish region.

These opportunities are sources of new and lucrative contracts, which primarily benefit dominant parties and politicians who have enforced themselves as business partners. These new avenues of wealth and corruption have provided rival parties a win-win situation by helping them further consolidate their dominance over all aspects of life in the Kurdish enclave. Leezenberg points out: "Post-1991 Iraq under Saddam developed a form of crony capitalism, where the new economic elites were in part protected by tribal and mafia-like networks that could use violence to protect their markets. In many respects the same situation holds in the north."[16] These structural similarities reflect the fact that victims often imitate the actions and behaviors of the victimizers. Not unlike the past regime, the previous victims are also prone to violence and intimidation. It is important to recognize the fact that both the preceding regime and the victims are products of the same culture of violence predominating society and political culture.

Maintaining politics of victimization will most likely lead to the creation of new victims in Iraq in a perpetual and vicious cycle of victimhood and violence. Makiya warned of the all-too-human mistake we might have fallen into, "of allowing ourselves to believe that there is something morally redeeming in the quality of victimhood itself. There isn't. The very opposite is likely to be the case: victims of cruelty or injustice are not only no better than their tormentors; they are more often than not just waiting to change places with them."[17] The past victims and now rulers of the country (the Shiite and Kurdish elites) are actually creating an extensive list of new victims, in a continuation of earlier policies inherited from the ex-regime.

Ironically, the majority of the Shiites and Kurds are victims of the elitist Shiite-Kurdish ruling alliance. It is paradoxical that the victims continue to be victimized, but this time, by their own elites. Both Shiite and Kurdish ruling elites perpetuate the previous politics of monopolizing decision making, power, and wealth at the expense of public interest. Nepotism, corruption, partisan governmental appointments, intense partisan rivalries, the intervention of political parties in the governmental affairs, lack of the rule of law, and the supremacy of militias all contribute to a situation where the majority of Kurds and Shiites are losers.

Although security in the south is relatively better than in other areas of the country, Shiites do not benefit much from the dominance of Shiite parties and militias in southern Iraq. Survivors of 1988 poison gas attack in Halabja have protested several times against the willful neglect of their city and corruption by the city's chief executive. They even boycotted many official memorial ceremonies for the massacre. Ironically, Halabja is often used by Kurdish politicians as a symbol of the victimization of the Iraqi Kurds. This paradox signifies the glaring difference between being a survivor of atrocities on one hand, and being a politicized victim (i.e., a dominant elite) who largely benefits from the situation, on the other. Even basic services and decent living standards—despite huge revenues—are not secured in both Kurdish- and Shiite-dominated regions.

Iraq as a nation seems to be the most serious victim of the alliance of previous victims. The dominant Shiite-Kurdish political alliance, which is benefiting from the new reality where militias are effective ground forces, is using the Iraqi state to advance sectarian and ethnic policies at the expense of genuine national interests. Since 2003, the Kurds have been adamant about enforcing a rather debatable kind of federalism, which is a clear example of a policy that seeks to weaken the Iraqi state. Shiites who themselves were once interested in advancing their own federalism in the south went along with the Kurdish

agenda in a politics of granting mutual concessions. However, this is a
dangerous game played under the name of victimization, when the
interest of Iraq as a nation is at stake.

It is also important to remember that Iraq as a nation was victimized
in the past when it was created on the basis of violence and exclusion.
The new ruling class maintains this earlier trend for the benefit of
sectarian and ethnic extremism. Humphrey states: "The idea of reconciliation is politically focused on the social recovery of the victim with
the purpose of reconstituting the national whole."[18] Thus the social
recovery of victims should be linked to the rehabilitation of the nation
as a whole, and national interests should be prioritized. A politics that
tends to grant mutual concessions to the newly ruling elites denies the
majority of the Iraqis real access to power, wealth, and decision making.
The politics of victimization, which states that "we are the victims and
hence we deserve to monopolize wealth and power," only leads to the
continued marginalization of most Iraqis and the continuation of an
old form of violent politics.

Indeed, the list of the victims of the new Iraq is extensive. Apart from
minorities and women, which will be discussed in the next chapter, the
Ba'thists have been prosecuted and victimized since regime change in
2003. This new victimization reached its pinnacle in the campaign to ban
several influential politicians from participating in the 2010 elections on
charges of connection to the Ba'thism. Hiltermann argues: "Indeed, the
campaign's initiators are exploiting two key vulnerabilities in the current
order: ambiguities in the law, and the acquiescence of many Kurds and
(religious) Shiites, whose sense of injury from the previous regime's trepi-
dations is a powerful undercurrent driving much of today's revanchist
politics."[19] De-Ba'thification resumes the politics of victimization by creating new victims, the victims of new Iraq.

POLITICIZING VICTIMHOOD

Victimization seems to be an integral part of Iraqi rule, whether old or
new. The legislation that allows the eradication of the Ba'thists abruptly
places individuals into positions—abusers and victims—that are
equally unhealthy and detrimental to making sound judgments and
reflecting and contemplating on life experiences that should naturally
follow dramatic events.

Nevertheless, even the previous victims (i.e., the abusers of today who
dominate the new regime) miss a similar opportunity to contemplate on
the root causes of the cycle of perpetual violence that confuses the

boundary between victims and victimizers, two groups who are merely changing places in the vicious cycle of victimization. Instead of using victimhood as an opportunity for constructive reflection, victims of the old regime seem to play the politics of victimization to a maximum level in new Iraq. Clearly, victimization as a form of politics has become an important consideration in new Iraqi politics.

The insistence on preserving the status of victimhood tends to result, by implication, in a reality where others have no choice but to keep their status and sense of being victimizers, even after losing power. Consequently, the previous abusers continue to hold feelings of guilt. This phenomenon does not serve to redeem abusers or to help them overcome their undesirable situation. Rather, it serves to keep them in this situation continuously, and exploit their feelings of guilt to extract from them as many benefits and advantages as possible. Keeping the abusers in a perpetual feeling of culpability makes them weaker and more vulnerable. Thus a perfect situation is created for the maximum extraction of benefits. However, in this violent kind of victimization politics, the previous victims start to become victimizers. Kurdish and Shiite actions in new Iraq are good illustrations of this kind of violent politics.

In discussing the shortsightedness of politics that is grounded on victimhood, Hiltermann argues: "The current political elite may have invested too much in their narratives of victimhood and their use of revenge as a way to secure their own power to do this. But some may come to realize that their long-term survival lies in the political stability that would follow from a process of reconciliation."[20] Iraq's present political environment seems to usher the institutionalization of the politics of victimization. The new class that came to dominate Iraqi politics is ruling based on its status as the previously victimized group. In fact, this is becoming the most crucial factor in the new Iraqi rule, particularly with the miserable failure of the rulers to ensure decent public services and life standards.

There is no doubt that governance in new Iraq is legitimized by elections, but these elections are largely motivated by a sense of victimhood. Hence, they serve merely as a formal or a "democratic" way of confirming claims to power. Clearly, victimhood has become a source of political legitimacy in new Iraq. However, this legitimized rule by former victims is also a legitimate tool for the acquisition of wealth and power. Moreover, this approach to legitimacy through the politics of victimization tends to contradict democratic principles, the supposed foundations of new Iraq. In a democratic process, legitimacy is derived from serving the interests of the electorate. Indeed, the failure of this process seems to be a strong motive for the ruling elite to insist on politicizing victimhood.

An elitist approach to victimhood comes with a drive to monopolize access to wealth and power. The dominant elites of the victimized community not only politicize victimhood but also capitalize on this politicization. This situation of politicized victimization leads not only to exaggerated claims of victimhood but also to a struggle to monopolize feelings of victimhood. Motivated by their interests to gain wealth and power, ruling politicians insist on advancing the myth of the monopoly of suffering. Accordingly, they are those who suffered from the former regime. They also advance notions of those who have suffered most, or those who have suffered more than the others have. New Iraq seems to be an open "auction" for claims about the highest level of suffering in old Iraq, which would surely be translated into more advantages and benefits.

Thus whereas all Iraqis have suffered from old Iraq, specifically from the reckless and violent policies of the prior regime, Shiites and Kurds insist on being the champions of claims of victimization. Although no one denies that these communities have suffered greatly, there is still the question of why the politics of victimization is occurring at the expense of other communities and the rest of the Iraqis who equally have their own share of sufferings. The previous suffering of all Iraqis is something that should unite and inspire all Iraqis to build a new experience where suffering is much reduced or even eliminated. The new experience of building a new and democratic Iraq should be the price, if one insists on having a price at all, for all past sufferings. At any rate, these sufferings should not become a ground for differentiation and privileges.

In this drive for monopolizing victimhood, there is a persistence on identifying the Sunni community with the former regime and the Ba'th Party. In reality, however, the Sunnis were also victims of the old regime. The Ba'thists and the Ba'th Party were the first victims of the regime of Saddam Hussein. Only few people enjoyed power and wealth under the former regime while the rest of the Iraqis of all sects and ethnicities were marginalized. All Iraqis and Iraq as a nation have suffered from and were victimized by an ugly past. A new democratic system should recognize this reality and strive to overcome this legacy. Democracy, rule of law, and economic development for the benefit of all Iraqis are natural ways to put an end to this legacy and the claims of victimhood. Competition over victimhood, Makiya warns, is a road that can lead only to disaster.[21] Indeed, the contest over legacy of victimization produces misjudgments and miscalculations as the development of Iraqi politics since 2003 has demonstrated.

These wrong calculations that are motivated by politicized feelings of victimhood help to create a difficult, if not miserable, life for the Iraqis in the new Iraq, similar to the old days. If the entire history of Iraq is not ample enough to reflect on the relationship between victimhood and violence, then the ugly reality of the past eight years should be a wake-up call for the Iraqis to do so. When feelings of victimization are oriented toward the previous regime and that regime has been overthrown, adherence to these feelings would seem to lack sense of justification. There is no eternal or permanent victimhood, because victimhood has only a temporal status. If the Iraqis are serious about building a new Iraq, feelings of victimization should not be part of the new experience. The colorless language of victimhood, Makiya suggests, can only provide a false sense of collective reassurance.[22] Buruma concurs: "It becomes questionable when a cultural, ethnic, religious, or national community bases its communal identity almost entirely on the sentimental solidarity of remembered victimhood. For that way lies historical myopia and, in extreme circumstances, even vendetta."[23] A new democratic and prosperous Iraq that is inclusive to all Iraqis on the basis of citizenship and equality is the best way to overcome the cycle of violence and victimization.

Makiya argues: "The problem of Iraq is that everyone was a victim, and most people, especially the Shi'a majority, only know how to think and behave like victims."[24] This "mentality" of victimhood, which is practiced by both Shiites and Kurds, has only harmful and violent outcomes. Hanging on to feelings of victimhood is detrimental to the desirable process of national reconciliation that should inevitably come after an ugly past. These feelings fail to build bridges of trust between the various communities sharing existence in Iraq. Buruma observes: "The tendency to identify authenticity in communal suffering actually impedes understanding among people. For feelings can only be expressed, not discussed or argued about. This cannot result in mutual understanding, but only in mute acceptance of whatever people wish to say about themselves, or in violent confrontation."[25] The politics of victimization that creates a new list of victims would surely make national reconciliation an untenable process.

Victimization tends to elevate the politics of identity in new Iraq. Victimhood as an identity has a profound impact on the identity of victims. The victimization of the Shiites and Kurds was based on

religion and nationalism, a reality that complicates any possible questioning of their status as victims. In fact, the genesis of Shiism is
strongly linked to a perceived feeling of victimization. Shiism, as a
political ideology, has actually transformed victimhood into a religion.
Thus there is a situation of praising, elevating, and even sanctioning
victimhood to a level of obsession and uncompromising stand. In this
situation, the victims insist on demanding a price for their victimization, whether real or perceived.

This identity politics impedes understanding among different communities in Iraq, and it can hardly become the basis of democratic
politics. The sentimentality and emotionality that are associated with
victimization and identity politics are shaky grounds for public life
and politics in a democratic system. This focus on identity through
victimization fails to build common grounds and common interests
among communities. The insistence on a mentality of victimhood, or
the "egoism" of sticking to victimhood, helps create an unhealthy
and unnecessary trap for the Iraqi society. This trap of victimization
is detrimental to the interests of Iraq as nation, and to the interests of
the majority of Iraqis sharing this land.

Victimization creates a new dichotomy in society, particularly
between victimizers and victims as two mutually exclusive groups
with huge insurmountable differences. However, this rigid and static
categorization fails to capture the complex reality of violence and
responsibility. In reality, such a sharp distinction between victims
and perpetrators is more fictional than factual, and is certainly not
supported by a rigorous study of Iraqi history. Whether consciously
or not, all Iraqis have participated, and are still participating in creating the tragedy of Iraq. Hence, everyone must hold responsibilities
for what happened. Victimhood is not a linear process or a clear-cut
concept because perpetrators and victims may change places, and
the victims are partly responsible for their victimization.

However, labeling those who have suffered from violence and
atrocities as victims has been criticized as the wrong label. Instead,
the label of survivors that includes both victims and victimizers has
been suggested. On the need to redefine the entire society as survivors, Mani argues: "While everyone is a victim, everyone is also a perpetrator, making the distinction pointless. It is necessary to go beyond
a simplistic dichotomy between perpetrator and victim and adopt the
discourse of survivor, whatever one's individual past . . . the recognition of the shared identity of all members of society as survivors with
a common stake in rebuilding community and a shared future."[26]

One of the solemn problems of victimization is that it entails passivity and entraps the victims in a situation of insensibility and inaction. Yet passivity is not conducive to democratic politics that stipulates political action and agency. Victimization is a denial of agency while in reality victims always have a choice. This discussion does not intend to belittle the sufferings of the victims of Iraq. However, there is a need to put victimization into a constructive and historical perspective. After all, all truth is subjective. No one dares to deny that victimhood existed and still exists in the country, but victimhood poses a serious challenge for the new experience in Iraq.

One alternative is to politicize victimhood for the benefits of narrow personal, sectarian, or ethnic purposes. When the party of the Iraqi President Talabani, the Patriotic Union of Kurdistan, was criticized by the opposition, Talabani's niece and a member of the national parliament, Ala' Talabani, said that her uncle's opposition to the regime of Saddam before 2003 and his efforts to safeguard Kurdish interests should never be forgotten. "In Europe you always talk about the future," she said, "here you have to mention the past, our martyrs."[27] Martyrism, on the other hand, is an additional contributing factor to violence. The situation of being stuck in feelings of victimization will undoubtedly trap or imprison people in the past and blur visions for the future.

The other option is to be free from this overdetermining grip of victimization and deal with sufferings caused by victimization in a more constructive and future-oriented manner. Indubitably, there is no moral superiority in the status of victimhood. Buruma states that the extent to which many minorities have come to define themselves above all as historical victims is alarming and reveals a lack of historical perspective; it seems a very peculiar source of pride.[28] The new Iraq will unequivocally be better off without this false pride. The challenge is, then, to create more productive and constructive kinds of pride. Arguably, that will make all the difference and that is what the new Iraq is supposed to initiate and develop.

NOTES

1. Michael Humphrey, *The Politics of Atrocity and Reconciliation: From Terror to Trauma* (London: Routledge, 2002), 145.

2. M. E. Yapp, *The Near East Since the First World War: A History to 1995*, 2nd ed. (Essex, UK: Longman, 1996), 247.

3. Joost R. Hiltermann, "To Protect or to Project? Iraqi Kurds and Their Future," *Middle East Report*, no. 247, summer 2008, http://www.merip.org/mer/mer247/hiltermann.html.

4. Charles Tripp, *A History of Iraq*, 2nd ed. (Cambridge: Cambridge University Press, 2002), 256.

5. Marion Farouk-Sluglett and Peter Sluglett, *Iraq since 1958: From Revolution to Dictatorship* (London: Tauris, 2003), 289.

6. Faleh A. Jabar, *The Shi'ite Movement in Iraq* (London: Saqi, 2003), 270.

7. Sandra Mackey, *The Reckoning: Iraq and the Legacy of Saddam Hussein* (New York: Norton, 2002), 24–25.

8. Kanan Makiya, *Cruelty and Silence: War, Tyranny, Uprising, and the Arab World* (New York: Norton, 1993), 74.

9. Ibid., 90.

10. Ibid., 93.

11. Mackey, *The Reckoning*, 26.

12. Makiya, *Cruelty and Silence*, 79.

13. Ibid., 89.

14. Ibid., 88.

15. Phebe Marr, *The Modern History of Iraq*, 2nd ed. (Boulder, CO: Westview, 2004), 248.

16. Michiel Leezenberg, "Iraqi Kurdistan: Contours of a Post-Civil War Society," *Third World Quarterly* 26, no. 4–5 (2005): 634.

17. Kanan Makiyya, *Republic of Fear: The Politics of Modern Iraq* (Berkeley: University of California Press, 1998), xxix.

18. Humphrey, *The Politics of Atrocity*, 106.

19. Joost Hiltermann, "Playing with Fire in Iraq," *The National*, January 28, 2010.

20. Ibid.

21. Makiya, *Cruelty and Silence*, 226.

22. Ibid., 323.

23. Ian Buruma, "The Joys and Perils of Victimhood," *The New York Review of Books*, vol. 46, no. 6, April 8, 1999.

24. Makiya, *Cruelty and Silence*, 225.

25. Buruma, "The Joys and Perils."

26. Rama Mani, *Beyond Retribution: Seeking Justice in the Shadow of War* (Cambridge: Polity, 2002), 123.

27. Sam Dagher, "Bloc Takes on Entrenched Kurdish Parties in Iraq," *New York Times*, March 6, 2010.

28. Buruma, "The Joys and Perils."

3

Dwindling Minorities, Debased Women

DEFENSELESS MINORITIES

Ironically, the politics of victimization, which has been elevated in new Iraq by the victims of the old regime, is considerably harming the interests—if not the very existence—of other minorities in the country. Victims turned victimizers in new Iraq tend to create a rather difficult and vulnerable situation for minorities sharing existence in the country. Through the politicization of victimhood, previous victims aspire to find a niche in an authoritarian system of oppression rather than to ensure universal justice and prosperity. Apparently, the status of former victims entitles them to persecute other minorities in the country.

Sectarian and ethnic politics, which is sanctioned by the Shiite-Kurdish alliance and has dominated the Iraqi landscape since 2003, affects other groups in the country. There is an erroneous politics of associating the Sunnis with the Ba'th Party and targeting the Ba'thists under various slogans, such as de-Ba'thification. The Sunnis can easily claim that they are becoming the new victims in a perpetual and vicious cycle of violence and revenge. The Faili Kurds, who were expelled from Iraq in 1971 and 1980 for allegedly having Iranian rather than Iraqi nationality, is a large minority representing a problem for the Shiite-Kurdish alliance as far as victimization is concerned. On the one hand, although they are Shiites, they are not recognized as such by the mainstream Shiite Muslims because they are more associated with the Kurds. On the other hand, mainstream Sunni Kurds do not recognize them as Kurds because they are Shiites. Consequently, the Faili Kurds are doubly victimized.

International organizations warn about a dangerous situation for minorities in Iraq since 2003. A report from Human Rights Watch (HRW), issued in November 2009 to address the situation of minorities in northern Iraq, particularly the Nineveh province, one of the most ethnically, culturally, and religiously diverse regions of Iraq, is particularly critical of the policies and tactics pursued by the Kurdistan Regional Government (KRG) in the so-called "disputed territories" in northern Iraq that have been under effective control of the Kurdish security forces and the two dominant Kurdish parties since 2003. It declares that to incorporate these territories into the Kurdish region, the Kurdish authorities have embarked on a two-pronged strategy of inducement and repression. The report also criticizes the heavy-handed tactics, including arbitrary arrests, detentions, violence, and torture against those who oppose and resist Kurdish expansionist plans.

The Kurdish authorities, the report maintains, are establishing a pro-Kurdish system of patronage in minority communities with the intention of undermining and challenging the established authority in these groups, many of which oppose Kurdish rule. The report indicates: "The goal of these tactics is to push Shabak and Yazidi communities to identify as ethnic Kurds, and for Christians to abide by the Kurdish government's plan of securing a Kurdish victory in any referendum concerning the future of the disputed territories."[1] The report continues to say that Iraq's Kurds "deserve redress for the crimes committed against them by successive Iraqi governments, including genocide and the displacement of hundreds of thousands. The victims of Saddam Hussein's Arabization campaign deserve to be able to return to, and rebuild, their historic communities. But the issue of redress for past wrongs should be separate from the current struggle for political control over the disputed territories, and does not justify exclusive control of the region by one ethnic group."[2] Kurdish authorities, however, simply dismissed the report as "false."

The Kurdish authorities are working hard to impose Kurdish identity on two of the most vulnerable minorities in Iraq, the Yazidis and the Shabaks. The Yazidi community is a minority of about 500,000 people, particularly concentrated in the eastern parts of northern Iraq. Their religion contains a mixed of various religious traditions. They are falsely accused as devil worshipers, hence making them an easy target of violence and terrorist attacks. In August 2007, five synchronized truck bombings left more than 300 Yazidis dead and more than 700 wounded. The attack pulverized about 400 mud-walled homes. The Shabak, another minority that live in northern Iraq, is also a target of violence. In August 2009, a terrorist attack led to a casualty toll of at least 35 killed and 200 wounded. The Arabs and the Turkmen, the third-largest minority in the country, are also the target of intimidation by the Kurdish authorities and security forces, particularly in the contested province of Kirkuk.

The Christians of Iraq, one of the world's oldest Christian communities, live across Iraq, but with heavy concentration in big cities and the northern part of the country. They are also the target of a brutal campaign of murder, kidnapping, violence, attacks against churches, and home demolition, promoting thousands of Christian families to flee their homes. In late 2008 there was a systematic and orchestrated campaign of targeted killings and violence that left 40 Christians dead and more than 12,000 displaced within a three-week period. A renewed campaign against the Christians in the north has also started in the beginning of 2010. The many killings of targeted Christians led to a new exodus of more than 4,000 Christians in the last week of February 2010. In October 2010, a terrorist group stormed the Our Lady of Salvation church in Baghdad, taking more than 100 hostages. Amidst shouting of "All of you are infidels," the attackers started shooting at the hostages. The rescue operation by the Iraqi Special Forces ended the drama, but 58 people were killed because of this tragic event, which triggered a new wave of Christian exodus.

The Christians who once numbered about 1.5 million started to leave the country during the sanction years of the 1990s, but the mass exodus has accelerated after the rise of religious militias and the increased Islamization of Iraqi society after 2003. Presently, there are probably no more than 600,000 Christians left in the country. Numerous Christian-owned liquor stores have been firebombed and forced to close, and many owners have been killed. A leader of a community council representing Qaraqosh, a Christian-dominated town, expresses fear: "We are living as doves among wolves."[3] Another Christian continues: "We are weak and helpless, so we are made into scapegoats." Another fellow complains: "Saddam was a dictator, but he was not a religious fanatic. Religious fanaticism is a threat to us."[4]

Using violence and intimidation, the Islamist militias are deliberately targeting minorities in Iraq. These violent campaigns have led to mass migration of minorities who are the original population of Iraq. The small and peaceful minority of Mandaeans, the only surviving Gnostic community, would have probably faced the danger of extinction of their 2,000-year-old culture if it was not for their mass migration to other countries. The fact that they are known as goldsmiths makes them an easy target of killings, robberies, and kidnapping for ransom when lawlessness and organized crimes in collusion with the militias and security forces are high.

Moreover, the policy of enforcing the veil, *hijab*, on women by fanatic militias is not restricted to Muslim women only, but also extends to women from other religions. One day in May 2007, Youssif had an encounter with extremists, a shocking experience that motivated him to flee the city of Basra with his family. While he was walking with his wife, they were stopped by the extremists who asked why his wife was not wearing a *hijab*. "We were beaten so badly that day when I told them that we are Christians and they threatened to kill me if I would not respect Islam in this city."[5] Many women feel that their situation has actually worsened since the regime change in 2003. Women from minorities are subjected to the double burden of intimidating politics against women and minorities.

Furthermore, there are reports that the religious militias are engaged in a campaign of terror against homosexuals in Iraq, leading to many killings. Islamists death squads are hunting down gay Iraqis and summarily executing them or subjecting them to various brutal tortures. According to the *Guardian*, Ali al-Sistani, the most revered Shiite cleric issued a religious edict, *fatwa*, urging the killing of gays and lesbians in the "most severe way possible."[6] Even if this edict is not officially confirmed, the silence of Sistani on the campaign of terrorizing homosexuals in Iraq is questioned and criticized. Not only what is posted on the official site of Sistani is important but also what is not posted, particularly when there is a need for a clear opinion and position regarding disturbing issues such as the brutal killing and torturing of homosexuals. Silence is complicity. The homosexuals are becoming a newly added vulnerable minority in the new Iraq.

However, violence against minorities is hardly a new phenomenon in Iraqi history. History shows that increased religionization, militarization, and authoritarianism in the country are widely detrimental to the interests, if not to the very existence and survival, of minorities. However, the past also reveals two other things related to this issue. First, some of the problems of the minorities are self-inflicted by exaggerated demands or far-fetched nationalism. Second, minorities have also contributed to the sufferings of other minorities.

The first victim of the increased role of the military in Iraqi politics since the 1930s is the Assyrians, a Christian minority. The Assyrians were assertive militants who explicitly rejected integration into the newly emerging independent State of Iraq and demanded, instead, Assyrian national home in the north of the country. The militant role played by one of their leader, Mar Sham'un, enforced the uncompromising stand of this community. The killing and looting of several Assyrian villages by Kurdish and Arab tribesmen culminated in the massacre of the Assyrian village of Simmel in the region of Dohuk in the north of Iraq in August 1933. The brutality of the army and the police force led to the killing of about 300 men and few women and children on the day of the carnage. Rape of women by soldiers and policemen also occurred. The total number of Assyrian victims of these events was estimated at 600, according to British officials, and several thousands, according to Assyrian sources.[7] General Bakir Sidqi, a Kurd, whose popularity has increased tremendously because of this violent incident, led the massacre of the Assyrians by the army. He was celebrated as a hero when he returned to Baghdad.

The Jews lived in Iraq since ancient times, and they are probably the oldest diaspora in history. They played a significant role not only in developing Jewish religious traditions but also in enriching life in the country on multiple fronts. However, the Jews of Iraq is a community that came to a tragic end, and their experience is considered as one of the most disturbing chapters in Iraqi history. The increased militarization of politics and the rise of an extreme and violent nationalism have led to a dreadful pogrom, *farhud*, on the Jewish community in Baghdad in 1941. Simon explains: "The immediate effect of Britain's overwhelming defeat of the Iraqi forces, was the attack on the 'internal enemy,' a riot in Baghdad during Sunday and Monday, the first and second of June, in which 179 Jewish men, women, and children were killed and several hundred wounded. Property damage was assessed in the millions of pounds sterling."[8] Religious articles were stolen and synagogues and Torah scrolls were desecrated.[9]

The government appointed an investigating committee, whose report identifies several causes of this dreadful event, most notably: a politicized educational system and military; intensive Nazi propaganda; the destructive role played by the Mufti of Jerusalem, Hajj Amin al-Husseini, exiled in Baghdad at the time; and the role played by Yunis al-Sab'awi, reputed to be the most pro-Nazi member of Rahsid Ali's group that led the coup of 1941.

However, the destiny of the Jews of Iraq reached its pinnacle during the years 1948–51 when almost the entire Jewish population, 130,000 people, migrated to the newly formed State of Israel. The departure of a well-integrated community has been a great loss for the country and most probably an early indication of the degeneration of Iraqi politics and society. For the few Jews who have decided to stay in Iraq despite the major exodus, the ordeal was far from over. Instead of appreciating the fact that some members of this community have nevertheless stayed in the country, extremely politicized violence after the military coup of 1958 has caused further sufferings to the remaining Jews. According to Zubaida, the Iraqi Communist Party in 1959 demanded of its Jewish members to either convert to Islam or leave the party. Their protest that as Marxists they did not believe in religion did not help.[10]

However, the regime of Saddam Hussein implemented a final blow to the remaining Jewish community by executing many of them on the fabricated charges of spying. The 1969 executions and public display of the corpses of several Jews in downtown Baghdad is an extraordinary event that should be part of serious scrutiny of Iraqi history. The 10 or less remaining Jews finally left the country after the Iraq War in 2003. Additionally, although all the Jews have left the country, their legacy is under attack in new Iraq. There are reports that the government, under pressure from Islamist parties, has already embarked on a plan to turn the Jewish tomb of the Prophet Ezekiel, situated in the small town of al-Kifl south of Baghdad, into a mosque and erase all Jewish markings under the pretext of restoring the site. According to local sources, "a number of Islamic political parties insist on changing and Islamizing this historical religious site and eradicate any reference to the Jews."[11]

After the military coup of 1958 and the ascendancy of violent street politics and intimidation by armed militias, the Turkmen encountered their share of this increased violence against minorities. In mid-July 1959, a significant violent event took place in the town of Kirkuk, which was preceded by another violent event, an attempted coup and street violence in the town of Mosul. On both occasions the Iraqi Communist Party played an instrumental role during a period witnessing the ascendancy of Communism in Iraqi politics. On the event in Kirkuk that led to the killing of between 32 and 50 and the injury of 130, McDowall points out: "Once again, the spark was a rally by leftists. It will be recalled that the ICP in the north was preponderantly Kurdish . . . Mullah Mustafa's triumphal visit to the town the previous October had nearly resulted in bloodletting. On this occasion, however, Kurdish Communists and Kurdish members of the Popular Resistance Force (PRF) attacked shops and their owners. Officially 32 Turkmen were killed, but the real figure was more like 50."[12]

Batutu concurs by stating that the immediate blame falls clearly upon fanatic Kurds of differing tendencies; all but 4 of the 28 perpetrators of excesses who were executed because of this event were Kurds. "The Communists did take an active part in the outbreak, but *as Kurds*. The ends they sought were not Communist but Kurdish ends. Their communism was, in most instances, skin deep. What, in effect, seems to have happened was the bending by the Kurds of all the auxiliary organ- izations of the Communist party to their own needs, that is, to the pursuit of their deadly feud with their old antagonists, the Turkmen."[13] He con- tinues to say that order was not fully restored until after the arrival of military enforcements from Baghdad and the disarming of the Kurdish soldiers of the Fourth Brigade.[14]

The plight of the Kurds and the Shiites, particularly during the reign of Saddam Hussein, is a well-known fact that needs no elabora- tion. These two communities have suffered utmost brutality in one of the darkest and disturbing chapters of Iraqi history. However, the real- ity that new Iraq, which is ruled by these two communities, is a tragic Iraq for other minorities is much more difficult to digest. Minorities and women are the victims of the so-called new democratic Iraq, a fact that is antithetical to any genuine democratic process.

In truth, the "democratic" system of power sharing, *muhasasa*, adopted in new Iraq is detrimental to the interests of minorities. As a compensation for their political marginalization, minorities are perhaps more generally qualified in having better technocratic and managerial talents than the average population. Therefore minorities find them- selves in a disadvantageous situation in a power-sharing system where public positions are not distributed on the basis of meritocracy but instead on loyalty, partisan politics, and identity. A genuine democratic system that is grounded on citizenship and individuality is more con- ducive to the interests and aspirations of minorities.

No one denies that Iraqi history has witnessed many brutalities against minorities. However, there are also remarkable stories of toler- ance and peaceful coexistence among various communities in this coun- try. This history of peaceful coexistence is a manifestation of democracy, contrary to claims that democracy is impossible in Iraq. The nation is blessed with a mosaic of various communities that represent the rich- ness of the Iraqi social fabric. Nevertheless, dealing with the pluralistic Iraqi society is not an easy task. A society that appreciates its minorities as assets and creates an inclusive system for all its communities is truly worthy of the name new Iraq.

DISEMPOWERMENT OF WOMEN

The 1959 ratification of a new personal status law, known as the Law of 188, was a great achievement for Iraqi women. This law was founded on Islamic principles but contained a selection of woman-friendly interpretations from each of the legal schools of Islam: Sunni and Shiite. It was legislated by the state as a unified code applicable to all Iraqis with the exception of certain non-Muslim minorities. The administration of the Law of 188 was entrusted to the secular court system.

This law established that monogamy is the norm for the family and put serious restrictions on polygamy. It considered polygamy a commitment of a crime if it is conducted without the approval of a judge, who can agree to cases of polygamy only if there is a "legitimate" motive and if the husband is financially capable of supporting more than one wife. However, if there is reason to believe that injustice between the wives will occur, the judge will not allow the polygamous marriage. The law also stipulated that the consent of the first wife is mandatory for these marriages.

The Law of 188 also legislated sexual equality concerning cases of inheritance, a serious departure from the religious rules, *Shari'a*, which state that a woman is entitled to only half of the share of a man. The age of marriage was raised to 18 although a judge can also agree to a marriage by the age of 15. The consent of the girl to the marriage became mandatory. It stated that a marriage should always be documented in a court and punished those who conducted a marriage outside the court system. Forced marriages were not allowed, and offenders were criminalized. The legislation also ended the so-called *nahwa*, a prevalent tradition in rural areas that gives a male a right of priority to marry his female first cousin and allows him to even prevent her from marrying someone else if he desires to marry her. The law put restrictions on arbitrary divorce and the unilateral right of the male to divorce, and it made it easier for women to request a divorce. It also allowed voluntary separation and the so-called *khula'*, where the husband agrees to divorce his wife in exchange for financial compensation.

This legislation granted the right to alimony for divorced women to a maximum of two years. A later amendment gave her the right to keep the accommodation. The Law of 188 also gave priority to the mother in child custody cases. A later amendment made this priority valid even if the mother remarries. It stipulated that the stepfather should treat the children of his wife from an earlier marriage fairly and, should he fail to do so, the wife has the right to divorce him. The law also stated that, if the original father of a child dies, his immediate family is not allowed to demand custody of the child if the mother is fit to take care of the child. This issue remains a serious problem in family laws in the region.

Despite its shortcomings, the Law of 188 was considered one of the most progressive family laws in the Middle East. Susskind argues: "The 1959 law is not secular. Much of it is rooted in *Sharia*, but the code represents a liberal, as opposed to reactionary, interpretation of Koranic law. The law also helped mediate against sectarianism by synthesizing Shiite and Sunni interpretations of Koranic law into one code that was applied to all citizens regardless of sect. Thus, though the 1959 law utilized *Sharia* to adjudicate personal and family matters, it did so in a secular manner."[15] This law has opened up public life for the participation of women. Naziha al-Dulaimi became a minister of municipalities, the first woman cabinet member in the Arab world. In 1959, Zakia Hakki became the first female judge in Iraq, and perhaps the first in the Arab world.

After widespread suffering from decades of violence, wars, and sanctions, Iraqi women are expecting improvements in their situation. Iraqi women have expected that the liberal family code of the Law of 88 will further be liberalized to provide them with more, not fewer, rights. However, new Iraq has brought a great disappointment. The ascent to power of religious parties signaled a serious reversal in the situation of women.

To be sure, the disappointment started much earlier. Efforts to draft a family law were made in the second half of the 1940s, yet the resistance of the religious leaders, the *Ulama*, has prevented these efforts from materializing. The religious authorities, particularly the Shiite, raised serious protest against the Law of 188 immediately after endorsement. The objection centered particularly on the issues of a unified code for all Muslims without making a distinction between sects, sexual equality in inheritance, unified and higher age for marriage, and restrictions on polygamy. One of the senior members of the newly established Iraqi Governing Council (IGC), the cleric Muhammad Bahr al-Ulum, had as early as 1963 written a legal treatise condemning the personal status law.[16]

The influential Shiite ayatollah Muhsin al-Hakim was a staunch opponent of the law and called for its abrogation. Luizard points out that al-Hakim "opposed the attempt by central government to diminish further the *mujtahids'* [clerics] influence on sensitive issues such as matrimonial and family law. The promulgation of the Personal Status Code was received in Najaf with dismay, even by the well-established and apolitical *'ulama* such as Hakim, who played a paramount role in the opposition to Qassim's code."[17] Susskind elaborates on this religious resistance to the law by stating that another, less publicized though perhaps more germane Islamist grievance is that the 1959 law "transferred power from Islamic clerics to the state. Prior to 1959, family law was interpreted by individual religious judges, giving clerics great influence over people's lives. The 1959 law removed that authority. It limited the role of judges to applying the law and ended clerics' control of personal status courts by absorbing these courts into a national judicial system under the authority of the state."[18] Because of these pressures from the religious authorities, the new regime that came to power through a military coup in 1963 amended the law by annulling the sexual parity in cases of inheritance.

However, in new Iraq and barely a few months after the downfall of the old regime, the son of Muhsin, Abdul Aziz al-Hakim, the then head of the Islamic Supreme Council of Iraq (ISCI) used his turn in the monthly rotating presidency of the IGC, in December 2003, to issue a new resolution, so-called Decree 137, concerning personal and family status. The timing was perfect as many of the IGC members were not present due to the holidays at the end of December. The resolution did not profit from sufficient deliberations inside the governing council and was issued without the benefit of popular discussions outside the council. The new resolution basically deprives women of their previously won rights since it stipulates the application of the *Shari'a*, and the annulment of all contradicting laws, particularly the Law of 188.

An Iraqi lawyer commented on this new legislation: "This resolution will send us back home and keeps us behind closed doors, in a similar way to what happened to women in Afghanistan under the rule of the Taliban."[19] However, al-Hakim defended his decision by declaring that the new legislation respects all sects in Iraq and that this goes well with freedom of religion in contrast to the old legislation, which was dictating to people how to conduct their personal affairs. Nonetheless, thanks to the strong opposition from women's organizations, which were still active before the rise of religious militias, and American intervention, this proposal did not come into existence. The key question remains: why political Shiism prioritized this particular issue of women when the country confronted a depressing legacy of severe problems on multiple fronts.

Nevertheless, the victory of women in repelling Decree 137 did not last very long; the infamous decree has actually been resurrected in the new permanent constitution. Shiite political parties emerged triumphant in the January 2005 election, a natural outcome of the Shiite demographic prevalence and the ethno-sectarian focus of this election. Empowered by electoral success, the Islamists were successful in institutionalizing the previously aborted resolution in the drafting of the new constitution of Iraq. Article 41 of the constitution reads: "Iraqis are free in their commitment to their personal status according to their religious, sects, beliefs, or choices, and this shall be regulated by law."[20] Thus the constitution states that personal and family matters should be under the jurisdiction of religious laws applicable to any particular community.

In reality, this represents a major reversal in the status of Iraqi women and the abrogation of one of the most progressive family laws in the Middle East, which had been effective in the country since 1959. Brown raises the question: "If individuals may choose among different codes or laws, what will happen when litigants disagree over the law to be applied? Will 'forum shopping'—in which, for instance, a Sunni temporarily becomes Shiite to escape alimony or allow his daughters to inherit a more generous share—be allowed?"[21] He continues to comment: "It should be noted that it was precisely these sorts of problems that led many Arab states to adopt uniform codes and unified court systems for matters of personal status in the first place. From a religious standpoint, this was state encroachment on religious freedom, but from an official standpoint, a decentralized system seemed chaotic and confusing."[22] In support of this argument, we should bear in mind that the Law of 188 proclaims the following reason for its enactment: "Multiple sources of legislations and different legal provisions make unstable family and unguaranteed individual rights, and therefore is the legislation of this unified code of personal status."[23]

The new constitution of Iraq is a very controversial document. On the one hand, Article 2 pronounces that Islam is the official religion of the state and a foundation source of legislation, and that no law may be enacted that contradicts the established provisions of Islam. On the other hand, the same article also proclaims that no law may be enacted that contradicts the principles of democracy. Article 14 asserts that Iraqis are equal before the law without discrimination based on gender and the like, while Article 16 affirms that equal opportunities shall be guaranteed to all Iraqis. It is astonishing how the drafting of a document that is supposed to be the anchor for new Iraq has been allowed to contain so many contradictory and conflicting statements.

As with many other religions, Islam does not prescribe equality, definitely not gender equality, yet gender equality is a fundamental principle of democracy. A constitution that elevates provisions of Islam, no matter how these provisions are defined, and sets down the religionization of society cannot guarantee sexual equality before the law or equal opportunities. Moreover, Article 29 states: "The family is the foundation of society; the state shall preserve it and its religious, moral, and national values." Apart from the controversial and highly significant issue of the individual versus the family, the document is vague on what these values are and who actually decides in this matter.

Democracy is based on individual rights and choices, whereas the constitution stresses religious and sectarian rights and choices, which are not necessarily a guarantee to individual rights. Al-Ali and Pratt underline: "In the process of creating a post-Ba'th Iraq, family law became part of a 'social contract' that traded communal autonomy for women's rights. In this way, the constitution weakened women's citizenship rights while strengthening the significance of ethnic and sectarian 'communities' within the political-legal system."[24] Brown, on the other hand, observes that in the constitution, personal status issues are addressed in the chapter on "rights and freedoms," a rather telling choice, "for the Shiite religious parties that dominated the drafting process, the issue of personal status law is understood as one of religious freedom."[25]

Within identity politics, which dominates the political process in new Iraq, extending ethnic and religious rights to the individual level is not a straightforward issue. On the contrary, individual rights are often sacrificed in identity politics that mostly benefits the leaders of various communities. A women's rights activist, however, categorically dismisses the talk about freedom of choice as mockery of women. "There will be no choices for women if a man makes a decision that he wants to live a certain way. Step by step, we will end up in a religious state."[26] The claim that women are free to choose any religious law does not necessarily make the constitution a democratic document. Apart from the fact that this issue will further split society, which is already deeply divided, religious laws, written centuries ago, fail to reflect the basic human rights standards achieved by humanity since then and cannot, therefore, guarantee the rights of woman, regardless of which religious law is applied.

Nonetheless, the constitution also contains several positive provisions. Anyone who is born to an Iraqi father or to an Iraqi mother shall be considered an Iraqi (Article 18). This is a good provision considering that the right of the mother to confer citizenship rights to her children is still a problem in the Middle East, particularly for women marrying foreigners. All forms of violence and abuse in the family, school, and society shall be prohibited (Article 29). Iraqi citizens, men and women, shall have the right to participate in public affairs and to enjoy political rights including the right to vote, elect, and run for office (Article 20).

More tangibly, the constitution recommends that the election law should aim to achieve a quota of no less than 25 percent of representation for women in parliament (Article 29). While this recommendation is a positive achievement for women, it is still a controversial issue. During the drafting process, the Islamists rejected the principle of a special quota for women on the ground that this provision contradicts equality of men and women before God enshrined in the Qur'an. The claimed equality, however, is merely a spiritual equality not supported by tangible reality. Anyway, affirmative action in favor of women is observed in even more-advanced countries where women enjoy much higher status. The 25 percent quota was actually a compromise solution since the secularists demanded a much higher quota.

The specific quota for women in parliament secures the participation of women in politics. However, this raises several important issues. A few selected women are empowered to occupy the highest levels of politics within a contrary context where the majority of women in Iraq are disempowered and/or not empowered. The disempowerment of women is unfortunately enshrined in the constitution, and is enforced by the religious agenda of Islamizing the Iraqi society. Under these circumstances, the quota for women in parliament is an elitist solution that makes sense only within the politics of identity. Democracy, on the other hand, means ensuring human rights for women, gender equality, and the empowerment of all women, and not only a few women elites. Furthermore, the overall effectiveness of the participation of women, and even men for that matter, ultimately depends on the effectiveness of the national assembly itself and its role in the political process. A parliament that is controlled from the outside by leaders of the dominant political parties will not allow much room for legislators, men and women alike.

A quarter of parliament being dominated mainly by women who are indoctrinated by the conservative interpretation of Islam, the superiority of men and inferiority of women, and gender inequality does not automatically make the political process in Iraq more democratic and would certainly prove harmful to the empowerment of women in the long run. Most of these women come from dominant religious parties that are averse to gender equality and women emancipation.

To make matters worse, most of these "elected" women are staunch advocates of the patriarchal and misogynist ideologies that counteract efforts to elevate the status of women. A parliamentary woman states publicly: "I much prefer the Sharia for personal issues. I am very afraid of language saying men and women are equal."[27]

During the debate in the legislative assembly in 2008 on the security accord with the United States, one of the female legislators who opposed the agreement invited her male colleagues in parliament who consented to the agreement to wear *abay'a*, a long black women's dress in Iraq, instead of their manly dress.[28] This clearly shows that the degradation of women is not necessarily exclusive to men; many women share this patriarchal conviction about their very own inferiority. This is also a clear indication that women in politics can be very counterproductive as far as the emancipation of women is concerned. Some of them are even more staunch advocates of the vindictive politics of uprooting the Ba'thists, thereby contributing to more violence in society.

The infringement on women's rights by political Islam is not only enshrined in the constitution but also enforced on the daily life of women in Iraq. The country has witnessed a campaign of violence and intimidation against women, and indeed even men. In the name of religion, the religious Shiite militias that dominated the streets of Iraq after 2003 led an agenda of imposing a certain way of life on Iraqi citizens. Fanatic militias and organized crime created a climate of fear in the streets of Baghdad, and the rest of Iraq, as sexual violence and abduction of women and girls was on the rise in the aftermath of regime change in 2003, according to the HRW.[29]

Basra, the second-largest city in Iraq, which is religiously mixed and known to be a tolerant community, became practically under the rule of Shiite militias and organized gangs well until the middle of 2008. In an imitation of a Taliban-style Islamism, these militias strictly forbade music, theater, cinemas, certain styles of hairdressing, and the selling of alcohol. They also imposed a strict and rigid moral code and the veil on all women, including non-Muslim minorities. The imposition of this code was done in a most ruthless and violent way. A graffiti warning message in the city center reads: "Your makeup and your decision to forego the headscarf will bring you death."[30]

Women, Muslim or non-Muslim, were killed on sight for not abiding by the newly enforced dress code. The Basra police commander admits: "There are gangs roaming through the streets, pursuing women and carrying out threats and killing because of what the women wear or because they are using makeup."[31] According to official figures, at least 10 women are killed every month. Another source reports that 133 women were killed in Basra alone during the year 2007 for "violating Islamic teaching"; some of them are later found in garbage dumps with bullet holes while others are found decapitated or mutilated.[32]

However, the number of women killed by violence is much higher since many crimes against women go unreported either because of fear of reprisal by religious militias or because of perceived feelings of shame and violated honor brought to these families by the murdered women. The fanatics who rule the streets in the name of Islam do not realize how harmful and counterproductive the rule of terror is that they try to impose on women. This is reflected in what a high school Iraqi girl from Basra said: "I hate Islam and all the clerics because they limit our freedom every day and their instruction became heavy on us. Most of the girls in my high school hate that Islamic people control the authority because they don't deserve to be rulers."[33]

Political Islam is obsessed with issues concerning women, and the Islamists of Iraq are no exception. The Islamists focus on the politics of identity, and women are central to their ideology. As a marker of Islamic identity, women are elevated in this identity politics to a level of obsession. Whereas the domination of the deposed regime over society is a secular domination, the domination of Islamist parties takes a religious aspect in which gender has utmost significance. Right from the beginning of the new regime, Shiite parties made it clear that they have an agenda of Islamizing the Iraqi society—where women will surely pay a high price. The Islamization of society is enforced through government policies. For instance, the minister of education, one from the Da'wa Shiite religious party, is encouraging a policy of gender separation in elementary schooling, which is the only stage of coeducation prior to higher education. The parliamentary committee on education has already affirmed the legality of this policy. This kind of policies attempt to create a de facto system of gender apartheid in Iraq, which indubitably affects the psychological development of children and leads to potential adverse and severe consequences for society.[34]

The ceremony to install the first female judge in the Shiite city of Najaf was indefinitely postponed due to a fierce opposition from lawyers and religious clerics. The opponents presented three religious edicts, *fatwas*, including one from Grand Ayatollah Sistani, the most revered Shiite cleric, declaring that judges have to be mature, sane, and masculine. One of the protesting lawyers, a female, argues that women cannot be a judge because they are always ruled by their emotions. "We refuse the appointment of a woman judge, because it contradicts Islamic law. This is what the Americans wanted to achieve in the first place with their invasion, to undermine Islam."[35] On the other hand, Nidhal Nasser Hussein, who is the first female lawyer in the city and aspires to become a family court judge, disagrees by stressing that nothing in Iraq's legal code bars women from serving as judges and that the religious establishment would just have to learn to live with it. "There were demonstrations against the first elementary schools for women, too, but everything needs a beginning."[36]

Today, Iraq is ruled by an alliance between religious Shiite parties and secular Kurdish parties. Although the Kurdish parties do not share the agenda of the Shiites in Islamizing society, they nevertheless go along with this agenda. In return, they secure concessions regarding their nationalist agenda from the Shiite parties. Additionally, the Kurdish parties are not serious about counteracting the intention of the Shiites to degrade women in Iraq because they intend to ensure that Iraqi Kurdistan will be shielded from such an agenda. What applies in Iraq is not necessarily applicable to the north of the country. This is sanctioned by the constitutional provision stating that laws enacted by regional governments override federal law. We therefore have an unholy alliance of Islamist and nationalist agendas, where there is nothing in common but the desire to dominate the spoils of new Iraq, and a sense of victimhood. This alliance comes at the expense of women.

In spite of their achievements, particularly since 1959, women in Iraq are still degraded and considered second-class citizens, not unlike the situation of women in the rest of the Middle East. A sociological study on Iraqi women conducted in the early 1980s concludes that most of the interviewed women were unhappy in marriage life.[37] One might anticipate that unhappy marriages would have increased since then due to wars, sanctions, and violence. In a survey conducted by Women for Women International in 2004, 94 percent of the women in Iraq's three biggest provinces said they want to protect their legal rights in the new constitution, whether the framework is religious or secular.[38]

Consequently, Iraqi women highly expect that new Iraq will deliver them justice after long decades of suffering. However, in new Iraq, the situation is worsened and the status of women is further degraded. The unified and tolerant Law of 188 helped transcend the sectarian divide in the country to the extent that about 30 percent of Muslim marriages are mixed marriages between Sunnis and Shiites, particularly in Baghdad. Hence, the abrogation of this law seems to fit the agenda of imposing political sectarianism on a society known for tolerating cross-sectarian marriages. This sectarianism enforces the control of sects over their women who are the first victims of the lawlessness that is associated with political sectarianism, the sectarian divide, and religious animosity.

It is noteworthy that the constitutionally sanctioned reversal in the situation of women is marked by big words: "equality," "democracy," and "human rights." These words, however, no matter how appealing they may be, are bereft of reality. After all, the Middle East does not suffer from the absence of constitutions that seem nice and democratic on paper, but are harsh and authoritarian in reality. If the Iraqi society is serious about building a peaceful and tolerant society, gender relations must be given utmost importance. The dominant cultural values of shame and honor lead not only to violent gender relations but also to the overall violence in society and the authoritarian order. A forward-looking society should prioritize the issues of violence, injustice, and inequality that dominate the structure of gender relations. Assuming that the status of women is one of the most important indicators measuring the progress of any nation, then a society that continues to debase women is certainly a society not moving toward democracy, tolerance, and prosperity.

The 1959 legislation that helped advance the status of women was initiated under a military dictatorship. With a few exceptions, subsequent dictators kept this achievement intact and even made some improvements. Iraqi women won the right to vote rather later, in 1980, under the ruthless regime of Saddam Hussein. It is a sheer irony that women advanced their rights under authoritarian regime and are losing them under democracy! As far as women are concerned, old Iraq is much better than the newly constructed Iraq. Looking at the photograph of her mother from the 1960s, an Iraqi woman shook her head and indignantly commented: "I can't wear what my mother was wearing at that time. It's really sad. Women had better conditions then. Now, they are challenged every day."[39] If new Iraq is determined to disappoint about 60 percent of its population, a demographic reality due to wars and violence, then we have a truly new Iraq, a new Iraq facing regression.

NOTES

1. HRW, "On Vulnerable Ground: Violence against Minority Communities in Nineveh Province's Disputed Territories," November 10, 2009, 5, http://www.hrw.org/sites/default/files/reports/iraq1109webwcover.pdf.

2. Ibid., 9.

3. Steven Lee Myers, "In Northern Iraq, a Vote Seems Likely to Split," *New York Times*, February 9, 2010.

4. Patrick J. McDonnell, "After Years of Relative Peace, Christians Live in Fear," *Los Angeles Times*, November 14, 2004.

5. UN Office for the Coordination of Humanitarian Affairs (IRIN), "Iraq: Extremists Fuel Anti-Women Violence in Basra," November 26, 2007, http://www.irinnews.org/rerport.aspx?ReortId=75396.

6. Peter Tachell, "Sexual Cleansing in Iraq," *The Guardian*, September 25, 2008.

7. Sami Zubaida, "Contested Nations: Iraq and the Assyrians," *Nations and Nationalism* 6, no. 3 (2000): 370.

8. Reeva Spector Simon, *Iraq between the Two World Wars: The Militarist Origins of Tyranny* Updated version (New York: Columbia University Press, 2004), 147.

9. Moshe Gat, *The Jewish Exodus from Iraq 1948–1951* (London: Frank Cass, 1997), 21.

10. Zubaida, "Contested Nations," 379.

11. Ur News Agency, "Archeology Authorities Start a Campaign to Eradicate Jewish Markings at the Tomb of the Prophet Ezekiel," December 23, 2009, http://www.uragency.net/index.php?aa=news&id22=3450.

12. David McDowall, *A Modern History of the Kurds*, 3rd ed. (London: Tauris, 2004), 305.

13. Hanna Batatu, *The Old Social Classes and the Revolutionary Movement of Iraq: A Study of Iraq's Old Landed and Commercial Classes and of Its Communists, Ba'thists and Free Officers* (London: Saqi, 2004), 912.

14. Ibid., 918.

15. Yifat Susskind, "Promising Democracy, Imposing Theocracy: Gender-Based Violence and the US War on Iraq," March 2007, 5, http://www.madre.org/index.php?s=9&b=248p=86.

16. Noah Feldman, *What We Owe Iraq: War and the Ethic of Nation Building* (Princeton, NJ: Princeton University Press, 2004), 109.

17. Pierre-Jean Luizard, "The Nature of Confrontation between the State and *Marja'ism*: Grand Ayatollah Muhsin al-Hakim and the Ba'th," in *Ayatollahs, Sufis and Ideologues: State, Religion and Social Movements in Iraq*, ed. Faleh Abdul-Jabar (London: Saqi, 2002), 92.

18. Susskind, "Promising Democracy," 6.

19. Pamela Constable, "Women in Iraq Decry Decision to Curb Rights," *Washington Post*, January 16, 2004.

20. An English version of the Iraqi Constitution can be found at http://www.uniraq.org/documents/iraqi_constitution1.pdf.

21. Nathan J. Brown, "The Final Draft of the Iraqi Constitution: Analysis and Commentary," Carnegie Endowment for International Peace, September 2005, 7, http://www.carnegieendowment.org/files/FinalDraftofIraqi Constitution1.pdf.

22. Ibid.

23. Faleh A. Jabar and Hisham Dawood, eds., *Naqd al-dustur* [A Critique to the Constitution]. (Baghdad and Beirut: Publications of Iraq Institute for Strategic Studies, 2006), 116.

24. Nadje al-Ali and Nicola Pratt, *What Kind of Liberation? Women and the Occupation of Iraq* (Berkeley: University of California Press, 2009), 115.

25. Brown, "The Final Draft," 6.

26. Tina Susman, "Iraqis Divided by Constitution's Treatment of Women," *Los Angeles Times*, October 9, 2007.

27. Alissa J. Rubin and Asmaa Waguih, "Fighting to Preserve Women's Rights in Iraq," *Los Angeles Times*, August 7, 2005.

28. Al-Rafidayn.com, "Legislators against the Security Accord with the US," November 27, 2008, http://www.alrafidayn.com/Story/News/02_12_10.html.

29. HRW, "Climate of Fear: Sexual Violence and Abduction of Women and Girls in Baghdad," July 2003, http://www.hrw.org/en/reports/2003/07/15/climate-fear.

30. IRIN, "Iraq: Islamic Extremists Target Women in Basra," January 2, 2008, http://www.irinnews.org/Report.aspx?ReortId=76065.

31. Susman, "Iraqis Divided."

32. Susman, "Iraqis Divided"; IRIN, "Iraq: Islamic Extremists."

33. Sabrina Tavernise, "Violence Leaves Iraqis Doubting Clerics," *New York Times*, March 4, 2008.

34. For the psychological impacts of gender segregation see, for instance, David Ghanim, *Gender and Violence in the Middle East* (Westport, CT: Praeger, 2009), particularly chapter 5.

35. Neil MacFarquhar, "In Najaf, Justice Can Be Blind but Not Female," *New York Times*, July 31, 2003.

36. Ibid.

37. Sana al-Khayyat, *Honour and Shame: Women in Modern Iraq* (London: Saqi, 1990), 207.

38. Zinab Salbi, "Women's Rights and Islamic Law in the New Iraq Constitution," *Huffington Post*, August 1, 2005.

39. Rubin and Waguih, "Fighting to Preserve."

4

De-Ba'thification and Politics of Exclusion

DE-BA'THIFYING IRAQI SOCIETY

The Ba'th Party was initially founded in Syria in 1947 while its Iraqi branch was formed in the early 1950s. This secular nationalist party was inspired by the fascist Nazi ideology and the German kind of nationalism stressing animosity against foreigners. It believes in the unification of all Arab countries in one nation, under the leadership of the Ba'th, "One Arab Nation with an Eternal Message." The stated principles of this party are unity, freedom, and socialism. Nevertheless, these principles are merely rhetorical slogans that have not been respected by the very two experiences of the Ba'thist rule—those in Syria and Iraq. The long and bitter animosity between the same Ba'thist regimes in these two countries fails to lend support to the declared principle of unity. The Ba'thist perception of the principle of freedom is never intended to be in the sense of democracy and human rights but merely freedom from foreign interests and control. The principle of socialism has meant in reality the monopolization of power and wealth of the nation in the hands of the ruling family and the few loyal elites. The Ba'th ruled Iraq for more than three decades through the utmost violence and intimidation.

The Coalition Provisional Authority (CPA) was established on April 21, 2003, as a transitional government following the invasion of Iraq, and was dissolved on June 28, 2004, because of the transfer of sovereignty to the Iraqis. It was empowered with executive, legislative, and judicial authority during its working period. The very first action of this ruling authority was order number one, entitled

"De-Ba'thification of Iraqi Society," signed by Paul Bremer, CPA administrator, on May 16, 2003. This order declared the disestablishment of the Ba'th Party by eliminating the party's structures and removing its leadership from positions of authority and responsibility in Iraqi society. Senior Ba'th Party members holding the top four ranks—Regional Command, *Qiyyada Qutriyya*; Branch, *Far'*; Section, *Shu'ba*; and Group, *Firqa*—were removed from their positions and banned from future employment in the public sector. The order also stated that individuals holding positions in the top three layers of management in every national government ministry, affiliated corporations, and other government institutions, such as universities and hospitals, should be removed from employment if they proved to be full members of the Ba'th Party.[1]

This action was soon supplemented by yet another controversial and highly destructive order to the integrity and functionality of the Iraqi state, order number two, entitled "Dissolution of Entities," which was signed by the CPA on May 23, 2003, and aimed at disbanding the Iraqi military, security, and intelligence infrastructure of the discredited regime.[2] This was followed by another CPA order, order number five, entitled "The Establishment of the Iraqi De-Ba'thification Council," signed on May 25, 2003. The main objectives of this act was to investigate the most efficient and equitable means of eliminating the structure and methods of intimidation and patronage of the Iraqi Ba'th Party; the methods of identifying the Ba'th Party officials and members; and the means of reclaiming the Ba'th Party property and assets.[3] With these orders, the one-party rule in Iraq was over, the Ba'th Party was dissolved, and the process of de-Ba'athification was set in motion.

The new Iraqi ruling elites played an influential role in issuing these orders. The transfer of authority to the Iraqis and the formation of the Iraqi Governing Council (IGC) have accelerated the process of de-Ba'athification. The IGC established a special commission for this purpose, the Supreme National Commission for De-Ba'thification (SNCD), headed by Ahmad Chalabi who favors a thorough purging of the Ba'thists. In September 2003, the commission put into effect the orders regarding the discharge and interdiction of senior Ba'thists from positions of authority in state institutions.[4]

One million documents were made available to the commission to scrutinize the records of the Ba'thists. The new commission contains a section for education and culture to deal with the Ba'thist legacy in these domains, particularly educational curricula. It also contains a legal section for cases of appeal. The official site of the commission states that it works for the following targets: Ba'th Party prominent officials should be removed from of their positions in the public sector; all the resolved Ba'th Party remnants and vestiges must be removed from life and society; the Ba'th Party cadre should be rehabilitated by adopting new democratic ideas like respect for human rights and public opinion, and rejection of the "old and queer ideas."[5]

The commission defines de-Ba'thification as the "uprooting of morality, politics, and applications of the defeated Ba'ath Party from the Iraqi society." The commission works for the rehabilitation and enlightenment of the Ba'thists and reintegrating them into the new Iraqi society "as good, suitable, organs of society respecting democracy, freedom, justice, equality, supremacy of law, and human rights working in the necessary transparency and integrity for reconstruction of the new civilized Iraqi society."[6]

It is difficult to know exactly the number of people affected by these orders but the official site of the commission gives a figure of 60,000 Ba'thists, of which 80 percent (i.e., the rank of Group in the Ba'th Party membership) have the right to appeal.[7] Another source claims that an estimated 150,000 senior civil servants, lecturers, teachers, health professionals, and managers were flung from their jobs due to Ba'thist membership between May and September 2003. This source also states that it was reported that 28,000 teachers were sacked in 2003 alone.[8]

However, the large number of people affected by these measures, the increase of violence and resistance to the new regime and American occupation of Iraq, the aggravated sectarian strife, the rhetoric of national reconciliation that is often repeated by the ruling elites, let alone American pressures, all contributed to a reconsideration of the process of de-Ba'thification. This has resulted in new legislation, the Accountability and Justice Act (*qanun al-musa'ala wa al-adala*), which was passed in parliament (only 140 out of 275 members were present) on January 12, 2008. This act proclaims that the old commission would be dissolved and a new commission, named the Commission for Accountability and Justice, should be established on a power-sharing basis. Nevertheless, this commission did not come into existence when the parliament failed to approve the move of the Prime Minister Maliki of nominating one of the leaders of his party to the position of the head of the commission. However, the new act emphasizes that the new commission should aim to realize the following objectives:

1. Prevent the return of the Ba'th Party to power or to the public life in Iraq whether in its ideas, culture, administration, policies, or acts under any name.
2. Cleanse state institutions, mixed-sector institutions, civil society institutions, and Iraqi society from any form of the Ba'th Party system.
3. Refer any member of the dissolved Ba'th Party and repressive agencies who is incriminated through investigations of committing criminal acts against the Iraqi people to the competent courts to be fairly dealt with.
4. Enable the victims of the dissolved Ba'th Party and the repressive agencies to claim compensation for the damages that have resulted from such crimes.
5. Participate in revealing the assets that were illegally seized by elements of the former regime whether inside or outside the country and return them back to the public treasury.
6. Serve the Iraqi memory by documenting all of the crimes and illegal practices committed by members of the Ba'th Party and its repressive agencies and provide a database regarding those elements in order to strengthen the future generations against falling into oppression, tyranny, and repression.[9]

The new act is both a continuation of the old legislation regarding de-Ba'thification and an introduction of some changes, both positive and negative, from the previous act. Article 11 of this act insists that the dissolved Ba'th Party shall be prosecuted as a party and a system for committing crimes against the Iraqi people. Articles 2 and 15, on the other hand, stress that all persons implicated by the act shall have the right to appeal against the decisions of the commission before the Cassation Chamber for Accountability and Justice, to be formed in the court of cassation, which will be comprised of seven judges nominated by the Higher Judicial Council and ratified by the Council of Representatives. The fact that all cases would now be subject to an independent judicial review is a serious improvement on the old practices wherein decisions by the old commission had been final. The new act opens the door for the rank of Group Membership in the Ba'th Party, estimated to be around 38,000, to be reinstated in government positions. Group Membership is not an influential rank in the Ba'thist hierarchy; it is only one degree above ordinary members of the party. Group members had relatively little power and were often promoted merely for attending rallies or performing well at work.

However, a study with the aim of evaluating this act conducted by Sissons, on behalf of the International Center for Transitional Justice (ICTJ), clearly shows a continuation of major shortcomings. Some of the serious negative aspects of this act are: while the act introduces elements of individual responsibility, it continues a system that is largely based on guilt by association; like the previous legislation, the new act does not set a time limit for the process or a deadline to complete the work; although the act is a major improvement by allowing the rank of Group Members to be reinstated in governmental posts, this enhancement is actually impaired by several restrictions and exceptions; the new act essentially preserves the same system of de-Ba'thification (objectives, staff, and structure), and the commission, which was widely criticized as secretive, all-powerful, and manipulative, is renamed rather than dissolved; the new act also strengthens the Commission's power and extends its reach to a number of organizations not previously affected, including the Iraqi judiciary. However, on the positive side, the study indicates that the creation of independent appeals mechanism is an innovation; pension rights are clarified and expanded to include the Section Membership of the Ba'th Party, a degree above the Group Membership and estimated to involve about 7,000–8,000 members. The study concludes that the new law establishes a clearer legal framework for dismissals and reinstatements and that it contains a number of significant improvements compared to the previous procedures, but many of the shortcomings of the previous system and the commission remain.[10]

Several others have also criticized the new legislation. Judge Juhi, known for indicting Saddam in 2004, expressed the need for more transparency within the workings of the commission to reduce corruption and inaccuracies. He also emphasized the need to create deadlines; otherwise it will no longer be considered transitional justice, and "there can't be transitional justice forever."[11] Others have criticized the fact that there is hardly a consensus on this legislation since only half of the number of legislators was present when it was approved in parliament. Some argue that expanding pension rights to more Ba'thists is in fact a kind of systemic purge of the previous top officials, who were mostly sent into retirement and thus denied active role in the public sphere. This legislation, however, denies any pensions for members of the Ba'th Party who continued to be members after the regime change in 2003.

Although Group Members, which is a simple rank in the Ba'thist hierarchy, were allowed back into government, they were kept out of the top presidential posts—the presidential council, prime minister,

head of parliament—and the supreme judicial council, security ministries and agencies, and ministries of foreign affairs and finance. Additionally, this reinstatement is limited by the fact that ministries are
distributed among the ruling political forces through a system of
power sharing that excludes the former ruling bureaucrats. Moreover,
the return of the Ba'thists can even prove to be harmful because it
helps to locate them easily, a risky outcome when militias and politics
of vengeance are dominant. A former education ministry bureaucrat
told the Associated Press: "This law is meaningless to me because
I cannot work again in a ministry controlled by Shiite parties and militias . . . I prefer to stay at home living the rest of my life in peace rather
than getting killed while heading to work."[12]

The process of de-Ba'thification is also enshrined in the new
constitution. Article 7 of the constitution prohibits the presence of
"Saddamist Ba'th" in political life and calls for the uprooting of Ba'thism as thought and practice; while Article 135 prohibits Ba'thists from
holding sensitive positions in the government and declares that the
SNCD is an independent commission under the supervision of
parliament.[13] The constitution also stipulates that the provision on
the eradication of the Ba'th should be reconsidered only after two elections have elapsed, that is, eight years after the endorsement of the
constitution. Even so, the move should be supported by popular referendum, with the consent of the absolute majority in parliament, and
only with the approval of the presidential council, or the president.
Nonetheless, it is noteworthy that while Article 7 of the constitution
criminalizes not only Ba'thism but also sectarianism, political sectarianism is in reality allowed and it dominates the current political system. Selectiveness in using convenient constitutional provisions for
political expediency is apparent.

The new political order in Iraq has institutionalized a divisive and
destabilizing constitution that includes fundamental contradictions,
among which is the process of de-Ba'thification that contradicts the
principle of equality of all citizens, regardless of their religion, ethnicity, or opinion. This conflict between different provisions poses a serious contradiction, which is not isolated from the many problems
created by this contentious constitution. Taking advantage of the
clearly stated constitutional provisions concerning de-Ba'thification,
many dominant politicians have argued that reconciliation with the
Ba'thists is against the constitution, a charter that should be respected
because it has been approved by the people. This clearly shows that
what has actually been approved by the Iraqis is merely a constitution

for the victors. It has been used by the new ruling elites as a pretext for obstructing the much needed reconciliation and for a serious reconsideration of the politics of uprooting the Ba'athists.

Thus the de-Ba'thification campaign finds a "legitimate" basis in the country's constitution. This charter provides for the eradication of the Ba'thism in thought and practice. If Ba'thist practices are considered violent and authoritarian, and have no place in a democratic political life, then de-Ba'thification is not only understandable but also desirable. However, the charter should have condemned these practices in general terms and not necessarily with specific reference to the Ba'thists. After all, these practices are part of the dominant political culture and are common to all political parties, including the ones that drafted the constitution.

Nevertheless, condemning practices is one thing and condemning or calling for the eradication of a thought is quite another. The criminalization of thoughts is a serious issue that is neither helpful nor sensible in a democratic system. Generally speaking, thoughts are not necessarily responsible for actions. Ba'thist thoughts are primarily nationalistic, and nationalism, particularly Kurdish nationalism, is part of the current Iraqi political system. At this point, one should note that sectarian thoughts and practices that have come to dominate the new experience in Iraq are no better than nationalist thoughts.

Provisions on uprooting the Ba'thists make the constitution an exclusive charter, which is hardly characteristic of democratic and inclusive processes. The constitution that is supposed to replace the politics of exclusion in the old regime seems to fall into the same trap under different contexts. The constitution, as an ultimate authority in the country, should reflect inclusiveness. Hence, the exclusionary provisions exist as paradoxes in the democratic charter. The negation of the Other, which comes from both sides, does not work to build a democratic and tolerant system. Amidst de-Ba'thification, the Ba'thists also fail to recognize the current political process and the ruling government. Meanwhile, a sweeping lustration process of limiting the participation of former bureaucrats in the new administration tends to reinforce hard-line positions.

LUSTRATION AND HUMAN RIGHTS

Many societies emerging from a horrible past preceded Iraq in confronting the problem of how to deal with abusers of human rights. Germany and Japan in the aftermath of their defeat in the World War II faced the conflict between the need for lustration on the one hand and the need for technocrats to reconstruct their devastated countries on the other. The new government in Germany was forced to use the service of thousands of ex-Nazis not only for their technocratic talents, which were deemed to be of absolute necessity for the revival of the country, but also for the belief that marginalizing these people would lead to the reemergence of the new Nazis. Similar problems were also faced in South America after the downfall of the authoritarian regimes, and in Eastern Europe, after the demise of the Communist regimes. In former Communist countries, whole bureaucracies were left intact to avoid anarchy and smooth the transition to a new system. The need to reemploy the ex-bureaucrats in the rebuilding efforts instigated this acrimonious comment by Ian Buruma: "Unscrupulous operators, who thrive in dictatorships, have a disturbing knack of surviving the wreckage when dictators fall, and of thriving, just as unscrupulously, under new regimes."[14] However, the survival of the technocrats is a much more complex issue than just the smartness or the dishonesty of these people.

Governance must differentiate between the state and the government—a distinction that seems blurred and overlooked. State bureaucracy is supposed to be a durable, depoliticized, and distinct realm from the constantly changing and highly politicized government. Authoritarian politics, however, tends to subjugate state bureaucracy to the politicized agenda of the government, to an extent that the government and the state become conflated. The Iraqi experience shows that there is a huge price to pay for confusing the boundaries between these two categories. First, after the dramatic regime change in 2003, the country has witnessed the collapse not only of the government of Saddam Hussein but also of the entire Iraqi state, which is supposed to survive changes in governments. Second, the demobilization of the army, in addition to de-Ba'thification and the disqualification of former bureaucratic elites from political participation, largely contributed to anarchy, violence, and the lack of basic services, hence further weakening the functionality of the Iraqi state.

The deterioration in the efficiency of the state, caused by wars and more than a decade of paralyzing sanctions, requires special attention. Currently, there is a pressing need to improve public services and enhance the functionality of the state. In addressing these needs, Iraq must recognize yet another reality, that is, the urgent and great need for technocrats, a much needed recognition hampered by relentless campaign of lustration and de-Ba'thification.

Many of the Ba'thists are technocrats and bureaucrats who are desperately needed in rebuilding the country. The sweeping purge of the Ba'thists has almost irreversibly struck a large section of the Iraqi professional class. This extensive de-Ba'thification is too indiscriminate to be fair. It implicates many of the country's most talented professionals who, unlike the current government, were able to prove their professionalism during the wars and sanctions. In this sense, it is no accident that the government falls short of delivering decent basic services and economic recovery; the blanket purge of the Ba'thists has obviously backfired. Hence, de-Ba'thification must take its share of responsibility for the continued regression of Iraq.

Lustration is simply draining the Iraqi society of scarce human resources. The loss of administrative and managerial elites involves serious risks and severe consequences. The use of technocratic talents can explain, at least to a certain extent, why Japan and Germany rose again after their total destruction following their defeat in World War II. The miraculous development of these two countries within a very short period has something to do with their careful utilization of scarce talents available and accessible in society.

Relatively speaking, the success of Iraq in rebuilding within a few months a totally destroyed infrastructure following the disastrous adventure in Kuwait, was mainly due to the efforts of the Iraqi, or the "Ba'thist," bureaucratic talents. This relative success was achieved in spite of crippling sanctions and deteriorating state capacity. This is often contrasted, not without justifications, with the miserable failure of the new regime to restore basic services even after several years since the regime change. Retaining and using existing talents is vital to any reconstruction efforts, and the de-Ba'thification process is slowing down the rebuilding of Iraq.

The Ba'thification of society in the old regime ensured that most of the bureaucrats and technocrats who work for the government were in some way affiliated with the Ba'th Party. Although it is true that the primary criterion for promotion was loyalty to the regime, the criteria did not exclude ability as well. Loyalty and ability are not necessarily mutually exclusive under authoritarian politics. In fact, many were promoted in their party membership simply because they had done their work well. Good performance was considered a nationalist duty for the employed Ba'thists (i.e., a "Ba'thist" duty). The removal from office of so many talented people, along with the collapse of the Iraqi state following the Iraq War, essentially resulted in the deterioration of public service delivery. The fact that the new order has focused on the negative task of de-Ba'thifying society rather than on the positive task of mobilizing all available resources for the revival of the country, is a strong point in explaining what went wrong in the so-called new Iraq.

To be sure, the deterioration of governmental services started much earlier, particularly since the 1990s due to wars and sanctions and coupled with the personalization of the rule by the dictator and the blurred boundary between the state and the government. Nevertheless, the early erroneous decisions by the CPA, particularly the demobilization of the army and the de-Ba'athification, have their own share of blame in the cause of this outcome. Scott Carpenter, a deputy assistant secretary of state whose portfolio in Iraq includes weeding out senior Ba'athists, considers that the process of de-Ba'thification should be the administration's "No. 1 priority," even if it slows the revival of government services.[15] Another American official affirms: "We recognize this is not going to be a very tidy process. De-Baathification will necessarily entail some inefficiency in the running of government. That's a price we are willing to pay to be sure that we extirpate Baathism from Iraq's society."[16] That price, however, proved to be very costly for everyone. The inefficiency of governmental services has led to unnecessarily prolonged sufferings for the Iraqi people and increased violence, thereby putting the entire American adventure and the experience of building a new Iraq in jeopardy.

The other important issue to discuss in relation to de-Ba'thification is party membership. According to Hiro, in mid-1950 when the Iraqi Ba'th Party was founded the party had only about 200 members. When they implemented their first coup in 1963, they had 850–1,000 active members and 15,000 sympathizers, and when they were successful in executing their second coup in 1968, the party had 5,000 members.[17] By the time they were overthrown in 2003, this figure jumped to an estimated 1.2 to 1.5 million members. This extraordinary rise in the party membership presents serious challenges to the objectives of the de-Ba'thification process.

To understand the unprecedented rise in Ba'thist membership, one must understand the nature of the overthrown regime and the accompanying social contract. After their debacle in the first coup, when the Ba'th Party was removed from power just a few months later, it became the party's first priority to avoid a similar fate when they came to power again in 1968. Several strategies were used for this purpose: expanding security and intelligence organizations tremendously; expanding membership and affiliation with the party; creating and spreading a climate of fear and terror; monopolizing all political, bureaucratic, and economic positions; and promoting people based on their party affiliation. In this authoritarian rentier social contract, the government became the primary, if not the sole employer in the economy. Given that the regime of Saddam Hussein meant in reality the domination of the ruling Ba'th Party over the state and the economy, living and surviving as members and affiliates of this party came to mean securing jobs, advancing careers, and getting educated. This affiliation had very little to do with ideological convictions; it had everything to do with survival instinct, at least for the majority. In other words, to have the right to lead a normal life in old Iraq, one must be affiliated with the ruling Ba'th Party.

This reality is explicitly reflected in the official slogans of the Ba'th Party: "Everyone who is born in Iraq is a Ba'thist and everyone who lives in Iraq is a Ba'thist" (*kul man youlad fi aliraq fahuwa ba'thi wa kul man ya'ish fi aliraq fahuwa ba'thi*); "all Iraqis are Ba'thi" (*kul aliraqieen ba'thiyeen*); "the Ba'th is fire against aggressors and light to the guided" (*al-ba'th nar liman ya'tadi wa nur liman yahtadi*); "those who are not from us, are against us" (*kul man laisa mina fahuwa alaina*). These were the slogans circulating in Iraq during the rule of the Ba'th and political messages coming from a regime obsessed with staying in power at any cost, adamant about dominating all aspects of life, and insisting on monopolizing all positions leading to earn a living in Iraq. Under these circumstances, there are not many options left for ordinary Iraqis to live their ordinary life under the Ba'thist regime. The price of defiance was often so high that it meant in reality a suicidal choice.

Many Iraqis joined the party out of fear or pragmatism, or both. Iraqis had joined the party perfunctorily to keep out of trouble. It was a necessity in order to survive and succeed in a system that seems to be enduring and all-powerful with no sign of ending. Ba'th Party membership was merely a career prerequisite.[18] The report done by Sissons for the ICTJ states: "Certain levels of membership entitled individuals to extra allowances and privileges that could make a real difference to a person's economic wellbeing. Party membership was also reportedly a condition of employment in some professions, and occasionally conferred to honor Iraqis for other reasons, as was the case for some Iraqi prisoners of war from the Iran-Iraq war."[19] Here is a story about how the regime used party membership or promotion within the party ranking as a reward for sacrifices during the wars: An Iraqi soldier who languished for 15 years in an Iranian prison was made a group member of the party when he came home in 1997. This has meant higher pay in his job at a government printing plant. Six years later, his promotion proved to be a disaster because of the de-Ba'thification procedures.[20]

These procedures are regarded as ill-conceived since the Ba'th was the only political outlet and one of the main instruments of Saddam's grip on power and society. Mere membership in the organization cannot be culpable behavior, and many feel they were pressured to join and therefore are unfairly punished by these procedures. Many feel that they become innocent victims of an indiscriminate purge, or a witch hunt. At any rate, everyone deserves and should get a second chance.

Iraq is not the only country where ordinary people living under totalitarian regimes have limited choices in their lives. People joined the ruling Communist parties because that was the only way to practice their profession successfully. In his study on Eastern Europe, Shwartz warns: "Condemnation of such people may be equivalent to judging past actions by present standards!"[21] This caution is also reflected in what a former Ba'thist had to say: "For 35 years, you had to be a Baathist to earn a living. That's how our children got extra points to get into college. That's how we avoided being bothered by the authorities. But we were not criminals. We did not get big houses and fancy cars. Maybe we were wrong, but why should they punish our children for it now?"[22]

Domination over the educational system was one of the utmost priorities for the deposed regime, an objective that has gradually led to the Ba'thification of education in Iraq, from primary schools to university level. The principal of one of the secondary schools for girls in eastern Baghdad said she joined the party at the age of 12 because she knew even then that she wanted to teach and that would be the only way for her to actually become a teacher. She was made a group member of the party and therefore lost her job in new Iraq. In protest, she says: "I'm sure Mr. Bremer and the new administration will understand this was our duty. We had to be Baathists."[23]

The irony about the de-Ba'thification process is that it fails to read well the reality and the nature of the authoritarian regime that ruled the country for decades. It is true that the Ba'th Party took power in 1968, but the regime had gradually become the personal rule of Saddam Hussein. In fact, de-Ba'thification started by Saddam himself when he liquidated the leadership of his party in 1979. He hijacked the Ba'th Party and transformed it into a security organization, and Saddam and the party became conflated. This party became a convenient pretext and cover for gangsterism, and it was transformed from an ideological political party into a tribal party under the leadership of Saddam. Therefore the social base of the regime became increasingly restricted to the immediate family and tribe of this leader, the *Tikritis*. Aburish confirms that Saddam's Tikriti relations and a handful of unthreatening followers used the party as a front; the Ba'th existed as a structure only: "Saddam and his small group ran its various aspects on all levels. It was a merger between the family and the party, with the former using the latter as a vehicle to control the country. The party reported to the family and justified its rule, but the family acted in the name of the party. Saddam, as head of the family, needed a personality to preside over the family's pre-emption of the party."[24]

Hussein's familial or tribal rule meant that access to wealth and power was reduced to a level of familial or tribal associations with the leader. This association secured many privileges and special treatments, but this option was restricted to only a few fortunate people. The rest of the society, the majority of whom were not privileged by any familial or tribal association with the president, were left with only the Ba'th Party to be associated with, not in the sense of getting the same privileges of the first category but merely of securing a normal, productive, and professional career and education. Although it sounds paradoxical, the Ba'th Party was transformed into some kind of popular or "democratic" alternative for millions of people not related to or associated with the president. In other words, in a life where society was tightly controlled by the regime, the Iraqis were faced with a situation of the tribe versus the party, where only the party was accessible to the majority. Thus the irony of the process that intends to eradicate the Ba'th Party is that it lacks a sense of differentiation between different levels of association with the previous regime and deals instead with the more "popular" aspects of the previous authoritarian regime.

Most Iraqis went along to get along in an authoritarian world where choices and options were increasingly and dangerously becoming scarce. To live an ordinary life, the only actual choice is to join the Ba'th Party. This meant the Ba'thification of life, or the right to life under an extremely ruthless regime that intends to dominate every aspects of life. This association with the previous regime through party membership does not make people accountable for the atrocities of the regime. For the more than a million Iraqis who joined the party, this hardly implied direct involvement or even complicity in crimes of the state simply because Saddam Hussein was so paranoid that only his very inner circles were entrusted with information on the dictator's plans and policies.[25] In Iraq under the rule of Saddam, party membership often signaled neither ideology nor criminal complicity, just normal human instinct of survival and family advancement. Therefore those people who had no choice but to join the party feel that they became victims of an unfair purging process.

To be sure, a choice does exist even in a very totalitarian regime, such as the previous one in Iraq. However, any choice against the mainstream is incompatible with staying in the country—alive and leading a successful professional life. There were people who refused. Many of them were subsequently physically liquidated; more were tortured, leading to their severe psychological damage. Others were not able to get jobs or secure career advancement and higher education. An Iraqi admitted that he joined the party only because he wanted to finish his higher education. His two brothers, however, were not able to find jobs simply because they chose not to become members of the ruling party. He said: "It was a choice, you step backward to guarantee two steps forward."[26] He earned a doctorate and worked at the university but was eventually dismissed due to the de-Ba'thification procedures.

There is, however, the choice of going into exile. Nevertheless, not everyone was fortunate enough to have the means, the connections, or the desire to live in exile. Many of those who have chosen exile were mostly involved in sectarian or partisan politics and they were supported by neighboring regimes. Many people would dispute the contention that these activities and the choice of leaving the country are essentially better than staying at home and choosing to get along with an aggressive and dominating regime. Those Iraqi politicians who were consumed by feelings of vengeance and who fled the country in exile, but returned to rule the country with revenge, violence, sectarianism, and corruption, are not necessarily better than those who chose to stay and went along with a regime that demanded complete political conformity. Staying and living in a system that was totally politicized meant an association with the Ba'th Party one way or the other. Now, who is in a position to judge which choice is "better," more "acceptable," or more "patriotic"? After all, no one has the monopoly of morality.

Thus although there was theoretically a choice, there were not so many real choices. It is astonishing, however, how the new ruling class failed to appreciate this reality and proceeded on a purging campaign. The American authority in Iraq shared the same perception with the native political elites. On people who claim that they had no choice but to get along, Carpenter apathetically comments: "There was also somebody who said no. It represents that fundamental human choice."[27] This remark reflects a disastrous failure of the American project in Iraq to understand the reality of life under brutal dictatorship, the complexity of the political culture, and the working details of the political economy of the social contract of rentierism. Real choices are tolerated and exercised only in a democratic system. However, naïveté, arrogance, or both characterize the whole American adventure in Iraq, leading to unintended and undesirable failure.

The Ba'thification of the Iraqi society seriously limited the choices available for people, and it seems that the opposite, de-Ba'thification, works on similar lines. Both of these processes are violent and aggressive; they are affecting the very survival of the Iraqi people and their right to lead a normal life with a wide range of accessible options. In defending their policy of de-Ba'thification, the CPA states that Ba'thist employment is banned only in the public sector. Clearly, the defense is more than naïve; how can people have the choice to work in the private sector when this sector is almost nonexistent? A flourishing private sector is a sheer contradiction in a strict authoritarian rule where a rigid state command of the economy is the norm.

The foregoing assumption shows lack of comprehension of the original Ba'thification policies. Expanding the state economy at the expense of private businesses was instrumental in Ba'thifying society. This ensured the absence of a competitive and accessible alternative, and guaranteed that people would surrender and accept Ba'thist affiliation and all the benefits that came with it. Thus when the Ba'thists are not allowed to work in the public sector, there is no private sector to turn to. This reality is not only a legacy of the old regime but also the result of the nature of the economic policies pursued by the new regime, aggravated by widespread corruption, nepotism, and inefficiency. Ending the legacy of state domination over the economy for the benefit of a flourishing private sector that can represent a real option for the Iraqis is still not a priority in the current regime.

As in the old days, de-Ba'thification limits the real choices of those affected; they might feel that they have no choice but to fight back when their ability to earn a living to support their families is compromised. It is no wonder that resentment against this policy and the politics of revenge has basically been feeding a lethal resistance and civil war during a critical period in Iraqi history. Both Ba'thification and de-Ba'thification are two sides of the same coin, and they share the same values of violence, exclusion, revenge, and intolerance.

According to de-Ba'thification procedures, all Iraqis who work for the government are required to sign a paper renouncing affiliation with the Ba'th Party. The paper is called "Agreement to Disavow Party Affiliation" and aims at relinquishing all ties to Ba'thism. One Iraqi woman smartly commented: "It is hilarious that Iraqis who had to pledge fealty to the party to get jobs in Saddam Hussein's Iraq will have to renounce the party to get jobs now."[28] The sophistication of this remark, though cynical, is that it refers to a situation of striking similarity between old and new Iraq. Although they lead in opposite directions, both the affirmation of affiliation with the Ba'th Party and later the denunciation of the party are two sides of the same process. It is a violent process of politicizing employment and the economy, and of confusing the state with the government—a process that infringes upon the right of Iraqis to employment and decent lives. Politicizing the simple right of earning a living in Iraq clearly shows that there are few differences between the old and the new experience.

Ironically, limiting the right to earn a living to those with a kind of affiliation with the ruling parties is still the case in the new Iraq. Unless one obtains a paper showing an affiliation with one of the religious and ethnic ruling political parties, it would be very difficult to secure a job in the public sector. In addition, the monopolization of governmental jobs in Kurdistan by the two leading Kurdish parties is no secret. Discussing the experience in the Kurdish region, McDowall observes: "Joining one or other party became the essential prerequisite to advancement. The patronage role of both political parties became disastrously entrenched in the fledgling administration undermining any chance of democratic institutional growth."[29]

When President Talabani visited Britain in October 2009, he was met with a protest demonstration by hundreds of Kurds, claiming that about 2,000 Kurds were dismissed from their jobs because they did not vote for the list of the two ruling parties in the July 2009 election in Iraqi Kurdistan. The demonstrators called on the British government to intervene and pressure the regional authority regarding this issue. Demonstrations were also organized in Sulaimaniya against arbitrary dismissing of teachers due to the same reason.[30] A 33-year-old nurse in a Sulaimaniya hospital was one of a very few health workers who refused to join the union sponsored by the Patriotic Union of Kurdistan. Because of this defiant action, his wages were cut by one-third.[31] Party control over people's lives extends down to all levels of government jobs in a well-entrenched system of political patronage, whether in old or new Iraq.

Affiliation with the Ba'thists is condemned and punished. In effect, the new regime insists on pursuing the very same policies it criticizes.

The new regime, which persists on pursuing de-Ba'thification, allows itself to ignore the paradox of the situation. Clearly, the new regime is following the same policies as the old. Therefore observers wonder whether the dispute between the new ruling elites and the old regime is a dispute over principles, policies, and procedures, or over something else. In this context, one cannot help but consider how the new regime is approaching de-Ba'thification—a mere exercise in politics of revenge and a manifestation of political power (not of differences over principles and issues). Given that the Shiite and Kurdish parties also practice the same policy of distributing jobs through partisan politics, it seems that resentment toward the previous regime is mainly motivated by a perceived consideration that the old regime was dominated by a "wrong" sect or ethnicity, let alone by a wrong dictator (in the sense of why this particular dictator is ruling the country when Iraq is full of other dictators who aspire to be rulers!). The rise of identity politics in the aftermath of the regime change is an illustrative point in this regard.

NOTES

1. CPA, "Coalition Provisional Authority Order Number 1: De-Ba'athification of Iraqi Society," May 16, 2003, http://www.iraqcoalition.org/regulations/20030516_CPAORD_1_De-Ba_athification_of_Iraqi_Society_.pdf.

2. CPA, "Coalition Provisional Authority Order Number 2: Dissolution of Entities," May 23, 2003, http://www.cpa-iraq.org/regulations/20030823_CPAORD_2_Dissolution_of_Entities_with_Annex_A.pdf.

3. CPA, "Coalition Provisional Authority Order Number 3: The Establishment of the Iraqi De-Ba'athification Council," May 25, 2003, http://www.cpa-iraq.org/regulations/CPAORD5.pdf.

4. SNCD, "The Mission," http://www.debaath.com/site/page/ka_h/1_h.htm; http://www.debaath.com/site/page/ka_h/2_h.htm.

5. SNCD, "The Targets," http://www.debaath.com/site/page/ENG/the_commission_target.htm.

6. SNCD, "About the Commission," http://www.debaath.com/site/page/ENG/about_the_commission.htm.

7. SNCD, "Accountability and Justice Law," http://www.debaath.com/site/page/ajt_s/index.htm.

8. James Cogan, " 'De-Baathification' Laws Modified by Iraq's Parliament," January 17, 2008, http://www.wsws.org/articles/2008/jan2008/iraq-j17.shtml.

9. ICTJ, "Unofficial Translation of Iraq's Accountability and Justice Law," January 2008, http://www.ictj.org/images/content/7/6/766.pdf.

10. Miranda Sissons, "Iraq's New 'Accountability and Justice Law,' " ICTJ, January 22, 2008, http://www.ictj.org/images/content/7/6/764.pdf.

11. Ayala Falk, "Judge Discusses Debaathification in Iraq," *The Cornell Daily Sun*, October 31, 2008.

12. Cogan, " 'De-Baathification' Laws."

13. SNCD, "The Constitution," http://www.debaath.com/site/page/h _distor.htm.

14. Ian Buruma, "How Iraq Can Get Over Its Past," *New York Times*, May 9, 2003.

15. Amy Waldman, "In Search for Baath Loyalists, U.S. Finds Itself in Gray Area," *New York Times*, July 22, 2003.

16. Peter Slevin, "U.S. Bans More Iraqis from Jobs," *Washington Post*, May 17, 2003.

17. Dilip Hiro, *Iraq: A Report from the Inside* (London: Granta Books, 2003), 52–53.

18. Ghassan Atiyyah, "Wanted in Iraq: A Roadmap to Free Elections," *Open Democracy*, October 16, 2003. http://www.opendemocracy.net/conflict -iraqivoices/article_1541.jsp.

19. Sissons, "Iraq's New," 4.

20. Waldman, "In Search for Baath."

21. Herman Schwartz, "Lustration in Eastern Europe," in *Transitional Justice: How Emerging Democracies Reckon with Former Regimes*, vol. 1, *General Considerations*, ed. Neil J. Kritz (Washington, DC: Institute of Peace Press, 1995), 463.

22. Pamela Constable, "Idled Iraqis Cry Foul Over Firings," *Washington Post*, July 27, 2003.

23. Waldman, "In Search for Baath."

24. Said Aburish, *Saddam Hussein: The Politics of Revenge* (London: Blooms-bury, 2001), 161–62.

25. Frederick W. Kagan, Jack Keane, and Michael O'Hanlon, "Making Iraq Safe for Politics," *Washington Post*, January 20, 2008.

26. Waldman, "In Search for Baath."

27. Ibid.

28. Slevin, "U.S. Bans More Iraqis."

29. David McDowall, *A Modern History of the Kurds*, 3rd ed. (London: Tauris, 2004), 385.

30. Shadha al-Juburi, "Protest Demonstration Meets Iraqi President in London," *Asharq al- Awsat*, October 11, 2009.

31. Sabrina Tavernise, "After the War: Northern Iraq; Trying to Set up Democracy in a Divided Kurdish Region," *New York Times*, July 1, 2003.

5

Uprooting the Ba'th and Sectarianism

DE-BA'THIFICATION AND SECTARIAN POLITICS

Iraq is not alone in confronting the dilemma of dealing with socially destructive political parties. Europe faced, and is still facing, problems with fascist and extreme rightist parties. However, both available options in dealing with these parties entail serious risks. On one hand, allowing these parties to conduct their activities publicly brings the benefit of easy monitoring, and the risk of promoting their popularity. On the other hand, outlawing them brings the risk of encouraging their secrecy and extremism. There is also the risk of allowing undemocratic parties to take advantage of the democratic electoral system, and jump into power and cancel democracy, as was the case for the Nazi Party of Hitler and some of the parties of political Islam. The risk may materialize in Iraq because most Iraqi political parties, not only the Ba'th Party, are undemocratic. Commitment to a democratic game and system is an absolute necessity in allowing parties to participate in political life and elections. This stipulates the enactment of laws to regulate, organize, and monitor the work of political parties, laws that are still missing in Iraq even after many years since the regime changed.

One of the most important problems with de-Ba'thification is the politicization of this legislation, in addition to entrusting politicians from the ruling political parties rather than judicial authority to be in charge of the implementation of this law. In so doing, the independence of the commission entrusted with de-Ba'thification is compromised. Deliberate politicizing of the work of de-Ba'thification persuaded the then-prime minister Ayad Allawi, who himself was a former Ba'thist, to try to install a court system to replace the commission. His aim was to readmit former senior Ba'thists unless criminal charges were brought against them and they were found guilty in a court. Yet the influential Shiite parties resisted his attempt. Prime Minister Maliki of the Da'wa Party said that what Allawi was trying to establish was "outside the law" and that the commission had every right to "remove all trace of the Baathists."[1]

It is true that de-Ba'thification, as well as the constitution, aims at banishing the Ba'thists from political life in the country. However, there is a tendency to accuse anyone who criticizes the government of supporting Ba'thism or working for Ba'thist agenda. In addition, there are repeated talks about the threat of the return of the Ba'th Party to power, and there are calls for unity to prevent this from happening. Apparently, exaggerating and exploiting the public fear of the Ba'th Party or a Ba'thist return to Iraqi politics is politically expedient. Many of the politicians or electoral lists that seriously competed with the ruling parties in the 2010 national elections were accused of Ba'thist connections. When contests during the days leading to the elections became fierce, the recourse to discrediting politicians and the political liquidation of unwanted candidates under the pretext of their Ba'thist connections became even more widespread.

The ruling Da'wa Party accused the cross-sectarian electoral list, the Iraqi National Movement (known as Iraqia), headed by the secular Shiite former prime minister Ayad Allawi as a "Baathist list with the agenda of preparing for the return of the Baath."[2] Undoubtedly, this sort of accusation causes grave damage to the political process and fair democratic contest among candidates. Nevertheless, not all politicians share in this political "hysteria" about the return of the Ba'th. One Iraqi politician declared: "The Baathists are Iraqis. We want them to live in peace in Iraq and we might even benefit from those who are qualified among them."[3]

Moreover, a crisis developed only six weeks before the March 2010 parliamentary elections. The de-Ba'thification Commission decided to ban 511 candidates and 15 political factions from participating in the election on charges of Ba'thist connections. Among those disqualified was the defense minister, abdul-Qader al-Obaidi, and Salih al-Mutlaq, a secular nonsectarian prominent Sunni politician who is a member of the parliament. Mutlaq dismissed the allegation: "How could I nominate myself as a Baathist when I know that it is illegal? I am wiser than that."[4]

The decision to ban selected candidates has solemn electoral ramifications. Most of those who were banned are secular and nonsectarian politicians. As such, the banning seemingly reflects the intensifying struggle between the Islamists and the secularists. It also reflects a fear that venturing beyond the "safety" of sectarian politics, which is sanctioned by the rulers, is still not electorally rewarding. This is particularly true, considering the poor electoral programs and the dismal achievement records of contending politicians. One Iraqi academic remarks: "Our political parties don't have real political and economic programs. So instead of struggling over programs and candidates' capabilities, they are trying to exclude each other—even within the same party or alliance."[5] Thus under these circumstances, sectarian politics seems to be a secured and proven method of gaining power. The crusade against the Ba'thists provides a platform on which sectarian politics is expressed, and in this sense, it is an attempt from the top to counter the popular rejection of political sectarianism. The way to power seems to go through repopularizing sectarian politics once again, similar to what happened in the 2005 elections.

Ahmad Chalabi heads the de-Ba'thification Commission with the assistance of Ali al-Lami. Both are candidates in the election and members of the Shiite religious electoral alliance, Iraqi National Alliance. Chalabi is a controversial figure who aspires to become a prime minister but was humiliated earlier when he failed to secure not even one parliamentary seat for himself or his party in the 2005 elections. One Iraqi politician who knows Chalabi well comments: "Even if it kills him, he's going to stay in Iraq to try to become prime minister. This issue [of de-Ba'thification] is the only tool he has, because he has nothing else going for him."[6] Chalabi himself admits: "On the issue of the Baath, I don't think anyone can match me."[7]

The U.S. military detained Ali al-Lami for a year on suspicion of ties to *Asa'ib Ahl al-Haq*, League of the Righteous, an Iranian-backed violent militia and a breakaway from the militias of Muqtada al-Sadr. Lami was detained after he was accused of organizing a bombing that killed two American Embassy employees, two American soldiers, and six Iraqis at a district council meeting in Baghdad in 2008. The Iraqi government released him in a deal to stop violence.[8] Obviously, this kind of record is an incongruous background for working in a commission entrusted with addressing justice.

The fact that both Chalabi and Lami are candidates in the election indicates that the decision of disqualifying selected candidates is an attempt at political liquidation of rival candidates. The conflict of interests in this action is rather evident. A spokesperson for Chalabi, who is also a candidate, admits: "It's made the Baathist danger an imminent national issue, and that will motivate people to vote."[9] However, the journalist abdel-Rahman al-Rashed cynically commented on this development: "Thanks to the commission of Lami, Iraq will become like the rest of the Arab democracy circus where a committee decides in advance who is the winner even before the start of the vote."[10]

The de-Ba'thification commission seems to follow the Iranian model where the religious "guardian of the constitution" actually decides who from the candidates in the elections are allowed to participate and who are not. The commission has even issued another list preventing the participation of some male and female candidates due to accusations of homosexuality and prostitution. It appears that the commission is influenced by the fanatically religious aim of "preventing vice," which is observed in some countries. Analogous to the political atmosphere of McCarthyism in the United States during the 1950s, the disqualification of some candidates in Iraq is a clear misuse of power. It is an arbitrary process of exclusion facilitated by an exclusive and controversial constitution. Excluding people for alleged Ba'thist ties clearly shows the extent to which democracy in Iraq is an illusion. The campaign against the so-called Ba'thist return dominated and defined the outcome of the 2010 elections. Consequently, issues of corruption, services, and the economy were once again sacrificed. The success of the de-Ba'thification campaign in changing the focus of the elections will surely give the dominant political class a four-year respite from confronting real issues that directly affect the general welfare of the Iraqis.

Slogans demonizing the Ba'th were among the posters that appeared during the electoral campaign. The provincial councils of Baghdad and several southern provinces started to declare that it is high time to purge the Ba'thists from administrative jobs. The head of the Basra provincial council states publicly: "The Baathists can't return to Iraq. There is no place for them among us. There is no place for criminals."[11] The local council of Baghdad initiated a campaign for the eradication of art in the capital city by removing several monuments that had been made by famous Iraqi artists. The campaign even included the removal of some monuments that have no direct linkage to the Ba'th but were taken down just because they were erected during the rule of the Ba'th Party. Furthermore, Prime Minister Maliki has threatened to use his "constitutional rights," whatever these might be, to prevent the Ba'thists from coming to the next parliament.[12] Noteworthy, there is an active civil society organization by the name of the "The Movement People for Debaathification." This organization declares that "we are a nation that does not forget its martyrs" and that "uprooting the Baath is our message to humanity."[13]

Whether or not they have previous connections with the Ba'th Party, many politicians are peacefully participating in the current political process and are willing to play by the new rules of the game. In so doing, they have distinguished themselves from other Ba'thists who do not yet recognize the regime change and the resulting political process, and who still use violence against the government. A more inclusive politics and an approach to dealing with the Ba'thists, which considers differences among Ba'thist groups, will isolate all those who still believe in violence, including some Ba'thists. Although the political expediency behind disqualifying candidates is obvious, such can affect the already fragile political process and jeopardize national reconciliation, which is a crucial step in strengthening an inclusive and democratic system. In this sense, what needs uprooting is the very policy and legislation of de-Ba'thification. After all, such policy was earlier implemented in the old regime against the Islamists, the Communists, and the Kurds, and its futility has been proven at the expense of many lives. One may pose the issue that indeed the Ba'th Party is evil, but who can judge that the current replacement is better? If one is to question the Ba'th Party, then one should also question all other players in the Iraqi political culture that are responsible for perpetuating violence.

Several years since the regime change, the Ba'th Party may have increased its appeal to the Iraqi society. This increasing appeal is ironic, given the wars, violence, and destruction that transpired under the name of Ba'thism. Interestingly, it has very little to do with the party itself, and very much to do with the current political process and the nature of the ruling political elites. There are several factors that contribute to this new appeal. After many years in power, the ruling parties have proven that they are not really better than the discredited Ba'thists. It is true that the Ba'th Party failed in Iraq but so did many of the other parties. Generally speaking, party politics is a failure in both old and new Iraq.

The ruling parties have failed to deliver their promises or to meet the expectations of the Iraqis. In particular, they have failed to improve basic services and ensure decent living standards. With its secular nature, the Ba'th Party is increasing its appeal under the backdrop of the failure of the religious parties in power. The new politics implemented in new Iraq seems to reflect primarily a continuation of old politics, whether this politics is associated with the Ba'th Party or other parties. Thus the politics of victimization, revenge, exclusion, militarization, and corruption are all continuations of old Iraqi politics. In other words, the current political experience has failed to represent a serious interruption in or a departure from the Ba'th-dominated old politics.

Moreover, the many risks, including the specter of civil war, associated with political sectarianism and destabilizing federalism tend to augment public disappointment with current politics, thereby making alternative politics attractive. Close relations between the dominant sectarian parties and Iran, as well as the growing influence of the latter in the internal affairs of Iraq, have led to an increase in nationalistic feelings across the country. There is a feeling that the anti-Ba'thist campaign is actually benefiting Iran rather than Iraq. This is particularly true, considering the bitter memories of the eight-year war with Iran.

Uneasy feelings about the de-Ba'thifying campaign have also been reinforced by the increasing role of Kurdish nationalism in Iraqi politics, which is primarily oriented toward serving clearly defined ethnic interests. There is a perception that discrediting the Ba'th Party and de-Ba'thifying Iraqi society and politics lie in the hands of one particular type of nationalism, i.e., Kurdish nationalism, which is perceived by many as a threat to Iraqi nationalist interests. This makes sense when Kurdish nationalism is taken to a rather extreme position and is aggressively pursued by dominant Kurdish politicians.

Furthermore, the de-Ba'thification campaign has perhaps thrown the Ba'thists into the light of being seen as victims of new Iraq, and consequently boosted sympathy toward them. Nevertheless, a society that oscillates between destabilizing and destructive nationalism, whether Arab or Kurdish, and unfeasible political Islam and radical Shiism is nothing but a doomed society.

Thus de-Ba'thification became one of the most important features of the new political experience in Iraq in the aftermath of the regime change in 2003. Uprooting the Ba'thists and the struggle to prevent a Ba'thist return have become the raison d'être of the ruling regime. Similar to the old regime, revenge politics—not the advancement of the country on many fronts—characterizes high politics in Iraq. We are left wondering if this is the right start for a society with a violent past or for a society struggling to achieve a prosperous and democratic future.

UPROOTING THE BA'TH AND VENGEANCE

The drive to purify society from the previous elites comes in stark conflict with the democratic principles that the new regime is supposed to initiate. This is clearly paradoxical. Albon summarizes critics to lustration as the followings: lustration is based on principle of collective rather than individual guilt; it considers whole categories of people guilty; it is based on the presumption of guilt rather than innocence; it does not distinguish among varying degrees of implications; it does not provide citizens proper protection by the judiciary; and it contradicts international covenants on discrimination.[14] People are targeted not as individuals but as members of a group, even when it is obvious that the price of defiance during the old regime was very high. De-Ba'thification is a form of collective punishment, a practice that is often used by discredited regimes, where whole families, villages, and towns are punished. It is noteworthy that the first trial against the former regime is the Dujail case, a case involving the punishment of a whole village following the failed assassination of Saddam. This trial is believed to be a case against the use of collective punishment, which ironically continues to be practiced in new Iraq.

By considering that the Ba'thists are guilty pending proof of their innocence, de-Ba'thification contravenes one of the most basic elements of justice and democracy. Guilt by association and collective responsibility, which leads to collective punishment, promotes lustration and contravenes the principle of inclusive citizenship, a highly cherished and desirable democratic ideal and objective. The absence of inclusive citizenship, which the new political regime is expected to remedy, is one of the strong features of the authoritarian politics that dominated Iraq for decades.

At this juncture, it is tempting to explore why the new ruling elites deal with the Ba'thists as a group and not as individuals. The concept of group, in this respect, is a reflection of tribalization that still characterizes political life in the country. The concept of group is also essential to the new Iraqi political landscape. Within the context of identity politics, the new elites have initiated the political process on the premises of "us as a group" (i.e., the Shiites or the Kurds) and them (i.e., the Ba'thists or even the Sunnis). In this sectarian and ethnic political configuration, there is no space for individuality, except perhaps when competing for important and prestigious political positions, particularly the three most prestigious positions: prime minister, head of state, and speaker of parliament.

Thus new politics in Iraq is primarily defined in terms of groups, and the Other is perceived as an enemy group. The Ba'thists are discredited as a group and are therefore vilified, delegitimized, and prosecuted. In contrast, the new elites are legitimized as a group, particularly in their "right" to govern the country. This legitimization is derived from their being victimized as a group by the previous regime. Today, the situation is reversed, and victims and victimizers are merely changing places in a vicious cycle of victimization. In the end, all will be victims. Ironically, ruling the country by entitlement as a previously victimized group—not on the basis of individual merit—is creating more miseries in Iraq.

To purge the Ba'thists, a process of fair and unprejudiced vetting is needed. Hiltermann argues: "One of the principal deficiencies of the post-2003 order has been the absence of transitional justice, including an impartial vetting mechanism that would have judged former-regime adherents on their conduct rather than mere membership in a mass party which the regime used as an instrument of political control."[15] According to the ICTJ, it is vital that the vetting process be based on individual responsibility rather than assumption of collective guilt, and be transparent, protected from manipulation, and subjected to a clear time limit. Vetting is a process of assessing an individual's integrity in order to determine his or her suitability for public employment. Integrity refers to a person's adherence to human rights standards and his or her financial propriety.[16]

However, this definition of vetting points toward double-standard practices in the case of Iraq. Vetting of Ba'thists to determine their appropriateness for public employment will immediately pose many questions on the aptness of the currently ruling elites for the same positions. A lot has been said about the inefficiency of the new governments in recent years. Even basic services were not restored after years of promises and billions of dollars of investments. The obvious wisdom of the right person in the right place has, regrettably, no credibility in the new Iraq yet.

Furthermore, the reference to financial propriety in the definition of vetting is also revealing, given the widespread and systemic corruption that plagues politics and public administration in new Iraq. Many of the new ruling elites contend that the inclusion of Ba'thists in public governance could promote corruption.[17] This contention is rather ironic, although we do not imply that the Ba'thists cannot be corrupt. Moreover, the argument is indicative of flawed Iraqi politics, whether old or new. The Other, which is frequently an enemy, is perceived as always corrupt, whereas the Self is viewed as constantly honest, even when bare reality shows that the Self is possibly more corrupt than the vilified Other. The old regime also vilified its numerous enemies in similar ways.

Additionally, adherence to human right standards, in the above definition of vetting, is something that not only the Ba'th Party miserably failed to exercise. The same failure taints the whole political culture that came to dominate the country. The key question is whether new Iraq represents an interruption with—or a continuation of—this culture. Leaving aside the rhetoric about new democratic Iraq, even the new ruling elites have failed to institutionalize new and highly needed premises for political practice in the country. It would be naïve to expect democracy and respect for human rights from sectarian, hard nationalist, and authoritarian politicians who do not initially believe in democratic concepts.

Most, but not all, of the Ba'thists joined the party out of fear and pragmatism. For certain, some were also enthusiastic about Ba'thist ideals, although this does not necessarily exclude apprehension and expediency. Believing in certain Ba'thist ideals could perhaps be considered as the rationalization of a rather forced or inevitable association with the Ba'th Party. However, some of these people do differentiate between Saddam Hussein and Ba'thism, asserting that these two entities are not necessarily the same. One Ba'thist puts it this way: "When I was young I sympathized with Baathist ideas, but Saddam had nothing to do with them. He represented only power."[18] Another political science student elaborates: "We didn't become members of this party for Saddam's sake. We found in this party and its aims, and what it wishes for, things we liked, particularly Arab nationalism."[19] Arab nationalism had, and still has, a strong appeal to Iraqis, and nationalism is still a generally viable ideology and feeling in the country. In this sense, one wonders why Kurdish nationalism, for instance, is considered heroism, whereas Arab nationalism is discredited in new Iraq just because of its association with Saddam Hussein or the Ba'th Party. New Iraq should find new ways to orient strong feelings of nationalism toward more peaceful and productive purposes, rather than elevate one kind of nationalism and dishonor another.

Many of the Ba'thists feel regrets and repentance for their association with the Ba'th Party, partly due to a new pragmatism of the new situation since 2003. After all, they joined the party out of the pragmatism of the old days. But many repent out of genuine feelings about the many disasters that befell on Iraqi society because of the rule that was associated with this party. Yet not all Ba'thists get the many lessons associated with this experience. There is the case of a Ba'thist university administrator who "conceded passing reports about people up the party chain but said he could not be held accountable for how the

security services used the information. Even now, his greatest regret
about Mr. Hussein's rule is not gross violations of human rights but
his betrayal of the party's pan-Arabic ideology by the invasion of
Kuwait."[20]

To combat a stubborn and violent insurgency, the government decided
to use the help of former Ba'thist military officers and so the Falluja Brigade was formed in April 2004, which has been regarded as a reversal
in the de-Ba'thification policy. But many of the recruits fled to the side
of the insurgents with their equipment and weapons, leading to more
violence instead. A similar experience also occurred in Mosul in the north
of Iraq. Thus there are incidents to show that reinstating some of the
Ba'thists could backfire and exacerbate violence even further. These
events, however, were used by the new regime as a demonstration of
unrepentant and unchanged Ba'th Party and, hence, an excuse for not
trusting or reconciling with the Ba'thists. Rubin comments on these new
experiences: "While it's fashionable to say de-Baathification caused the
Sunni insurgency, in reality terrorist violence is proportional to that policy's reversal . . . It has not assuaged insurgency. Not only does offering
concessions to violence encourage violence, but also by extending an
olive branch to unrepentant Baathists, diplomats may have furthered Iranian influence and worsened militia violence."[21]

One surely wonders whether all the disasters during the last two decades that culminated in the U.S.-led occupation of the country has
induced the Ba'thists to reflect on this experience and their role in this
calamity. If not, what else will do the trick? Ba'thist leaders who
escaped into exile are still talking about their "legitimate right" to rule
Iraq, yet there are no efforts to evaluate critically their experience of ruling and ruining the country. The stubbornness and the uncompromising stand of the Ba'thists are in reality an exercise of the politics of
revenge against the new regime. However, this politics is, at least partly,
a reaction to de-Ba'thification, which is also motivated by vengeance
politics. The politics of revenge from both sides, which involves all
political players, reflects the lack of a culture of apology in Iraqi politics.
Iraq needs upright Ba'thists who are not afraid to condemn the past
atrocities of their party. However, the difficulty of apologizing is hardly
restricted to the Ba'thists alone because this seems to be a constant fea-
ture of the dominant political culture in Iraq, if not in the whole of the
Middle East. A scrutiny of Iraqi history reveals that many political parties are responsible, to varying degrees, for the misfortune of Iraq, yet
there is not a single political party that has so far critically and honestly
evaluated its role and apologized to the Iraqi society.

The failure to forward sincere apology badly hampers efforts at realizing the very desirable and inevitable process of genuine reconciliation. The Ba'thists and the new ruling elites are both to blame for not taking reconciliation seriously. Mithal al-Alusi, a former legislator, was a member of the Ba'th Party but fled to Germany in the mid-1970s when he was sentenced to death by the regime. He became a general director in the de-Ba'thification commission, and in 2004 he had this to say about reconciliation: "Those of the Iraqi politicians who talk about reconciliation can not be described but with naivety. Reconciliation with the Baath is rejected by the Iraqi street. Any call for reconciliation with the Baath is a danger for present and future situation in Iraq."[22] Rubin criticizes the efforts of reconciling with the Ba'thists: "Sometimes, premature reconciliation, no matter how well-meaning, can do far more harm than good. For the sake of appeasing 40,000 Baathists, proponents of reconciliation risk antagonizing 16 million Shiites."[23]

It is this appeasement to the majority Shiites for electoral purposes that made Prime Minister Maliki relinquish earlier efforts at reaching out to Ba'thists by repeatedly and categorically rejecting any reconciliation with the Ba'th Party. In April 2009, he said that this party is "filled with hate from head to toe."[24] Readmitting the Ba'thists is like putting a cobra snake in the bed, as one Iraqi politician publicly stated. When a legislator was asked about her opinion whether the parliament should discuss the inclusion of the Ba'thists in the political process and amend the constitution accordingly, she ardently replied: "This is impossible. I will not recognize this parliament anymore and will not stay in it one hour more. If this will happen, it signifies the day of judgment."[25]

Reconciliation starts with the recognition of the Other. It is difficult to deny the existence of the Ba'th Party when this party is part of Iraqi history, society, and political culture. In this sense, condemning the Ba'thists is, by implication, a condemnation of the Iraqi political history and the entire dominant political culture that is shared by all the political parties, including the currently ruling parties. Reconciliation and de-Ba'thification are incompatible processes and sharp contradictions. A democratic regime that aims at positively confronting the ugly past and secures a bright future for the country should have been resolute at promoting serious reconciliation right from the very beginning. Such a step entails forgiving and reaching out to the Ba'thists, and integrating them in the state administration and political process.

The nature of the regime change in 2003 made reconciliation with the Ba'thists a more difficult option to accomplish. The sweeping

American military victory and the swift and total collapse of the regime threw the Ba'thists into a disadvantageous position in the new regime. However, it must be noted that the regime change was made possible only due to foreign intervention and not due to the struggle of the new ruling elites. This total collapse deprived the old regime any power to negotiate more favorable terms for them. Although waging a violent and destructive "resistance" intends to remedy this unfavorable situation for the Ba'thists, using armed violence and indiscriminate killing is a dangerous and condemned policy. These are unjustified and unwarranted criminal acts, although it is an equally destructive policy to kill, force into exile, or target Ba'thists as a group, and deny them their rights as citizens.

These kinds of attitudes toward reconciliation coupled with the stated principles and objectives of the de-Ba'thification procedures would seem to indicate in reality a politics of revenge. Calling all Ba'thists Sadamite, or repentant, *tawabun*, or those returnees to the nationalist block, *al-a'idun ila al-saf al-watani*, are all humiliating to the Ba'thists and not unlike what Saddam used to do in his malicious and revengeful politics. This name-calling is anyway against the principles of citizenship and equality. The first word that was used for the campaign against the Ba'th, *ijtithath*, or uprooting, is rather a cruel and violent term to use and is a contradiction in a supposed-to-be-new Iraq. Politics of retribution, however, is hardly an innovation; it is a continuation of an old tradition in Iraqi politics of revenging the deposed regime.

Disqualification of the Ba'thists is a political process susceptible to the influence of partisan, sectarian, and revenge politics. Discussing the politicization of the purging process, Schwartz argues that there is a tendency of using lustration for partisan political purposes, to win political battles or settle old scores.[26] Huyse agrees: "Lustration operations tend to become highly politicized. Sometimes, the eagerness to purge society results from the political calculation of parties and factions."[27] This is also the experience of Iraq concerning the issue of what to do with the Ba'thists. Less than a year after instigating the banning of the Ba'thists, Bremer, who was initially proud of this policy, admitted: "Many Iraqis have complained to me that de-Baathification policy has been applied unevenly and unjustly. I have looked into these complaints and they are legitimate."[28]

De-Ba'thification is seriously criticized because it has been influenced by the politics of sectarianism that has come to dominate Iraqi politics since 2003. Two critical points have led to this criticism. First, leadership in the de-Ba'thification commission has been restricted to the Shiite sect.

The Kurds, who fought for every small and big division of the spoils in new Iraq, were not privileged to participate in this leadership. At any rate, however, they were influential in writing the constitution, which basically institutionalized the whole process of de-Ba'thification. The monopoly of the Shiites in the commission gives the impression of a sectarian group that intends to take political and sectarian revenge. This fact has dangerous implications. Many of the Shiite former Ba'thists have been admitted in the new regime, e.g., Jawad Bulani, the minister of interior, and Sharwan al-Wa'ily, the minister of national security. Sunni former Ba'thists, on the other hand, did not get the same chance in the reemployment of ex-Ba'thists as did their Shiite fellows. Ambassador Istrabadi, who played a role in the constitutional drafting process, discloses: "A very high proportion of the Shia who were members of the Baath party were allowed to continue to function in their positions. The burden of being removed from office fell disproportionately highly on Sunnis, to the extent that the Sunnis of Iraq began to call it 'de-Sunnification' rather than de-Ba'athification."[29] Under the impact of the dominant sectarian politics, there is a risk of a sect-inspired de-Ba'thification process that can lead to the undesirable outcome of failing to alleviate legitimate sectarian concerns.

Second, the policy of de-Ba'thification has erroneously considered the Ba'th as a party representing the Sunnis. The reality is far from this accusation. Right from its formation, the Ba'th Party included Sunnis, Shiites, Kurds, and other minorities. In fact, the majority of the Ba'thists are Shiites, and this is hardly surprising because the Shiites comprise the majority of the population. The unjustifiably enforced association between the Ba'thists and the Sunnis indicates a rather unhelpful and counterproductive approach to Iraqi politics in the aftermath of the regime change. Paradoxically and ironically, the currently ruling political parties are either sectarian or ethnic in nature. The Da'wa Party of Prime Minister Maliki, the ISCI, the Sadrists, and the Fadhila are all sectarian Shiite parties and movements; the two dominant Kurdish parties, the Kurdistan Democratic Party (KDP) and the Patriotic Union of Kurdistan (PUK) are ethnically Kurds; and the Islamist Party is a sectarian Sunni party. The sectarian and ethnic profiles of these parties serve as primary obstacles to a veritable transition toward democracy and to inevitable changes in the dominant political culture. It seems that there is a connection between the ethnic and sectarian characteristic of these parties and their unwarranted insistence on giving the Ba'th Party a sectarian makeup.

Moreover, the inception of the de-Ba'thification procedures was accompanied by a campaign of physical liquidation of the Ba'thists. One of the many risks associated with sectarianizing the de-Ba'athification process is the risk of smuggling the lists of the Ba'thists compiled at the de-Ba'thification commission to the active and violent sectarian militias for the purpose of liquidating them. This is a feasible outcome considering the absence of rule of the law and the dominance of politics of revenge and sectarian militias. However, whether they were organized through death squads or "voluntarily," the assassinations of Ba'thists appear to have picked up after regime change, particularly in the Shiite-dominated areas such as Karbala, Najaf, Basra, and the Sadr City in Baghdad. A piece of graffiti in the Sadr City reads "Oh Baath Party, there is no place to hide." A resident of this city said: "We want the Americans to kill them, but we don't think they are going to. I will kill Baathists myself. This is my right."[30] This perceived "right" to kill enemies is callously revealing in the sense that regime change is inevitably and unquestionably considered to be an opportunity for revenge and violence. Hundreds of civilian and military Ba'thists were assassinated in these areas, driving many more to flee the country to the safety of exile. Incontrovertibly, these killings contribute to suspicions and lack of trust that are antithetical to reconciliation and peaceful coexistence. These killings are against the necessary supremacy of the rule of law, an essential key to any democratic process.

Most Iraqis are angry about how the Ba'thists destroyed their country, but revenge politics is not a solution. The Ba'th Party seriously harmed the country, and so did many other parties. The Ba'th Party is, in a sense, a crystallization of the degeneration of Iraqi politics. It is a natural product of a violent political culture that dominated Iraq for many decades, particularly since the mid-1930s. However, in judging the previous regime, one should also ask what the new regime has provided for the Iraqis. It seems that both the prior and the current regimes should be brought to accountability for both have failed to satisfy the needs and aspirations of the Iraqis. In this context, it is important to stress that the mistakes of the old regime should not justify the mistakes of the new regime, inasmuch as current mistakes should not justify the mistakes of the former regime.

The nearly absolute domination of the previous authoritarian regime over all social aspects of life and its monopolization of all access to wealth, power, jobs, and education have contributed to a bizarre situation where the right to a normal life was seriously constrained. This situation led to various ways of complicity, a destiny that very few people were able to escape. Nevertheless, the arrogance of the dominant political culture tends to blur this reality. The Ba'th Party is not the only violent party in the Iraqi political culture, which can easily be described as violent and intolerant. Taking into consideration the violent history of Iraq and its intolerant political culture, it would be futile to identify who are responsible for the disaster of the country and who are not. Any such efforts would succumb to sectarian, ethnic, and partisan politics, which is bereft of objectivity. Instead of starting a process of blaming and vengeance, Iraq must focus on a conscious self-critical investigation of its history and start to institutionalize processes and measures capable of arresting the reoccurrence of its ugly, violent, and authoritarian past. In discussing the experience of the post-Communist regimes, Elster dares to argue: "One should target everybody or nobody. And because it is impossible to reach everybody, nobody should be punished and nobody compensated."[31]

De-Ba'thification is an expression of politics of revenge that came to dominate the vision and philosophy of the former opponents and now ruling elites. Through repressive measures, the victors are taking revenge against the old oppressive regime. Paradoxically, although Americans have a vision of democracy for Iraq, they too were enthusiastic about this vindictive politics by institutionalizing and encouraging the process of de-Ba'thification. Just few days after his arrival in Baghdad, Paul Bremer announced that the Iraqi Army would be disbanded and not paid and that all ministries would be de-Ba'thized. He even used the word "extirpating" the remnants of the old regime. In an interview with *Newsweek*, Bremer maintained that "the de-Baathification decree is the singly most popular thing I've done since I've been in Iraq."[32]

Nevertheless, the politics of revenge contradicts the more desirable and more beneficial vision and objective of establishing a veritable democratic system in Iraq that is based on institutions, individuality, citizenship, the rule of law, and a system that respects and preserves the culture of human rights. Achieving these objectives would ensure another way of de-Ba'thification, and pursuing this other option entails changing priorities and focuses. Hence, the main issue should not be the eradication of Ba'thism as such, but instead, the eradication of the whole authoritarian politics and culture that produces the Ba'th Party and all other violent parties that dominate the Iraqi political landscape. This inevitably calls for a critical reevaluation of the whole constellation of sociocultural values that dominate Iraqi social existence on various levels: childhood, family, gender, society, culture, and politics. The alternative route, *de-authoritarianization*, is a process that de-emphasizes all forms of violence in society and promotes instead a culture of tolerance, the peaceful resolution of conflicts, and working for national interests. From all angles, de-authoritarianization makes much more sense in new Iraq than vengeful de-Ba'thification.

NOTES

1. Edward Wong and Erik Eckholm, "Allawi Presses Effort to Bring Back Baathists," *New York Times*, October 13, 2004.

2. Osama Mahdi, "The Ba'ath Challenges: Exploiting the fear of candidates in the elections," *Elaph Electronic Paper*, November 20, 2009, http://www.elaph.com/Web/Politics/2009/11/504997.htm.

3. Ibid.

4. Liz Sly, "Iraq Bars Major Sunni Party from Election," *Los Angeles Times*, January 8, 2010.

5. Steven Lee Myers, "Candidate Bans Worsen Iraqi's Political Turmoil," *New York Times*, January 18, 2010.

6. Ernesto Londono and Leila Fadel, "Ahmed Chalabi's Renewed Influence in Iraq Concerns U.S.," *Washington Post*, February 27, 2010.

7. Liz Sly, "Iraqi Politician's Star Rising Again," *Los Angeles Times*, February 28, 2010.

8. Rod Norland and Sam Dagher, "U.S. Will Release More Members of an Iraqi Militia," *New York Times*, August 18, 2009.

9. Sly, "Anti-Baath Campaign a Spur to Iraq Shiite Voters," *Los Angeles Times*, February 12, 2010.

10. Abdel Rahman al-Rashed, "Petraeus, Lami, and the Farce of Integrity," *Asharq al-Awsat*, February 1, 2010.

11. Nada Bakri, "Biden Visits Iraq Seeking to Resolve Political Dispute," *New York Times*, January 23, 2010.

12. Nasir al-Ali, "Fears of Liquidating Rivals," *Asharq al-Awsat*, November 14, 2009.

13. For details, see the official website of this movement at http://www.no-ba3th.com.

14. Mary Albon, "Project on Injustice in Time of Transition," in *Transitional Justice: How Emerging Democracies Reckon with Former Regimes*, vol. 1, *General Considerations*, ed. Neil J. Kritz (Washington, DC: Institute of Peace Press, 1995), 50–51.

15. Joost Hiltermann, "Playing with Fire in Iraq," *The National*, January 28, 2010.

16. Miranda Sissons, "Iraq's New 'Accountability and Justice Law,' " ICTJ, January 22, 2008, 3, http://www.ictj.org/images/content/7/6/764.pdf.

17. Peter Slevin and Rajiv Chandrasekaran, "Iraq's Baath Party Is Abolished," *Washington Post*, May 12, 2003.

18. Pamela Constable, "Idled Iraqis Cry Foul over Firings," *Washington Post*, July 27, 2003.

19. Amy Waldman, "In Search for Baath Loyalists, U.S. Finds Itself in Gray Area," *New York Times*, July 22, 2003.

20. Ibid.

21. Michael Rubin, "Misguided Reconciliation with Baathists," *Philadelphia Inquirer*, October 19, 2006.

22. SNCD, "Accountability and Justice Law," http://www.debaath.com/site/page/ajt_s/index.htm.

23. Rubin, "Misguided Reconciliation."

24. Sam Dagher, "Iraq Resists Pleas by U.S. to Placate Baath Party," *New York Times*, April 26, 2009.

25. Huda Jasim and Nasir al-Ali, "No Reconciliation and No Return for Those Who Caused the Destruction of Iraq," *Asharq al-Awsat*, March 30, 2009.

26. Herman Schwartz, "Lustration in Eastern Europe," in Kritz, *Transitional Justice*, 464.

27. Luc Huyse, "Justice after Transition: On the Choices Successor Elites Making in Dealing with the Past," in Kritz, *Transitional Justice*, 346.

28. Quoted in Michael Rubin, "The Price of Compromise," *New York Sun*, August 8, 2005.

29. "Seven Questions: The De-Bremerification of Iraq," interview with Ambassador Feisal al-Istrabadi, *Foreign Policy*, January 2008, http://www.foreignpolicy.com/story/cms.php?story_id=4139.

30. Scott Wilson, "Iraqis Killing Former Baath Party Members," *Washington Post*, May 20, 2003.

31. Jon Elster, "On Doing What One Can: An Argument against Post-Communist Restitution and Retribution," in Kritz, *Transitional Justice*, 566.

32. *Newsweek*, October 6, 2003.

6

Deficient Justice

CONTEXTUALIZING JUSTICE

Preoccupation with justice is one of the most important aspects of the historical development of mankind. However, social consensus on the centrality of justice does not make justice less controversial or an easy issue to tackle. This is particularly true for countries confronting a horrible past. Questions on the meaning of justice, such as how to achieve it, who are the winners and the losers, and who are the victims and the perpetrators, are all difficult to settle. Addressing these complex questions depends on what definition of justice to adopt. In a general sense, justice implies rectifying the wrong and making things right, but then the contingent question is how to achieve this objective. Arendt stresses: "Men are unable to forgive what they cannot punish."[1] Punishment appears to be interrelated with and significant to justice, at least to punitive or retributive justice, which focuses on individual culpability.

This limited notion of justice has been questioned lately in favor of adopting a much broader sense of justice that focuses on society. This issue has been taken by Kiss, for instance, who argues that the tendency to equate justice with retribution must be challenged; justice should not be seen merely as retribution; and that "prosecutions would have yielded much less truth about what happened and why, and far fewer opportunities for closure, healing, and reconciliation."[2] Instead, Kiss calls for the alternative expansive notion of justice, restorative justice, "which is concerned not so much with punishment as with correcting imbalances, restoring broken relationships with healing, harmony and reconciliation."[3] Thus, restorative justice is the rehabilitation of perpetrators and victims and the reestablishment of relations based on equal concern and respect.

In this societal sense, restorative justice is strongly linked to distributive justice that entails addressing the underlying causes of conflict, inequitable distribution of and access to political and economic resources. Both restorative and distributive justice are feasible within a context of rule of law, equality, and democracy. What is more helpful for societies that are serious about burying a terrible past is to adopt an approach to justice that is grounded on institutional reforms and reflecting societal concerns. It is in this vision of justice where the notion of transitional justice makes sense. According to Dworkin, transitional justice is "the idea that legal accountability for atrocities committed by an outgoing regime can help to heal divided societies."[4] Undoubtedly, accomplishing justice is a desirable objective as such, but it is even more functional to use justice as an instrument for societal reforms. In this sense, authentic justice needs to go beyond punishment to national healing, particularly for a wounded nation like Iraq, emerging from the trauma of dictatorship and long history of violence.

Trials are not necessarily the optimum means to ensure national healing. After all, the Nuremberg trials did not lead to the healing of Germany, and there are serious doubts that the case of Iraq would prove otherwise. However, the new ruling elites consider that trials are indispensable in any approach to serving justice. In this respect, trials are regarded as a symbol of new Iraq and the end of the old regime. However, the challenge for new Iraq is certainly a much more complex than just putting an end to the previous regime. The challenge is putting an end to the multiple vicious cycles of violence, victimization, and revenge by altogether changing the rules of the game that govern social existence in the country. A more constructive vision of justice entails reevaluating Iraqi history, the entire political culture, and the dominant social, cultural, and gender norms and values that feed cycles of violence and intolerance. In contrast, an approach that reduces justice to merely punishing the former rulers is a deficient justice that comes into conflict with a much more broader and productive notion of justice. The new Iraqi experience since 2003, which is dominated by the supremacy of partisan politics, sectarianism, corruption, monopoly of resources, and revenge and victimization politics, tends to promote the inevitable adoption of a limited notion of justice. A vision of justice that is solely based on trials not only fails to end a chapter in the history of violence in Iraq but also takes violence to another level.

However, the seriousness of the atrocities of the deposed regime makes trials an unavoidable outcome. Human rights officials have estimated that more than 300,000 bodies were buried in mass graves across the country during the rule of Saddam. Creating the paradox of rich land/poor people by wasting the national wealth through extensive militarization, wars, and corruption is an equally serious crime. It is also important to put an end to the culture of impunity where government officials, security agents, and military officers break the law without fear of punishment. Lack of accountability should be replaced with a culture of responsibilities and rights. Humphrey stresses: "The primary aim of trials after mass atrocity is to re-establish the rule of law by establishing truth and justice about the past. Trials are an important mechanism to re-establish the authority of law and thereby engender people's trust and confidence in national institutions . . . the burden of trials is not just restorative but constitutive of national law."[5]

Thus it is important to hold the untouchables accountable. However, achieving this objective will inevitably confront a difficult question: who is really responsible for the atrocities and who should stand trial? In no way can the prosecution of a handful of scapegoats cleanse the past, and the prosecution of every guilty individual would render the state inoperable. In this respect, providing individuals with protection from liability for previous acts (i.e., amnesty) would have appeared to be an attractive alternative. Amnesty could be helpful in buying societal peace and advancing reconciliation, which are badly needed in a fragmented society. Amnesty for perpetrators could also be beneficial for those on the other side of the conflict—the "victims"—who themselves might have committed atrocities against the previous regime or against innocent people. Iraqi history is full of incidences of such violence, from several assassination attempts to horrifying atrocities during the revolt of 1991. Nevertheless, amnesty could be interpreted as destructive to ethics and morality, and harmful to justice. It may simply extend the impunity that the perpetrators once enjoyed under the old regime.

Prosecuting all those responsible for the atrocities is as contentious as the issue of amnesty. This is particularly true when the history of violence is interpreted as a shared responsibility of many opposing parties, although this explanation is less acknowledged as such. This interpretation is still valid even when the primary focus is on the atrocities of the regime. Responsibility is a thin concept; under seductive circumstances, anyone can in fact do evil. Goldhagen's book, *Hitler's Willing Executioners*, where he holds the entire German society responsible for what happened during that violent period, has instigated a heated academic debate. Many have criticized the book in the sense that no society deserves such sweeping, indiscriminate moral characterization. Discussing shared guilt, Arendt warns: "Where all are guilty, no one is; confessions of collective guilt are the best possible safeguard against the discovery of culprits, and the very magnitude of the crime the best excuse of doing nothing."[6] However, the question raised by this Goldhagen's book is too controversial an issue to be dismissed easily.

What is important in this respect is that this question is very relevant to the case of Iraq, and it implies serious repercussions to visions of justice in the country. Makiya explains this predicament for Iraq: "Almost any post-Ba'thist future in Iraq is going to be like walking a tightrope, balancing the legitimate grievances of all those who have suffered against the knowledge that if everyone is held accountable who is in fact guilty, the country will also be torn apart. Iraq after Saddam is going to be a country in which justice is both the first thing that everybody wants and the most difficult thing for anyone to deliver."[7] Perito expands:

> During its rule, the all-pervasive reach of the Baath Party and security organs has involved vast numbers of Iraqis in the apparatus of abuse. As a consequence, the number of individuals implicated in the crimes of the regime may run into the tens or even hundreds of thousands. The decisions on who will be held accountable will have to be made in a fully transparent manner, conscious of the very significant practical limitations of the renascent justice system. Such decisions must also be made with the awareness that the entire process will fail if it appears such trials are a means of taking revenge or of assigning collective guilt or if the ultimate result is not reconciliation and the promotion of national unity.[8]

When responsibility is a debatable concept and complicity in violence is more common than is readily admitted, selective trials become necessary. Maier suggests: "Trials must be highly selective, and the relatively few culprits must serve as proxy for a broader group of offenders. Complicity is diffuse, and it is impractical to try what may be close to an entire population."[9] On the other hand, Minow argues that selective prosecutions jeopardize the ideals of accountability and the hope for deterrence; prosecuting only high-level officials leaves the impression that those lower in the chain of command are excused.[10] Trials are about the individualization of responsibility and guilt, which is important for retributive justice. However, individualizing the legal process of responsibility and guilt has its own drawbacks. According to Humphrey this process can lead to "a polarized division between the innocent and guilty. Trials then produce a post-conflict solution which tends to overload responsibility on certain responsible figures, effectively making them scapegoats. The polarizing outcome has the negative effect of disengaging the public from reflecting on their responsibility for allowing the erosion of law and individual rights to take place."[11]

Trials can have additional shortcomings too. Trials are financially and emotionally costly and can be easily perceived as political retribution, which could possibly lead to further resentment and division in society. At the trial, atrocities might be reduced to wrangling over legal technicalities by the perpetrators and their lawyers. When a trial is mocked or exploited, the law can seem helpless and inadequate. There is also a big discrepancy between the horror of mass murder and the dispassionate proceedings of a courtroom. Minow elaborates: "Trial procedure make for laborious and even boring sessions that risk anesthetizing even the most avid listener and dulling sensibilities even in the face of recounted horrors. The simplistic questions of guilt or innocence framed by the criminal trial can never capture the multiple sources of mass violence."[12]

One of the serious limitations of trials is that the main focus is on the perpetrators, and not the victims. The role of the victims in a courtroom is to testify in order to establish the guilt of the defendants. This is even more so when the perpetrator is a politically important figure, as Saddam Hussein for instance. Humphrey argues: "The political priority of national trials is to re-establish the principle of justice and authority of the law rather than to achieve individual justice for many victims who, as a consequence of the selectivity of prosecution, remain unrecognized, unreconciled and uncompensated."[13]

Despite limitations, trials help advance justice, particularly if these trials are incorporated into a broader vision of justice that is linked to the future of the country. Trials can serve educational purposes and can strengthen justice, the rule of law, and accountability. Bringing political leaders to accountability is a new achievement in Iraq and in the rest of the Middle East. Notwithstanding the fury of the Arab world, with their claims that the U.S.-sponsored trials are tainted with illegitimacy and that putting an Arab president on trial is an insult to the Arabs, this achievement remains an inspiring development in a region still ruled by stubborn authoritarianism. An Iraqi citizen says: "Of course we are deeply affected when we see him on television in front of a judge. This man ruled us for 35 years."[14] To secure the right to defense to everyone, even to an infamous perpetrator, such as Saddam Hussein, is a new legal routine. Trials offer a medium for listening to the story of other sides of the conflict. Despite the serious atrocities committed and the strong political opinions about these crimes and the trials, listening patiently to what the defendants have to say in the courtroom is an exercise of democracy and tolerance. In a sense, trials can function as a cathartic forum.

New trials in Iraq represent a serious departure from staged trials under the old regime. In the past, even telling a joke about the president could lead to torture or execution, without the benefit of standing trial. It is because of this bloody history that trials and justice in Iraq should take a new turn and meaning. Although it is true that the new trials could be considered a serious improvement in the record of Iraqi justice, it would be an insult to a truly new Iraq to compare these trials with the arbitrary justice of the deposed regime and be content with the comparison. New Iraq should aspire much further to establish a culture of human rights and adopt modern standards of international law and justice.

However, the timing of the trials poses serious problem; they were held under intense sectarian violence. The ruling political elite believes that a quick move to trial and punishment will publicly signal the end of a discredited regime, thereby deterring any insurgent force that aspires for a return to the previous order and signaling the beginning of a new Iraq. Meanwhile, many people believe that new Iraq is about putting an end to the vicious cycles of violence and intolerance. For them, the trials are nothing but disappointments that miserably fail to put an end to a violent chapter in Iraqi history. Moreover, starting a trial in the midst of deteriorating security and sectarian strife makes the trial itself an exercise of violence, destabilization, and further social divisiveness. The contradiction and the paradox of the timing of the trials are apparent when they are viewed from the perspective of continued violence. They may have the negative consequence of blurring boundaries between old and new Iraq. Mani suggests: "Sometimes it may be detrimental to the cause of justice to rush trials in volatile, vulnerable postconflict situations with weak criminal justice systems. It may be preferable to postpone trials until government is more stable, and the rule of law is better equipped to provide formal justice."[15]

The time of the trials is as important as the trials themselves, and the time chosen by the ruling politicians was questionable. To hold a trial while the country is still under a state of insecurity and violence is both undesirable and insensible. Rushing trials under these circumstances certainly jeopardizes the security of the court; the resulting threat poses a grave problem with somber implications. In fact, one judge and three defense lawyers were killed during the course of the trials. The meaning and the message of trials are lost when they are held under conditions of violence. Moreover, the connection of these trials to the rule of law, democratic transition, reconciliation, overcoming the cycle of violence, and hoping for a better future becomes disappointingly weak and dubious.

However, the rulers have decided to initiate a limited number of trials and to indict only the top leaders of the former regime. This makes sense, considering the complexity of political and economic life under the regime of Saddam. Even the famous Nuremberg trials prosecuted only 24 defendants despite the graveness of the Nazis' atrocities. However, the decision to seek justice through trials has immediately encountered the dilemma of holding these trials locally or internationally. At this point, it is necessary to emphasize that what is important in a locally convened trial is avoiding the subjugation of the trial to political pressures or turning the trial into a political exhibition. This is particularly true, given that there is a history of staged trials in Iraq since 1958 and especially after 1968. Trials that are not an integral part of a wider vision of justice, especially since revenge is deeply rooted in Iraqi political culture, face the risk of being reduced to a mere exercise of revenge.

FLAWED TRIAL

The Iraqi Special Tribunal was established by the IGC on December 15, 2003, to prosecute the leaders of the deposed regimes for crimes committed between 1968 and 2003. In January 2005, the parliament approved the court and changed its name to the Iraqi High Tribunal (IHT), *al mahkama al iraqiyya al jana'iyya al ulya*. The IHT has jurisdiction over individuals residing in Iraq accused of committing genocide, crimes against humanity, or war crimes during the rule of the Ba'th Party 1968–2003. Since Iraqi laws do not enclose this type of crimes, the definitions of these crimes were taken from international criminal law.

The trial of Saddam Hussein and his close associates opened on October 19, 2005, with the Dujail case, which was the first investigation completed in a series of 14 cases. This case is about an assassination attempt against Saddam by members of the banned Shiite religious Da'wa Party who fired on his motorcade while in a visit to the village of Dujail in 1982. It is noteworthy that this trial is a case of assassination against Saddam, who himself participated in an assassination attempt against a former prime minister, abdul-Karim Qassim, in 1959, for which Saddam was sentenced in absentia to a prison term.

The aborted attempt against Saddam, however, was followed by indiscriminate reprisal and a campaign of retribution. Nine people were immediately killed and hundreds were arrested. A revolutionary court sentenced 148 people to death, including 10 who were under the age of 18; 4 people were hanged by mistake; 46 of the sentenced died under torture while in detention; 700 residents were banished to a remote detention center in Iraq's southern desert; in addition to the destruction of the village's livelihood by eradicating date palm groves and fruit orchards and razing hundreds of homes. However, Saddam eventually returned the confiscated farms to the residents. Altogether, seven defendants were charged for this case, including Saddam Hussein himself: Barzan Ibrahim al-Tikriti, Saddam's half brother and former intelligence chief; Taha Yassin Ramadan, a former vice president and leader of the Popular Army; and Awad al-Bandar, former chief judge of the Revolutionary Court. The other three were lower-level defendants from Dujail.

About 600 lawyers volunteered to defend Saddam. Most of these lawyers were Arabs, including for instance Ai'sha, daughter of Qaddafi, and Najib al-Nuaimi, a former Qatari justice minister; but there were others as well, including Ramsey Clark, a former U.S. attorney general. The paymaster of the lawyers was Raghad, daughter of Saddam. Many of these lawyers publicly stated that they were honored to defend Saddam. However, one can still argue that there are more decent and constructive sources of honor for these lawyers than the defending of a notorious dictator, such as playing an active role in improving the dismal records of human rights culture in the Arab world. Their own record at the court was so poor and disappointing that even Raghad was angry and bitter at their performance. Her disenchantment was also shared by international organization that monitored the trial.

HRW states that the observed performance of the defense counsel was generally poor and that it was difficult to discern any coherent defense case developed by the lawyers. The absence of any training or instruction in principles of international criminal law was evident in the failure to raise or discuss any of the relevant principles during the course of the trial. HRW also stresses that the common use of boycotts by the lawyers not only would appear to contravene their professional obligations under Iraqi law, creating the strong impression that they deliberately sought to delay or obstruct the court; but also did not advance the interests of their clients since this tactic greatly diminished their ability to raise legitimate and serious procedural concerns. The defense counsel "seemed more concerned to make political statements through their questioning of witnesses than to serve the interests of their clients by addressing the substance of the case against them."[16] Another organization, the ICTJ, concurs: "The defence repeatedly failed to use the opportunities afforded to it by the tribunal. Privately retained counsel would often resort to politicized and unhelpful tactics such as staging walkouts."[17]

During the trial of Saddam, instead of staying to litigate complaints, defense counsels opted for the tactics of frequent walkouts and politicizing the trial by focusing on the legitimacy of the court. They even went as far as questioning the legitimacy of the American invasion and occupation. The defense insisted that their client should not be prosecuted because he is still the legitimate ruler of Iraq. In one of the many tirades against the United States, Khalil Dulaimi, the Iraqi lead lawyer, asserted that Americans "want to blame Saddam for the mass graves and killing Kurds, but they forget that they supported Saddam back then."[18]

Politicizing, boycotting, and disrespecting the court, in addition to interrupting and insulting witnesses, showed a missed opportunity on the part of the defense to engage in improving legal standards and advancing justice in Iraq. One testifying victim said that he and his mother were detained for four years and that his 70-year-old father and 17-year-old brother never returned from detention. He later received a death certificate for them showing they had been executed. In cross-examination, defense lawyer al-Nuaimi asked if the witness had filed complaints with the government after their release. "Who am I going to file a complaint with?" the witness replied. "We could not say a word."[19]

Nevertheless, the man who designed the Iraq in which no word of protest could be raised in public was himself now on trial. When the judge referred to him as the "former" president after asking him to identify himself, he growled from the dock, "I didn't say 'former president,' I said 'president,' and I have rights according to the Constitution, among them immunity from prosecution."[20] Thus according to Saddam, impunity should continue even when he is not in power. When the judge asked him how to plead to the charges against him, he replied "I can't reduce my answers to 'yes' or 'no,' I cannot say 'guilty' or 'not guilty. You are in front of Saddam Hussein, the president of the republic," to which the judge replied: "You are a defendant."[21] In one of his many outbursts he scoffed at the charges of the killing of 148 people in the case against him by saying: "Do you think Saddam Hussein has no work? I have no time."[22] For some leaders, the death of one citizen is a serious problem; for others, the killing of 148 people is a trivial matter.

As expected, the defendants often tried to disrupt the court with misbehavior, interrupting and insulting witnesses, fierce but irrelevant outbursts, and turning the court into a theater for political discourse. Judge Rizgar Amin resigned in January 2006 amid criticism that he was too soft, too lenient on eruptions and theatrics from defendants and their lawyers. Discipline was somehow restored with the appointment of a new chief judge, Raouf abdel-Rahman. In a trial of this type, courtroom management tends to face serious problems in curtailing political speeches, disruptive behavior, and disorderly conduct. However, turning the court into a theater for political and anti-American diatribes occurs even in internationally held trials, as the case of Milosevic clearly showed. There is a dilemma in how to deal with such a distracting and unruly strategy without jeopardizing the fairness of the trial. Allowing political discourse to dominate the court in the name of defendant's rights will surely compromise the victim's rights to witness a fair trial and to bring perpetrators to accountability.

The Dujail trial ended on July 27, 2006, and a verdict was announced on November 5, 2006. Saddam, Barzan, and Awad were sentenced to death; Taha was initially sentenced to life imprisonment but the decision was changed to the death penalty by the Court of Appeal; two lower-level defendants received jail sentences and one was acquitted. Posner comments: "The trial of Saddam Hussein will have the same structure as a certain type of detective novel: we know who did it, and we know how it will end; the only mystery is how we will get there."[23] In reality, however, the important question is not really whether or not Saddam was guilty of crimes against humanity; the public record is full of his unforgivable atrocities.

Fortunately, the deposed regime documented its own atrocities, mainly to check if orders were executed to ensure loyalty and subordination but also to introduce terror and fear in others. The former Iraqi regime documented its acts in minute detail and archived these in central and local government ministries as well as the offices of intelligence and security agencies.[24] Unimpeachable evidence from the regime's own archives directly linking the chain of responsibility for the Dujail case to Saddam himself was found by the court. Strong evidence was presented at the court including documents bearing his signature for the approval of the executions. There was even a written order showing that Saddam approved the secret execution of

10 juveniles whose ages ranged from 11 to 17. Many lawyers in criminal law observed that the prosecution marshaled surprisingly convincing documents. A legal expert, Scharf, observed: "Saddam was convicted on the strength of his own documents."[25] During the course of the trial, Saddam eventually admitted responsibility, but he denied committing any crime, stating that he took the actions lawfully as Iraq's president in response to an assassination attempt. "Where is the crime?" he protested.

However, the Dujail trial triggered somewhat mixed reactions and evaluations. On behalf of the ICTJ, Sissons and Bassin point out that the greatest failing of this trial is the lack of judicial independence associated with the power of the council of ministers to transfer judges from the tribunal and the provision preventing former Ba'thists from being members of the tribunal's staff. They continue to indicate that while it was better than any previous Iraqi trials, it failed to meet the minimum fair-trial guarantees. "The Dujail trial was a missed opportunity in the search for Iraqi justice."[26] Elsewhere, Sissons was more conceding by revealing: "This was not a sham trial. The judges are doing their best to try this case to an entirely new standard for Iraq."[27] Other legal experts have similar mixed feelings about the trial. Drimmer provides the answer no to the question whether the trial met the standards of international justice: "But to look at the ultimate verdict, it certainly is consistent with the evidence presented"; and he continues, "But ultimately having Saddam Hussein prosecuted in a transparent proceeding is a major step for Iraq."[28]

One of the solemn critiques of the trial is the political interference and pressures on the trial that contravene the ideal of impartial justice and compromise the notion of judicial independence. HRW asserts: "The statements of officials indicate that the Iraqi government has not only failed to promote a climate of public opinion conducive to a fair trial, but has actively encouraged the prejudgment of the outcome of the case . . . In creating an environment in which judges feel intense pressure to be seen as dealing severely with the accused, such behavior undermines the guarantee of presumption of innocence at trial."[29] Similar criticism is also made by ICTJ: "Political leaders made public remarks assuming the guilt of the accused throughout the process, and gave the impression that verdicts and sentencing were foregone conclusions."[30] While it is true that there are strong opinions on these crimes and the responsibility of Saddam, the ruling political elites should have refrained from making political statements regarding these issues during the course of the trial. Respect for the independence of the court is utterly important for building a new experience in Iraq.

Political meddling in the trials was also evident in other aspects, with serious consequences for the cause of justice in Iraq. After the confirmation of the verdict in Saddam's case, the court ordered that the sentence be carried out in thirty days. This practically meant the execution of Saddam before the conclusion of other, even more important pending trials. Indeed, Saddam was hastily executed while his second trial was ongoing. This second trial involves the so-called Anfal case, the code name for Iraq's military attacks on Kurdish villages and towns in the north of the country. The attacks were considered crimes of genocide and ethnic cleansing. The term "Anfal," which means "spoils" in Arabic, is a Qur'an-inspired name used for this genocide. Committing atrocities under religious names shows how religion is currently perceived and exploited in the Middle East. Anfal is a well-documented case; there are detailed records of officers responsible, execution orders, and lists of victims. Anfal shows the arrogance of the previous regime, which lived under the illusion that it would enjoy eternal impunity and would never collapse or be held accountable.

In audio recordings presented at the trial, one officer was telling Saddam about plans to drop napalm bombs on Kurdish towns, to which Saddam replied: "Yes, in areas where you have concentrated populations that would be useful." At one point, he was heard telling a general to summarily execute field commanders who fail to adequately prepare their defenses against Kurdish guerrilla attacks. In one of the recordings, he was heard justifying the use of chemical weapons against Kurds and praising the effectiveness of these weapons. In conversation with his deputy, he said: "Yes, they will kill thousands. I don't know if you know this, comrade Izzat, but chemical weapons are not used unless I personally give the orders."[31] Saddam is the first president in history to use chemical weapons against his own people.

Saddam's cousin, Ali al-Majeed, popularly known as "Chemical Ali," was put in charge of committing these horrifying atrocities. In June 2007, he was sentenced to the death penalty for the crime of Anfal, in addition to two other death penalty convictions for his role in the atrocities against the Shiites in the south. In December 2008 another trial started, the case of Halabja, a small Kurdish town near the border with Iran that came under poison gas attack in March 1988, leading to the death of 5,000 people. The trial was concluded on January 17, 2010, with yet another death sentence for Ali. He was executed on January 25, 2010. McKiernan comments: "Imagine looking down on thousands of little creatures and then spraying them with a giant can of Raid. This is essentially what Saddam Hussein's air force did in 1988, when pilots doused the Kurdish town of Halabja with a cloud of deadly toxins, including large quantities of nerve gas."[32] Halabja became a symbol of Kurdish sufferings and a shameful image of the extreme brutality of the authoritarian rule of Saddam.

Saddam Hussein stood trial and was punished for just one case. Paradoxically, the case involves the least of all of his crimes. Despite the horrifying scale of his crimes over many years, Saddam was convicted of the murder of just 148 people in 1982.[33] The Dujail case is a good start but not a good finish.[34] After he was hanged, the interest in following the rest of the trials has dropped significantly, although these trials are far more important than the case for which he was executed. As one legal expert, Scharf, puts it: "The world will see in this first trial as something less than a genocidal monster."[35] Despite Saddam's terrifying acts against the Kurds, Kurdish politicians allowed him to be executed before the conclusion of other cases, particularly the cases of Anfal and Halabja. This position is rather strange, considering that Kurdish politicians usually fight fiercely for their rights, whether real, exaggerated, or imagined.

Although the Dujail case involves crimes against the Shiites, the atrocities against them were reduced to just one case, the case that particularly concerns the Da'wa Party (the ruling party since 2005). This proves that even with the supremacy of ethnic and sectarian politics, partisan politics is still very important in new Iraq. Makiya reveals that the Shiite village of Dujail is known for its political militancy and a stronghold of the Islamic fundamentalist underground.[36] Sissons and Bassin argue: "The political sensitivity of the case was reinforced by an alleged connection between events in Dujail and the Ba'th regime's persecution of the al-Dawa party, a leading Shi'a political party of which the current and previous Iraqi prime ministers are both members."[37]

Thus Saddam was tried and hanged for one case, for the benefit of one sect, or more precisely, for the benefit of only one political party. Authentic justice would be to have Saddam stand trial for all the intended cases against him. Although Saddam was indiscriminate in his violence, justice was reduced to a revengeful mix of partisan and sectarian politics. All Iraqis suffered from his crimes, including the Sunnis and even the Ba'thists. The trial of Saddam and his associates would have had a different impact if the 1979 massacre of top Ba'thist leaders, for instance, was included in the series of trials against him. If so, justice will then be considered as belonging to all Iraqis, not just to a few. Instead, many Iraqis feel they have been cheated when national justice was turned into partisan and sectarian vengeance. Establishing the fact that Saddam victimized all Iraqis is vital to the new order in the country. This could have positively influenced how the new regime would deal with old Iraq's legacy of violence and authoritarianism; it could have offered a fresh perception of reconciliation and justice. In this sense, the trial of Saddam failed to achieve a desirable outcome; therefore only deficient justice was served.

NOTES

1. Hannah Arendt, *The Human Condition* (Chicago: University of Chicago Press, 1998), 241.

2. Elizabeth Kiss, "Moral Ambition within and beyond Political Constraints: Reflection on Restorative Justice," in, *Truth v. Justice: The Morality of Truth Commissions*, ed. Robert I. Rotberg and Dennis Thompson (Princeton, NJ: Princeton University Press, 2000), 69.

3. Ibid.

4. Anthony Dworkin, "The Trials of Global Justice," *Open Democracy*, June 15, 2005, http://www.opendemocracy.net/globalization-institutions _government/war_crimes_2604.jsp.

5. Michael Humphrey, *The Politics of Atrocity and Reconciliation: From Terror to Trauma* (London: Routledge, 2002), 125.

6. Hannah Arendt, *On Violence* (New York: Harcourt, Brace and World, 1969), 65.

7. Kanan Makiya, *Republic of Fear: The Politics of Modern Iraq* (Berkeley: University of California Press, 1998), xxxii.

8. Robert Perito, "Establishing the Rule of Law in Iraq," United States Institute of Peace, Special Report 104, April 2003, 7, http://www.usip.org/ files/resources/sr104.pdf.

9. Charles S. Maier, "Overcoming the Past?" in *Politics and the Past: On Repairing Historical Injustices*, ed. John Torpey (Lanham, MD: Rowman and Littlefield, 2003), 296.

10. Martha Minow, "The Hope for Healing: What Can Truth Commissions Do?" in Robert and Thompson, *Truth v. Justice*, 238.

11. Humphrey, *The Politics of Atrocity*, 145.

12. Minow, "The Hope for Healing," 238.

13. Humphrey, *The Politics of Atrocity*, 132.

14. Borzou Daragahi, "Hussein Trial Inspires Fixation, Fury in Iraq," *Los Angeles Times*, December 8, 2005.

15. Rama Mani, *Beyond Retribution: Seeking Justice in the Shadow of War* (Cambridge: Polity, 2002), 100.

16. Nehdal Bhutta, "Judging Dujail: The First Trial before the Iraqi High Tribunal," *Human Rights Watch* 18, no. 9 (November 2006): 70–71, http://www.hrw.org/en/reports/2006/11/19/judging-dujail.

17. Miranda Sissons and Ari Bassin, "Was the Dujail Trial Fair?" *Journal of International Criminal Justice* 5 (2007): 280.

18. Jim Hoagland, "Put Iraq's Story on the Stand," *Washington Post*, October 23, 2005.

19. Louise Roug, "Iraq Trial Marked by Chaos, Drama," *Los Angeles Times*, December 23, 2005.

20. Neil MacFarquhar, "The Defiant Despot Oppressed Iraq for More Than 30 Years," *New York Times*, December 30, 2006.

21. Borzou Daragahi, " 'Not Guilty' Plea Is Entered for Hussein," *Los Angeles Times*, May 16, 2006.

22. Doug Struck, "In Courtroom, Hussein Acts Out Old Role with Flourish," *Washington Post*, December 7, 2005.

23. Eric Posner, "Justice within Limits," *New York Times*, September 26, 2005.

24. ICTJ, "Briefing Paper: Creation and First Trials of the Supreme Iraqi Criminal Tribunal," October 2005, 14, http://www.ictj.org/images/content/1/2/123.pdf.

25. Julia Preston, "Hussein Trial Was Flawed but Reasonably Fair, and Verdict Was Justified," *New York Times*, November 6, 2006.

26. Sissons and Bassin, "Was the Dujail," 273.

27. Preston, "Hussein Trial Was."

28. Ibid.

29. Bhuta, "Judging Dujail," 44.

30. Sissons and Bassin, "Was the Dujail," 278.

31. John F. Burns, "Hussein's Voice Speaks in Court in Praise of Chemical Atrocities," *New York Times*, January 9, 2007.

32. Kevin McKiernan, "Justice in Iraq," *Boston Globe*, February 9, 2005.

33. Richard Seymour, "The Man Who Knew Too Much," *The Middle East*, February 2007.

34. Gary J. Bass, "Try and Try Again," *New York Times*, September 26, 2005.

35. Richard Boudreaux and Borzou Daragahi, "More than Hussein Is on Trial," *Los Angeles Times*, October 14, 2005.

36. Makiya, *Republic of Fear*, 107.

37. Sissons and Bassin, "Was the Dujail," 275.

7

Sectarian Execution

CAPITAL PUNISHMENT

The IHT concluded that Saddam Hussein was found guilty in the Dujail case and awarded him the death penalty on November 5, 2006. At age 69, he was hanged in the early morning hours on December 30, 2006. Two other close associates, including his half brother Barzan, met the same fate few days later. His two sons and a grandson were killed in a shootout with U.S. troops in July 2003. As a symbol of utmost cruelty and violence, there is no question that Saddam deserved the harshest penalty possible for his many crimes and destructions against Iraqi society. No punishment in the world, not even the death sentence, is fair enough for such an extremely ruthless tyrant as Saddam. "He was just a death grip imposed on our neck," as one Iraqi citizen put it.[1] Even joking about him could have brought death or torture. When he was asked about the mass graves, he said that they were thieves who deserted the terrain of wars in Iran and Kuwait. However, the well-documented criminal record of Saddam does not mean that his execution was a straightforward case. On the contrary, the execution of Saddam proved to be highly contentious and open to much criticism.

The hasty execution of Saddam Hussein faces legal ambiguities on at least two grounds. First, by law, the president and his two deputies must sign the death sentence. Although the president, who opposes the death penalty on principle, failed to sign the death warrant, he executed a letter of consent in the end. Second, the law states that executions should not be held on public holidays. In violation of existing laws, the Iraqi government could not have chosen a worse time than the first day of *Id al-Adha*, a religious Muslim holiday that marks the end of the annual pilgrimage to the holy city of Mecca. The insistence on this timing brought widespread condemnation from the Arab world, which perceives the new political development and the rise of Shiite power in Iraq with suspicion and apprehension. It also aggravated the increasing sectarian polarization and antagonism in the Arab world between the mainstream Sunnis and the minority Shiites. In this context, there is a perception that the timing of the hanging was an insensitive gesture, if not an apparent insult to Muslims.

Paradoxically, Islamist politicians who hold religion at high esteem and whose worldviews are centered on religion committed this insult. It is noteworthy that the first Ba'thist regime in 1963 killed the then prime minister Qassim when he was fasting for Ramadan. Clearly, there is a history of religious inattentiveness when people are impelled to end the lives of their enemies. It is apparent that the vicious cycle of revenge feeds itself.

The insensitivity of the timing of Saddam's execution is a clear expression of the politics of sectarianism by the ruling elite. Instead of offering regrets and apologies, they dismissed the outcry of the Arab world as criticisms motivated by sectarianism and animosity toward the new Iraqi regime. It has also been claimed that the day of the execution is not normally a holiday as far as the Shiites are concerned. The Shiites usually celebrate the religious holiday one day after the Sunnis do.

In defending the time of the execution, an Iraqi judge claimed that the official religious holiday is celebrated not on the day of the execution but on the day thereafter. In an unconcealed sectarian tone, he added: "Saddam is not Sunni. And he is not Shiite. He is not Muslim." Perceptibly, this remark intends to silence all controversies over the time of the execution as nonsensical because the hanged man was not even regarded as a Muslim. This remark is a typical method of vilifying the enemy, which is an integral part of the politics of violence and revenge. To complicate matters, the insistence that the mainstream Sunni celebration of the religious holiday has nothing to do with the Shiite sect was taken by orthodox Islam as a further proof of the accusation that the Shiites are not truly Muslims, thus further aggravating sectarian polarization.

Regardless of this sectarian divide, one can still argue that celebrating the religious holiday one day later does not change the fact that the whole period was a time of religious festivity that should have been respected by everyone. In fact, deferring the execution of convicted criminals on account of public holidays is an accepted global tradition. Thus the ruling Shiite politicians not only unnecessarily violated this universally held tradition, but were also extremely insensitive to their fellow Iraqi Sunnis and to approximately 1 billion Sunni Muslims worldwide. The timing of the execution is an avoidable ugly act of violence. Unfortunately, the new ruling elites insisted on reproducing the politics of violence and revenge, as well as the mentality of the ruler they executed. The execution bears a clear sectarian message that makes the often talked about reconciliation a mere empty slogan. Many vainly expected the new rulers to invoke religion and religious festivities as a symbol of tolerance, forgiveness, and reconciliation.

Saddam Hussein was in the custody of the Americans, to be handed over to the Iraqi authorities for the execution. During the few days prior to the hanging, intense negotiations occurred where the American side insisted on clarifying some legal ambiguities and respecting Islamic religious sensitivity. On the Iraqi side, Prime Minister Maliki insisted that Americans should respect Iraq's right to decide matters for itself. One American official replied to him: "Forget about us. You're in front of the international community here. People will be watching this."[2] This is the same old argument of national sovereignty that Saddam and all dictators play in international politics and under which many atrocities and crimes are committed. Paradoxically, it is the same inculcation of national sovereignty that toppled the executed tyrant and brought Iraqi opposition politicians to power. However, to end the deadlock and reinforce the desirable solution, the unyielding Maliki secured the approval of the supreme authority in Iraqi Shiism, *the Marji'iyya*. The other side finally gave up.

Observers remain to question why the Iraqi government insisted on this timing and the hasty hanging when it was obvious that delaying the execution for a few days would have been a safer and more sensible approach. One Iraqi official, who was critical of the timing of the hanging, argued: "According to the law, no execution can be carried out during the holidays. After all the hard work we have done, why would we break the law and ruin what we have built?"[3] The religious holiday, however, was a feast of sacrifice, and executing the previous despot was the symbolic sacrifice implemented by theocratic rulers. The hurried hanging was a sacrifice, a gift to the Iraqi people, particularly to the Shiites, when there was nothing or very little to celebrate amidst violence, sectarian killings, high unemployment, and the lack of basic services. This explains why the head of the inefficient government, Maliki—contrary to the appeals of wisdom and prudence—rushed the execution.

Another explanation suggests that Saddam was hanged just for the Dujail case, which directly concerns the ruling Da'wa Party, Maliki's party. Interestingly, the Dujail crime was triggered by a violent act in itself (i.e., an assassination attempt against Saddam), and it is the least of Saddam's crimes. Saddam was not punished for the rest of his crimes, which were even more horrendous. He was executed despite a pending trial that involves far more important and serious charges where at least 100,000 were killed (only 148 were killed in the Dujail case). Sissons and Bassin bitterly comment: "The botched execution of Saddam Hussein undid in moments what the trial chamber had laboured hard to achieve."[4] The particular case for which the deposed ruler was hanged shows the sectarian nature of the new ruling elites. Turning national justice into sectarian vengeance shows that those who are now ruling the country harbor a mentality of opposition politics, not the mentality of the state they run and represent.

One of the most serious troubles with the execution of Saddam is the principle of capital punishment itself. One of the first rules of the CPA was the suspension of capital punishment, which is perhaps the first attempt at such in the Arab world, if not the whole Middle East. However, this was soon reversed by the Iraqi authority, who argued that the death penalty is valid for crimes committed before the decision of suspension. There are alarming reports of increasing use of death sentences and actual executions in the administration of justice in the country since the reinstitution of capital punishment. Amnesty International reports that Iraq has one of the highest rates of execution in the world. At least 120 people are known to have been executed in Iraq between January and early December 2009, and over 900 people including 17 women are waiting to face the same fate.[5]

However, the IHT is empowered to sentence the convicted guilty to death. Article 27(2) of the status of this special court makes the carrying out of death sentences handed out by the tribunal mandatory, by prohibiting the commutation of death sentences by any government official. This appears to infringe upon the constitutional authority of the president, who is required by the constitution to ratify death sentences before they are implemented. According to HRW, the mandatory application of the death penalty without any opportunity for clemency directly violates Iraq's human rights obligations under the International Covenant on Civil and Political Rights particularly Article 6(4): "Anyone sentenced to death shall have the right to seek pardon or commutation of the sentence. Amnesty, pardon or commutation of the sentence of death may be granted in all cases."[6]

The status of the special tribunal also requires that a sentence be executed no later than 30 days after a final decision is handed down.

This means that death sentences should be carried out even if other trials or charges for the same defendant are still pending. In doing so, justice and the accountability of the defendants are compromised. The question is why this conflict or contradiction was allowed to be drafted in the status of IHT when this is a tribunal specially established for the crimes of Saddam and his henchmen who were accused and charged for multiple crimes. For the sake of avoiding incomplete justice, the appeal court could have deferred the carrying out of the death penalty long enough to allow the completion of the rest of the trials addressing charges against Saddam.

International organizations oppose the death penalty as an inherently cruel and inhumane punishment. The insistence of the IHT on applying the death sentence triggered broad reservations and critics by these organizations. According to the ICTJ: "The application of the death penalty is a cause of major concern for many international human rights groups and has led many governments and international organizations, including the UN, to conclude that they are unable to lend the Tribunal moral, technical, or financial support."[7] In reality, however, although these critics are valid and significant, the decision to boycott the Iraqi trials has also been motivated by a politicized stand and critics of the Iraq War and the legitimacy of these trials under American occupation.

Notwithstanding the politicized rationales behind them, reservations and criticisms on the death penalty by international groups are serious and valid. Criticisms against the capital punishment do not in any way diminish the seriousness of the atrocities committed by the previous regime. There are arguments claiming that the suspension of the death penalty would lead the families of the victims to take revenge on their own, or that the Iraqi insistence on the death penalty is but a usual feeling of a wounded nation emerging from the trauma of dictatorship.

Nevertheless, the reinstitution of the death sentence is a big mistake and an unfortunate development that contradicts the objective of creating a culture of human rights. To facilitate the national healing of a traumatized nation, it is important to look beyond revenge and punishment. It is important for new Iraq to abrogate the death penalty, regardless of the nature of crimes and the social stature of criminals. Alternative options always exist, such as life imprisonment, different prison terms, or even community service. Imprisonment might lead to a prolonged state of contemplation on the part of convicted criminals, and it may even result in protracting their sufferings. In principle, this is a valid possibility, although there are serious doubts whether this can possibly be the case for Saddam and his close associates, judging from their behaviors in and out of power.

DEATH AND SECTARIAN POLITICS

The moment of the hanging of Saddam was an extraordinary instant indeed. It was undisguised crystallization of politics of revenge, and a moment of revenge par excellence. Order and law were replaced by Shiite confessional chants: "The tyrant has fallen! May God curse him," "Go to hell," "Long live Muhammad Baqir al-Sadr," "Long live Muqtada al-Sadr," or the repeated chants of "Muqtada, Muqtada" during the execution.[8] These chants reveal the poverty of the justice that was implemented that day. Chanting the name of Muqtada, an extremist religious leader, is only ironic given that there is an arrest warrant against him for the charges of murdering a rival senior Shiia leader, Khoei, in Najaf in 2003. This irony is reinforced by the fact that his sectarian militia, the Mahdi Army, is one of the militias that are responsible for the bloodshed during the sectarian conflict and for terrorizing the streets.

Krauthammer comments, disappointedly: "Worse was the content of the taunts: 'Moqtada, Moqtada,' the name of the radical and murderous Shiite extremist whose goons were obviously in the chamber. The world saw Hussein falling through the trapdoor, executed not in the name of a new and democratic Iraq but in the name of Moqtada al-Sadr, whose death squads have learned much from Hussein."[9] The executioners let Saddam drop in the midst of repeating a prayer of religious confirmation. There were even reports of revenge dancing around the corpse of Saddam. Trying to justify this behavior, the then security adviser who was present in the room said that the dancing is simply an Iraqi tradition!

The primitive sectarian chants, the vengeful dance, the taunting during execution, and the unruly, mocking atmosphere turned a supposedly dignified execution room into a jungle of reprisals. The fact that such a behavior came from religious people is ironic given that Islam calls for respecting the dignity of the dead. It is true that the brutality of Saddam caused thousands of Iraqis to face undignified death, but the new Iraq is supposed to be about breaking this cycle of revenge.

The ceremony of sectarian revenge was filmed surreptitiously on mobile phones. The images were not unlike the many videos terrorists take of beheadings in Iraq and elsewhere that are also accompanied by religious chants. The world has condemned these images of beheading and killing, yet the Iraqi government produced its own bloody and violent images. An editorial in the *New York Times* comments: "Saddam

Hussein deserves no one's pity. But as anyone who has seen the graphic cellphone video of his hanging can testify, his execution bore little resemblance to dispassionate, state-administered justice. The condemned dictator appeared to have been delivered from United States military custody into the hands of a Shiite lynch mob."[10]

Video images of Saddam's execution reveal something extraordinary. In the face of death, Saddam was calm, confident, and brave. He refused the offer of a hood to cover his eyes. He came out more dignified than his executioners did; he appeared a victim and even a hero for some. Many consider that these last moments are the good moments in Saddam's life that can transcend decades of his violent life and brutal rule. The dictator was overly rehabilitated, and the sectarian execution gave him a second chance he did not deserve. He lost the chance of apologizing to the Iraqi people during his trial, and with his death, that chance has gone forever. A ruthless mass murderer was allowed to win unearned victory. "They changed him from a criminal into a martyr," as one Iraqi teacher put it.[11] This event unfortunately reveals that the new rulers failed to raise themselves above violence, revenge, and intolerance. A convicted murderer emerged restrained and dignified, while his executioners, his former victims, appeared as bullying street thugs. This exchange of places in a perpetual cycle of hate and violence is nothing but a paradox, an ugly and destructive paradox.

The Arab world strongly reacted to Saddam's execution. The predominantly Sunni Arab world maintains that what they have witnessed was a calm and composed Sunni leader, and a spiteful and abusive Shiite Iraqi leadership. This has led to a resurgence of admiration, with the effect of eulogizing and even lionizing the late dictator. His dignity and pride are intact, if not enhanced. Meetings and conferences to glorify Saddam have been held by civil society organizations. The killing of Saddam was even regarded as the killing and the destruction of an Arab dream of renaissance and development. It was also seen as an act intended to block the road leading to the liberation of Palestine! Saddam was made a mythical hero of Pan-Arabism. Libya was considering the erection of a monument for Saddam, next to the statue of Omar el-Mukhtar, the hero of Libyan resistance against Italian colonialism.

While there were strong reactions against Saddam's beheading, there was complete silence about his countless atrocities, his responsibility for the destruction of Iraq, and what happened to the Middle East because of his foolish policies. This silence is astonishing, given that Saddam's atrocities were highly exposed, particularly after the invasion of Kuwait. The Arab Journalists Union glorified someone

who killed journalists and denied free press in his country. The Arab
Lawyers Union glorified someone whose rule was the very antithesis
of the rule of law and justice. Although it is true that this reaction in
the Arab world is partly motivated by the wrong timing and the disorderly atmosphere of the execution, it nevertheless shows a complete
lack of empathy and insensitivity to the sufferings of the Iraqis for
the benefit of a ruthless ruler who is now regarded as an "Arab hero."

The death of Saddam was a day of mourning in the Arab world. His
pictures were on display, and he was considered a martyr. From sociological and psychological viewpoints, this reaction is equally astonishing
and interesting. After watching this reaction toward the death of the dictator, one just wonders why people in the Arab world complain about
dictators in their countries. The death of a dictator is supposed to be
a time for reflection and thinking, a time for a critical evaluation of
Middle Eastern problems and the role that dictators play in aggravating
these problems. Thus a moment of great significance was lost in a region
well known for scoring missed opportunities. It is noteworthy that this is
not the first time the Arab world mourned the death of a dictator. The
same mourning happened earlier with the death of the Egyptian dictator,
Nasser. The fact that the Arab world mourns, this time for the death of a
very ruthless dictator with countless documented atrocities, only shows
the recent degeneration of this world on many fronts.

Thus the timing and the sectarian nature of the execution of
Saddam not only denied the Arab world a historic opportunity for
reflection but also aggravated sectarian polarization in the Middle
East. Ironically, the missed opportunity and the intense sectarian
divide are more evident in Iraq than anywhere else. The timing of
the hanging, coupled with the chanting of the Shiite militia, had serious repercussions on political sectarianism in Iraqi politics. The
circumstances of the hanging clearly show the extent to which the current government is controlled by sectarianism. The hanging was supposedly a formal proceeding carried out by a dispassionate state.
Instead, the ruling elites chose to behave not as state officials but as
mere sectarian politicians. Once again, the government and the state
became one and the same in perpetrating a rooted tradition in modern
Iraqi history. It is evident that the Shiites are running the state under a
sectarian banner, sometimes disguised and sometimes even undisguised, as shown in the case of Saddam's death.

There are those who claim that the hasty execution was motivated
by the aim of suppressing violent resistance. Accordingly, the execution was designed to purge a rallying point and symbol. In reality,

however, violence escalated as a result of the execution. Absurdly, one of the strong reasons behind the escalation of violence is that sectarian militias, which are connected with the ruling politicians, have been officially tolerated within the ethnic and sectarian political system that has dominated Iraq since 2003.

Although all Iraqis have suffered from the countless atrocities and disastrous adventures of their late dictator, the Shiites alone secured the "privilege" of benefiting from the dictator's trial and execution. No one has a monopoly on claims of sufferings in a terribly violent Iraqi society. The Shiites, Kurds, Sunnis, and even the Ba'thists were all victims of Saddam's atrocities, yet what occurred in Iraq was a sectarian application of justice. Many Iraqis feel that they have been cheated in this inconsistent application of justice.

The execution shows that the ruling Shiite politicians are trying to use populist politics to win legitimacy within the Shiite sect. Expressing his happiness over the hanging of Saddam, a 46-year-old Shiite citizen ecstatically says: "I feel like my mother delivered me for the first time. It's my birthday."[12] However, this kind of populist politics is associated with violence and vengeance. Populist politics has become increasingly instrumental in new Iraq, particularly under dire conditions of chronic corruption, a debilitating economy, and poor public services. For this reason, many ruling politicians claim that the hanging of Saddam is a victory for Iraq and for democracy. Alternatively, one can argue that a real victory for a democratic Iraq entails a country free from endemic corruption, violence, revenge, and intolerance. A real victory is about the supremacy of the rule of law, tolerance, and a culture of human rights for all Iraqi citizens. A real victory is, incidentally, the abolition of the death penalty that led to this execution, a step that is beneficial to the future of Iraq and to the positive integration of the country into the international community.

The ruling government has notably failed to view execution as a violent and vindictive act. The hanging of Saddam showed little justice but more revenge, feeding more violence and bigotry in society. Some Iraqis, the Shiites in particular, celebrated the event with customary gunfire. This symbolically proves that the Iraqis are missing the entire issue of violence: what it is and how it should be addressed. As an illustration of violence, gunfire is the last way to celebrate how authentic justice is being implemented in new Iraq. Acts of vengeance that feed the vicious cycle of violence, producing deficient justice, are not the right recipe for a new democratic Iraq. Dealings with past atrocities that do not form part of a broader vision of justice could very well degenerate into an exercise of revenge politics. The priority given to the case of Dujail, an atrocity connected to the ruling Da'wa Party, and the hasty execution of Saddam at the conclusion of this case—without putting him to answer the charges in the other pending trials—might have created the perception that the trial and the execution are acts of vengeance. One can acknowledge the need to establish a national standard of justice to avoid the use of vengeful acts by families of victims. However, it is unfortunate to see justice degenerate into simple acts of vengeance.

Revenge politics is rooted in Iraqi history. It is noteworthy that Shiism, as a political ideology, is strongly linked to revenging the death of Imam Hussein, the grandson of Prophet Muhammad, who was killed at the Battle of Karbala in Iraq in 680 CE. Moreover, even earlier, the concept of compensatory justice, an eye for an eye and a tooth for a tooth, was established in Iraq by ancient Mesopotamian rulers. The famous code of Hammurabi was promulgated 4,000 years ago in ancient Babylon. Back then, this code was the first step to establish justice in society, but an eye for an eye in the modern era will surely make the entire world blind, and a tooth for a tooth will leave the world toothless. Vengeance kills politics, or in the words of Shriver: "Nothing eats away at the 'glue' of civic order so surely as cycles of escalating revenge and counterrevenge."[13] Revenge is the very antithesis of politics. While authoritarianism essentially means extraordinary politics, if not a process of depoliticization, a new democratic Iraq should be about ordinary politics where revenge has no place.

In a sense, death and end are not essentially the same thing. Death is an end but end is not necessarily death. Clearly, it is possible to end the rule of a dictator without killing him. One can perceive the death of a dictator as a symbol of the end of an old regime, and, by implication, a symbol of the beginning of a new regime. Yet in the case of what has happened in Iraq since 2003, the difference between the old and the new is merely a change in the people who rule, not a change in the mentality or the values that generate and feed violence. The focus is on changing rulers and not on governance; hence, the start of the new regime seemed unthinkable for the new rulers, without the hasty physical liquidation of the former ruler. In the continuation of a well-established Iraqi political culture, new Iraq has a place for only one ruler. In a planet where more than 7 billion share life, there is no room for two rulers of the same country to be alive at the same place in one lifetime, even when one ruler is deposed and has no power.

Sentencing the despot to life imprisonment without the possibility of parole is surely a worthwhile option that can, perhaps, break the cycle of vindictive justice. To see the former tormentor alive, respected as a human being—even when he is a convicted criminal and in jail—and to see justice preserved even for a victimizer would have, perhaps, helped the new rulers to come to terms with their state of victimhood. This would have resulted in helping the new rulers transcend their bitter feelings of victimization. Yet banishing the abuser for good is a way of reinforcing and protracting this state of victimization, if not making it more respected, justified, and perpetual. After all, victimization is one of the significant political premises in new Iraq. This is clearly reflected in what Prime Minister Maliki said: "Anyone who rejects the execution of Saddam is undermining the martyrs of Iraq and their dignity."[14]

There is a rich history of executions in Iraq, particularly since 1941, concomitant with an increased militarization of Iraqi society and the development of a violent political culture. This constructed culture appears to lack ambivalence and hesitation about the death penalty. During the reign of Qassim in 1958, thousands of people in the street shouted, "No conspiracy occurs when we have the ropes," *maku mu'a-mara tsir wa al-hibal maujuda*; or "Execute, do not say I do not have time, execute them tonight," *a'dim la tkul ma indi wakit idimhum illela*. The execution of the Jews by Saddam in 1969 was turned into a picnic day for the public to watch the hanged corpses in the main square in downtown Baghdad. It is this culture of easy and unhesitating acceptance of executions that the new experience in Iraq should overcome. However, new Iraq insists on preserving this violent aspect of the dominant culture by feeding cycles of revenge and intolerance.

It is true that the dictator is dead for sure, but the legacy of authoritarianism and violence is very much alive in Iraq. Social existence in Iraqi society is still dominated by ruthlessness and intolerance. An editorial in the *New York Times* bitterly comments on this outcome: "Mr. Hussein had now gone to his grave. But the outrageous manner of his killing, deliberately mimicking his own methods, assured that this cruelty will outlive him."[15] Hoagland concurs, just as acrimoniously: "He leaves behind a country successfully recast in his own ferocious image to a degree far greater than I had imagined. Before 2003, I believed that Iraqis were largely a people held hostage by Hussein, his murderous clan and the Baathist machine. But far more Iraqis turned out to be like Hussein, ready to use torture and assassination in pursuit of wealth and power."[16] It is great to see the end of the dictator, but it would have been far greater and entirely euphoric to see the demise of the entire autocratic system in Iraq. The execution of the culture of violence and authoritarianism is far more desirable, functional, and productive than merely executing one symbol of such culture by the newly emerging elites who rule the country as irresponsibly and violently as before.

NOTES

1. Sabrina Tavernise, "Hussein Divides Iraq, Even in Death," *New York Times*, December 31, 2006.

2. John F. Burns, "Before Hanging, a Push for Revenge and a Push Back," *New York Times*, January 7, 2007.

3. Marc Santora, James Glanz, and Sabrina Tavernise, "Dictator Who Ruled Iraq with Violence Is Hanged for Crimes against Humanity," *New York Times*, December 30, 2006.

4. Miranda Sissons and Ari Bassin, "Was the Dujail Trial Fair?" *Journal of International Criminal Justice* 5 (2007): 285.

5. Amnesty International, "Over 900 People on Death Row in Iraq Face Imminent Execution," December 4, 2009, http://www.amnesty.org/en/news -and-updates/news/over-900-people-death-row-iraq-face-imminent-execution -20091204.

6. Nehdal Bhutta, "Judging Dujail: The First Trial before the Iraqi High Tribunal," *Human Rights Watch* 18, no. 9 (November 2006): 87, http://www .hrw.org/en/reports/2006/11/19/judging-dujail.

7. ICTJ, "Briefing Paper: Creation and First Trials of the Supreme Iraqi Criminal Tribunal," October 2005, 9, http://www.ictj.org/images/content/ 1/2/123.pdf.

8. John F. Burns and Marc Santora, "Rush to Hang Hussein Was Questioned," *New York Times*, January 1, 2007.

9. Charles Krauthammer, "The Hanging: Beyond Travesty," *Washington Post*, January 5, 2007.

10. Editorial, "The Ugly Death of Saddam Hussein," *New York Times*, January 4, 2007.

11. Sabrina Tavernise, "For Sunnis, Dictator's Degrading End Signals Ominous Dawn for the New Iraq," *New York Times*, January 1, 2007.

12. Ibid.

13. Donald W. Shriver Jr., "The Long Road to Reconciliation: Some Moral Stepping-Stones," in *After the Peace: Resistance and Reconciliation*, ed. Robert L. Rothstein (Boulder, CO: Rienner, 1999), 212.

14. Santora, Glanz, and Tavernise, "Dictator Who Ruled."

15. Editorial, "The Ugly Death."

16. Jim Hoagland, "What the Dictators Can't Stop," *Washington Post*, December 31, 2006.

8

Elections and Illusive Democracy

A CARNIVAL OF ELECTIONS

The last free election in Iraq was held in 1954. The many authoritarian rules in the country prevented the Iraqis from experiencing any real sense of democracy and elections for the following five decades. However, the new experience in the aftermath of the regime change in 2003 has been projected in the dominant political discourse as a new democratic Iraq, where elections play a central role. In fact, the country was successful in holding several elections within a very short period. There was an election in January 2005 for drafting the constitution, accompanied by provincial elections and the election of the regional parliament in Iraqi Kurdistan. A referendum was organized for the approval of the constitution in October 2005, followed by a legislative election in December 2005. A provincial election was held in January 2009, and legislative and presidential elections in Iraqi Kurdistan were conducted in July 2009. A second legislative election was held in March 2010. The key question is whether this carnival of frequent elections would necessarily translate into a real democracy capable of serving national interests and the welfare of the Iraqis.

The constitutional election of January 30, 2005, reflected a clear preponderance of ethno-sectarian loyalties and identity. Because of the boycott by the Sunnis, the turnout for this election was very low, 58 percent. Seven thousand candidates competed for 275 seats in parliament. The Shiite bloc, the United Iraqi Alliance won 48.2 percent of the vote, securing 140 seats in the legislative assembly. The Kurdish bloc, the Kurdistani Alliance, representing the two dominating Kurdish parties: the Kurdistan Democratic Party (KDP led by Barzani) and the Patriotic Union of Kurdistan (PUK led by Talabani), won

25.7 percent of the vote, securing 75 seats, in addition to 2 seats captured by the Islamic Union of Kurdistan. The cross-sectarian secular list, the Iraqi Nationalist List, won 14 percent and 40 seats. The main task of the resulting government was to draft a new constitution for the country. This election was accompanied by the elections of the governorate councils in all of the 18 provinces and the election of the 111-member regional parliament in Iraqi Kurdistan.

The first legislative election after regime change was held on December 15, 2005. Thanks to the heavy participation of the Sunnis this time, the turnout was rather high, 79.6 percent. The Shiite bloc won 41.2 percent, securing 128 out of 275 parliamentary seats; the Kurdish bloc won 21.7 percent and 53 seats, in addition to 5 seats (1.3%) won by the Islamic Union of Kurdistan; the Sunni bloc was represented by the Iraqi Accord Front, which won 15.1 percent and 44 seats, and the Iraqi Front for National Dialogue, won 4.1 percent and 11 seats; the Iraqi Nationalist List won 8 percent and 25 seats. Similar to the previous election, it was a true expression of an increasing polarization of sectarian politics, resulting in the formation of ineffectual government. The national unity government that emerged from this election has lacked both unity and a national agenda and has barely governed.[1]

The provincial election of January 2009 was held in all the provinces with the exception of the three Kurdish provinces and Kirkuk. More than 14,400 candidates competed in the election for 440 posts. The turnout was rather low, 51 percent, and it was even lower in Baghdad, 40 percent. This election, however, reflected a certain level of dynamism in Iraqi politics after 2005. After boycotting the previous election, the Sunnis heavily participated in this election. The Shiite bloc became divided between two main groups, the Da'wa Party of Prime Minister Maliki and the ISCI, competing against each other for the Shiite votes. This election signaled a retreat of the religious discourse, most particularly sectarian politics. The fact that this positive development is coming in the aftermath of the sectarian fighting during the years 2006–8 clearly shows that sectarian feelings are not deeply rooted in society.

The election was also a setback for federalism, particularly in the south, which was mostly advanced by ISCI. Because of these new orientations in the political mood, the ISCI did rather poorly in the election. This party has relied on religious imagery and symbols, and the vision of a southern federalism and weak central government. Their poor result was also influenced by the poor performance and the corruption of the previous provincial councils dominated by this party. The relative defeat of the ISCI, however, has benefited the party of Maliki, who participated in the election under the slate of the "State of Law." This list promised the rule of law and basic services and a departure from the dominant sectarian politics. Maliki's resounding victory also benefited from a military campaign against Shiite militias in Basra and the Sadr city in Baghdad. Nevertheless, Visser warns: "If Maliki's steps in the direction of centralism are to have a lasting impact and mark a definitive break with Iran, they will need to be anchored in institutional reform and constitutional revision rather than flowery rhetoric."[2] However, voting for pledges of services and rule of law shows that the priorities of the Iraqis in elections are not different from that of the electorates in democratic countries. What is remarkable in this election is that an independent technocrat, Yusuf al-Habubi, was able to win a majority of the votes in Karabla, the holy Shiite city and stronghold of dominant religious parties. Nonetheless, subsequent political maneuverings bestowed upon him the post of vice mayor, a not very influential position.

The limited political dynamism that was manifested in the provincial election has had a repercussion in the north of the country, but this influence was only strengthening an already evolving political dynamism of its own in Iraqi Kurdistan. Presidential and parliamentary elections were held in this region on July 25, 2009. The undisputed leader of the Iraqi Kurds, Mas'ud Barzani, easily secured a victory in the presidential election by gaining almost 70 percent of the votes. However, the parliamentary election proved to be a more difficult and interesting contest. With a high turnout of 78.5 percent, Kurdish electorates voted 57 percent for the list of the Kurdistan Alliance, which consists of the two ruling parties, KDP and PUK. Thirteen percent of the vote went for the list of Services and Reform, an alliance of socialists and Islamists; and a surprising 24 percent of the votes went for the list of Change, Gorran in Kurdish. This list represents the newly formed movement led by dissidents who failed to impose internal reforms from within their PUK party. This list made a strong showing, particularly in Sulaimaniya, the stronghold of PUK.

However, accusations of fraud and undemocratic ways of influencing voters were raised not only by the opposition but also by independent organizations. According to the head of the Kurdish Institute for Elections, an independent monitoring and voter education group, "There were widespread reports during the campaign that the Kurdistani List had been distributing cash, guns and cars in an effort to influence voters."[3] One voter, a driver at the Ministry of Industry, informed that his manager had warned employees in his department that they would be fired if they did not vote for the Kurdistani List.[4]

In the aftermath of the invasion of Kuwait and the suppression of the failed Shiite and Kurdish uprisings that led to the establishment of free zones in the north and south of the country, Iraqi Kurdistan became a de facto autonomous entity since 1991. A year later, the Kurds held a parliamentary election that showed the clear dominance of the two main parties: KDP won 45.5 percent, PUK won 43.6 percent, while the Islamists won 5.5 percent. The emergence of the Islamists in Iraqi Kurdistan followed a familiar pattern in the Middle East where the Islamists spotlight and complain about the corruption of governments, then present themselves as an alternative. This election was stained by accusations of fraud and multiple casting of votes. The 7 percent threshold requirement for a seat in parliament practically meant shutting out every party except the KDP and the PUK.[5]

Thus the 1992 election initiated the institutionalization of the absolute dominance of the two main parties over all aspects of life in the region, including the parliament and the government. Exercising power outside the electoral system has hardly helped the development of democratic institutions and was the greatest damage done to the KRG.[6] However, the contest between the KDP and PUK over the spoils of the lucrative smuggling, black market, and transit trade routes has proved too difficult an issue to be settled peacefully. This led to an intense intra-Kurdish war and fighting for four years, 1994–97. These divides and struggles for control of wealth and power in Iraqi Kurdistan became less violent only with the specter of the Iraq War and the vision of overthrowing the regime of Saddam Hussein. In October 2002, the two parties agreed to cooperate to present a united front to maximize their gain in the upcoming big transformation of the political system in the country.

It is against this background of how the dominant Kurdish parties ruled the region by practically dividing government and economy on a 50-50 basis and their control over patronage, jobs, and economic benefits, that Gorran emerged and made a remarkable success in the 2009 election. Gorran's campaign manager states: "Yes, we have stability. But we also want services, transparency and better government."[7] Nosherwan Mustafa, a founder of PUK and now head of the Change List, points out: "There is a form of totalitarianism in our system. We believe the time is ripe to put our house in order."[8] He adds: "We don't want to change just the faces and the persons. We want to change the political system. We want to separate the political parties from public life."[9] The opposition focused on issues of corruption, cronyism, and nepotism that dominated the nature of governing the region by the leading parties. It is unsurprising that this new politics has especially appealed to the young population, who desire a better future, which seems to be unattainable in the quasi-feudal fashion of ruling the region. The 2009 election in Iraqi Kurdistan was a protest vote against the two parties that dominated Kurdish politics for a long time.

Furthermore, the emergence of a viable opposition in parliament will surely have serious implications for Kurdish politics. This could lead to real changes in parliamentary politics. The decision of Gorran and the Islamists to refrain from participating in the new government and to confine their role to a parliamentary opposition is indeed a new positive development in Iraqi politics that should be replicated in Baghdad. The Kurdish parliament, at least until this latest election, is considered a rubber stamp for the two dominant parties who make all the major decision behind closed doors. This is hardly different from the Iraqi parliament under the old regime.

However, it remains to be seen if the opposition will be able to make real changes to a tribal and undemocratic system. After all, the leaders of the opposition are the architects of the old system that they now denounce. It is also noteworthy how the dominant parties adjust to the new reality of the existence of a feasible opposition. Some reactions clearly indicate a lack of tolerance to an effective opposition in the region. Talabani, president of Iraq and head of PUK, said this about the leader of the Change List: "He is hostile to the PUK, and he is opposed and hostile to the KRG."[10] While this remark is induced by partisan rivalry between the two leaders, to perceive opposition as hostile and a threat is not a healthy sign of a democratic process where the opposition is supposed to be an integral part of the process. At any rate, the 2009 election and its results represent a major development in the region. One would have hoped that the political dynamism of the Kurdish election that was influenced by the 2009 provincial election would have had an impact on the 2010 parliamentary election in Iraq and bring issues of corruption and services to the fore in addition to the emergence of an effective and viable opposition, but events disappointingly took a different turn.

The second legislative election was held on March 7, 2010, where 6,200 candidates competed for 325 parliamentary seats, of which 82 were reserved for women. The cross-sectarian coalition list of Iraqiya, headed by former prime minister Ayad Allawi, won the highest number of seats, 91. This result gave Allawi a plurality but not outright majority. The second runner was the list of Prime Minister Maliki, the State of Law, which won 89 seats. The difference between these two lists was only 54,000 in popular votes. The other Shiite list of Iraqi

National Alliance came third with 70 seats. Within this Shiite coalition, the Sadrists faction, Ahrar, captured most of the votes, 39 seats, followed by the ISCI with 18 seats and the Fadhila Party with 8 seats. The total seats that went to the Kurdish parties were 57. Most of these seats went to the Kurdistani Alliance, 43, while the other parties won 14 seats: 8 for Gorran, 4 for Islamic Union of Kurdistan, and 2 for al-Jama'a al-Islamiyyia. The Sunni list, Tawafuq, won only 6 seats, while the list of the interior minister Bolani, Unity of Iraq, won 4 seats.

Yet the results of the elections have been contested by almost every politician in Iraq. Accusations of fraud and hard criticisms against the work of the Independent High Electoral Commission were expressed from every corner. The only praise in favor of the commission came from international observers, including the United Nations, and a few Iraqi politicians. However, the most serious challenge to the result of the election came from the incumbent prime minister Maliki, who made a rather strong categorical statement: "No way will we accept the results." He rejected the outcome and asked for a manual recount of the votes, to which the commission hesitated. Maliki has even invoked his position as Iraq's commander in chief of the army to warn about violence if his demand for a recount is rejected. Indeed, an Iraqi judicial panel eventually ordered a manual recount of about 2.5 million ballots cast in Baghdad, an action requested by Maliki. Nevertheless, the recount did not change the results of the vote. Other politicians were talking about similar action that should be taken in other provinces as well, where allegations of vote fraud have also been filed. However, the politics of doubting and disrespecting the results of elections, and the numerous calls for recounting is a very risky politics to pursue in a fragile democracy that can endanger the entire political process.

Moreover, adamant about securing a second term, Maliki has brought into the play the controversial constitution. He asked the federal court to interpret a rather ambiguous clause in Article 76 of the constitution: "the parliamentary bloc with the most members" will be the one to form the government. Yet the court's interpretation was even more controversial. It stated that it is either the bloc with most votes in the election *or* the bloc that succeeds in forming the biggest bloc in the parliament when it reconvenes after the elections. Pollack cautions that this is a recipe for political chaos in Iraq after every election: "If this opinion is allowed to become precedent, it means that the elections says nothing about which party gets the first shot at forming a government—all that matters is the politicking that follows—creating the potential for endless negotiations after every election."[11]

Nonetheless, acting on the interpretation of the federal court, Maliki did not waste much time as he promptly started to negotiate with the other parties the formation of a new government, presenting himself as a candidate for the post of the prime minister. An editorial in the *Los Angeles Times* comments: "In Iraq, winning the vote and winning power are two entirely different propositions."[12]

It is noteworthy that Ayatollah al-Sistani, the most revered Shiite religious authority, has refrained from intervening in the elections or backing any coalition at the expense of another. This is a positive development from the previous legislative elections. However, many irregularities occurred in this election, including vote buying by handing out blankets, stoves, or money, particularly to the poor.[13] Leaflets discouraging people from voting for Allawi were dropped from the air, and CDs were distributed in the streets to the same effect.[14] Journalistic Freedoms Observatory, a nongovernmental organization, registered more than 50 repressive actions against journalists and media institutions during the elections: 23 incidences were registered in Iraqi Kurdistan and 27 in Baghdad and the rest of the provinces.[15] This organization also stated that the army raided and closed three printing houses, leading to the arrest of several people on the accusation of printing "misleading information." The information was in fact a booklet with the title, "Where Has the Money of Iraq Gone," which was essentially a critique to the corruption and inefficiency that has marked the work of the government.[16] Moreover, there were reports of armed clashes between the supporters of Gorran and security forces in Sulaimaniya in north of Iraq, leading to several injuries and arrests.[17]

As mentioned earlier, de-Ba'thification was the dominant issue in this election. Many candidates were banned from participating in the elections on accusations of linkage to the Ba'th Party. The de-Ba'thification commission was even targeting some of the candidates who won in the elections to cancel their votes. Allegations of Ba'thism reinforced sectarian and ethnic polarization in this election, not unlike the preceding one. Once again, voting was based on identity politics rather than on political programs.

Like the previous one, this election also witnessed violence, leading to the death of 38 people. Yet violence played only a minor role in the electoral turnout, which was only 62.4 percent, a much lower number than that of earlier legislative elections. The turnout in the capital Baghdad was even lower, 53 percent, while the rate among the diasporas was only 14 percent. The rather low turnout figures clearly show a diminishing enthusiasm about elections in Iraq. Out of tangible experience, people started to realize that there is a weak correlation between participating in elections and improvements in their lives. People also wonder whether in the absence of decent services, participating in elections could legitimize a corrupt and ineffective governing that only benefits a few politicians at the expense of improving security and services immediately affecting the daily lives of the Iraqis.

It is estimated that the expenditure on the electoral campaign for this election reached a figure of $600 million.[18] An Iraqi citizen bitterly comments: "They are spending that much so they can make hundreds of millions more once they are in office."[19] Another citizen indignantly protests: "There are no services, we are without jobs, and poverty is killing us. What these politicians are waiting for. Do they want to see us begging in the streets to earn a living? Is this what they want?"[20] An Iraqi woman who participated in the election, on the other hand, is in a different mood: "I have got a good feeling that the coming years are going to bring us prosperity and a good life."[21] The Iraqis keep dreaming and hoping, which is part of existence as life has to continue despite everything. The question is, will the elected politicians listen to and respect these dreams and hopes, and honor them eventually?

After more than nine months, no complete government was in power in Iraq. Iraqi politicians took a very long time to jockeying and deliberating behind closed doors the formation of political coalitions, the formation of a government, and the distribution of the three presidential posts and the ministerial positions, in what appears to be, expectedly, a very protracted and frustrating process. Watching these negotiations closely, one cannot help getting the impression that the self-interested leading politicians are turning elections and democracy into a political bazaar where everything is on the table for selling and buying. Apparently, elections and democracy in the so-called new Iraq are exercised as, and reduced to, a political circus.

ELECTIONS OR DEMOCRACY

The global trend toward democratization appears to have reached every region in the world except the Middle East. The resilience of authoritarianism and the stubborn resistance to democratic change in the region have proved to be remarkable. The failure to seriously engage in democracy has instigated an academic debate about the "exceptionalism" of the Middle East.[22] This counterhistorical development seems to make little sense in a highly dynamic and changing world. Nevertheless, winds of change have reached even this region, leading to some democratic practices. This exploration in democracy is manifested in organizing elections that range from tightly controlled to free elections. The willingness of the dominant authoritarian regimes to engage in this process is based on the perception that holding a somewhat managed election not only would solve the embarrassing problem of the exceptionalism of the region but also could disqualify the authoritarian nature of these regimes.

Accordingly, well-managed elections not only keep autocratic rulers in power but also help them advance the claim of ruling democratically. However, this reduction of an entire system of democracy to the elections of officials only is very misleading. While elections are an indispensable and integral part of democracy, democracy and elections are not exactly the same. Elections are simply a mechanism for implementing democracy. Still, for democracy to function in the proper sense, there is a need for a whole set of democratic values and principles. An election without these values and principles is an empty shell that provides only an illusion of democracy, and seems to feed authoritarian politics rather than initiate the democratic process.

However, ventures in holding elections and the accompanying results seem to confirm rather than deny the exceptionalism of the Middle East. Thus recent elections in the region tend to raise a new set of contentious questions: Can an election necessarily lead to democracy? Can a democracy be built without democrats? Does a regime become legitimate by merely holding an election? Who is the real beneficiary of this experiment in elections and democracy? It appears that the entire political process in the region presently revolves around the controversies surrounding the election-democracy-legitimacy nexus.

Iraq has a special role in this debate concerning elections and democracy. The country has witnessed a carnival of series of elections since 2005. Yet the question is whether these elections have helped to establish or strengthen democracy in the country. The five years of elections in Iraq can hardly offer a positive answer to this question. On the contrary, the Iraqi elections have led to ethno-sectarian polarization, a weak and divided government, and ineffectual parliament. These elections appear to have resulted in an increased role of religion, strengthening of tribalism, weakening of national identity and common ground for all Iraqis, and increased violence. Elections are accompanied by the elevation of politics of victimization and vengeance politics, difficult and unattainable national reconciliation, rampant corruption and lack of improvements in basic services, and the unjustifiable failure to revitalize the economy, particularly the private economy. Indeed, considering all of these antidemocracy tendencies that the elections have contributed to, the entire democratic process in Iraq seems to be highly questionable.

The one-sided perception of the relationship between elections and democracy was clearly manifested in the circumstances leading to the first election in January 2005. The debate on the transfer of sovereignty to the Iraqis has led to a new debate about the timing of the elections. The American authority in Iraq wanted to delay holding any elections until certain conditions were ripe, while the Shiite religious authority, *marji'iyya*, insisted that no constitution would be drafted unless a national election was held first. Seen as a magic ticket to power, the Shiite perception of democracy was reduced to an unmistakable appreciation of elections. Other democratic values did not benefit from a similar appreciation and persistence by the Shiite religious authorities or Shiite politicians.

However, the Shiite insistence on prioritizing early elections has complicated the political process in the country. On the risks of premature elections, Diamond argues: "No issue is tougher than the timing of elections. Ill-timed and ill-prepared elections do not produce democracy, or even political stability, after conflict. Instead, they may only enhance the power of actors who mobilize coercion, fear, and prejudice, thereby reviving autocracy and even precipitating large-scale violent strife."[23] Wimmer concurs by pointing out that elections are likely to stir up ethno-religious conflicts, if democratic institutions are not designed to foster moderation and compromise; therefore elections should come last, not first in the process of institutional transformation.[24] Rushing elections in new Iraq has resulted in drafting a divisive and highly controversial constitution, complicating the process of national reconciliation that should have preceded any elections, accentuating ethnic and sectarian polarization in society, and the rise of the religious influence in politics. All of these results are hardly a healthy start for a genuine democratic political process.

The *marji'iyya* played a crucial role in rushing elections in Iraq in the aftermath of regime change. Shiite religious authorities, who control and influence the masses, organized mass demonstrations calling for early elections. Given their dominant position in manipulating people, it is unsurprising that the religious authorities claim that Iraqi political elites should obey the wishes of the "streets" and listen to people's demands. They even threatened to further agitate the streets and create turmoil in the country if their demand for early elections was not granted. For this purpose, religion has been played out to the maximum to ensure the mobilization of people to participate in elections that were projected as a religious duty. Ayatollah al-Sistani declared that holding free elections throughout the country is the only way to restore legitimacy to the Iraqi government.

Consequently, there was plethora of religious edicts, *fatwas*, and slogans about elections: "If you don't vote, your wife will be forbidden to you"; "Voting is more important than fasting and praying."[25] Sistani has also issued a number of *fatwas* demanding that the faithful should vote and persuading women to participate in the elections even without the consent of their husbands.[26] To encourage women to vote, Shiite religious history and the image of the Shiite female model, Zainab, the sister of Imam Hussein who was killed in Karbala in a bid for power, were brought into the electoral campaign. Religious flyers circulating in the Shiite holy cities read: "Truly, women who go forth to the polling centers on election day are like Zaynab, who went forth to [the field of battle at] Karbala"; "Congratulations on your role [in the elections], through which you will be joining Zaynab in establishing and in granting victory to the Religion of God, His Messenger, and His Progeny."[27] Thus voting was explicitly equated with the sacred act of promoting Islam. A senior aide of Sistani made this explicit: "Those who don't participate in the elections will end up in hell"; "We must bear the responsibility and we must all participate in the elections because it's a patriotic duty and not doing so is like treason."[28]

Although the intention of Sistani was to ensure legitimacy to the process of transferring sovereignty to the Iraqis, the outcome of the rushed elections was not necessarily a more legitimate political process. The role that Sistani played in uniting the Shiites in one political bloc for the elections has significantly contributed to the rise of a destructive and violent political sectarianism and sectarian violence for many years. It is important to recall that early and rushed elections in Iraqi Kurdistan in 1992 failed to prevent the occurrence of the Kurdish civil war between the two dominating parties. Even though Sistani is against the intervention of religion in politics, his role in enforcing the ill-timing and the sectarian nature of elections clearly showed how one man can decide the fate of the nation, which is a continuation of old politics in Iraq, a reality that is hardly compatible with democracy.

To be sure, the position of Sistani has been exaggerated and exploited by self-motivated Shiite politicians who wanted to come to power as soon as possible and at any cost. However, one can still ask why Sistani did not show the same enthusiasm and determination in addressing some of the dangerous aspects of the rushed electoral process that he personally contributed to, such as violent sectarian politics, rampant corruption, and inefficient government. This failure of Sistani is well reflected in an interesting slogan that appeared in the provincial election in 2009: "We have been fooled by the Marji'iyya, we have elected amoral people." The slogan is even more rhyming in Iraqi dialect: "qashmuratna al-marji'iyya, wa intikhabna al-sarsariya!"[29] The results of the rushed elections might suggest that there was a kind of persistent and deliberate "hijacking" of a fragile democratic process for religious and sectarian purposes, leading to a wrong start for the political and democratic process in Iraq.

The rush to election in 2005 has resulted in exasperating ethnic and sectarian divides in society. Discussing how the voters turned to their primordial loyalties in the two elections in 2005, Dawisha and Diamond observed: "Even in the large multiethnic cities—such as Baghdad, Mosul, and Kirkuk—there was little crossing of ethnosectarian lines. Rather, each alliance focused its energy on cementing support among its own base, while doggedly obstructing intrusions by other alliances into its home area. The logic of electoral politics as an identity referendum became further entrenched."[30] Thus sectarian and ethnic affiliation was a decisive factor in the elections. This fact has opened the door for demography rather than political programs to dictate the electoral process. The Sunni estrangement and their boycott of the constitutional election have led to the new reality that the Shiites and Kurds are significantly overrepresented in the parliament and provincial councils.

In turn, this overrepresentation is detrimental to the legitimacy of the newly initiated political process, an ironic outcome considering that the call for rushed elections was motivated by ensuring legitimacy for the political process. Undisputedly, fair representation of all communities is part of a credible and legitimate political process. However, overrepresentation, as for underrepresentation, leads to undesirable and negative consequences. The new political process in the country has resulted in the empowerment of Shiites and Kurds, a desirable outcome without doubt. The key questions remain: Who is benefiting from this empowerment and at the expense of whom? Is Iraq as a nation and are the majority of Iraqis, regardless of their differences, benefiting from this new ascendancy in the political process? These questions, however, are central to the discussion on new Iraq.

The demographic reality of the numerical majority of the Shiites always ensures that they will emerge triumphant in any and every election to be held in the country. This is particularly true when primordial loyalty is a key factor in deciding how to vote. While democratic elections usually result in a political majority, sectarian elections, by contrast, always lead to the triumph of a demographic majority, and these are two entirely different outcomes. The Shiite insistence on rushing the electoral process in 2005 reflects a convenient and one-sided perception of democracy, in the sense that elections are their route to power as a sectarian majority.

Undeniably, democracy is the rule of the majority, but it is only *the political majority*. Democracy also represents a constitutional guarantee to minorities and the supremacy of citizenship rights. It is true that elections are about winning and losing, but they are also about competing political programs for the benefit of the nation and its citizens. Lack of competing political programs tends to negatively affect the democratic process to the advantage of destructive demography and identity politics. What complicates the scene further is that many of the winners in the elections are Shiites with close ties to Iran, thereby further aggravating sectarian politics in the country. Many of these religious parties are founded and nurtured in Iran and get various forms of support from the theocratic regime in Iran. These ties contribute to an increased violence and complicate the relationship between elections and democracy on the one hand and the political landscape in Iraq on the other.

Elections in the present situation in Iraq tend to aggravate ethnic tensions as well. This is clearly manifested in the repeated attempts to bring ethnic disputes and ethnic politics to the electoral process, or rather bringing elections to these ethnic disputes. The sensitive issue of Kirkuk is a clear example of an attempt to solve a complex issue through the medium of elections. This issue has often been forced into the parliamentary deliberations regarding electoral laws. These efforts have led to the outcome of frustrating negotiations and causing a considerable delay in the approval of the electoral law in 2009.

Elections have also been perceived as a possible solution to ethnic conflicts regarding the so-called disputed territories. Referring to the disputed territories in the Mosul province, a Kurdish politician argues: "There's good evidence that these places belong to the KRG. People have been waiting for this election to know whether there's a majority of the population that wants to break away from the central government."[31] Another Kurdish politician from the same city makes the relationship between elections and ethnic identity politics more explicit: "We are looking not only to know our political size but our ethnic size. How can we know the truth? By democratic means: we don't want to force any identity on anyone. Voters will choose what identity they want."[32]

During the 2010 legislative elections, a leading Kurdish politician from Mosul accentuates: "First ethnicity, second political party."[33] Yet an Arab politician from the same province objects: "We think the elections are for political parties. It's not for nationalities to decide their final fate."[34] Nonetheless, there are Kurds who do not agree with the emphasis on identity politics by their ethnically affiliated politicians. For these Kurds, the most important priorities are better electricity and water, unblocked streets, more jobs, and greater safety. In a remarkable show of political pragmatism, a Kurdish businessman has even voted for the *al-Hadba*, a list that although includes Kurds is mostly dominated by Arabs, but that he considers as more capable of delivering: "Here we vote for the political party that would serve the interests of the city, regardless of ethnic identification."[35]

Politics of identity associated with holding elections that are mostly seen as a test of primordial loyalties is nothing but politics of violence. Ethnic conflict, which continues to be part of the new experience in Iraq, is a risky and dangerous politics. The rushed elections of 2005 have led to the ascendancy of sectarian politics. These elections helped to trigger a terrible sectarian violence for many years, causing the death and displacement of many thousands. Democracy that is based on a sectarian power-sharing system also triggered a terrible civil war in Lebanon that lasted for 15 years and caused the deaths of 200,000 people. It is a paradox that democracy in the Middle East leads to violence and conflicts while democracy and elections elsewhere help to build peaceful, tolerant, and prosperous societies.

The 2005 election occurred in a climate of confusion, chaos, violence, and the rise of ethno-sectarian identity politics. This seems to put the newly initiated democratic process on the wrong footing. The fact that the same atmosphere, this time taking the form of the fear of the return of the Ba'thists, repeated itself in the March 2010 legislative elections clearly shows that the year of the first elections was not an extraordinary event. On the contrary, the rushed elections with these footings seem to lock forever the entire political process in a futile and violent trap of ethnic and sectarian identity politics. Some people might still describe the game of ethno-sectarian politics as democracy. Yet the risks, as the experience of new Iraq demonstrates, are rather obvious. Identity politics inevitably comes at the expense of political, economic, and social issues that are more important, urgent, and relevant to a peaceful and prosperous future for Iraq. These are the issues that are, incidentally, more pertinent to the essence of any veritable democratic process.

An approach that reduces democracy to only a mechanism of conducting elections is not a guarantee for a real democratic change, if democratic values and principles are deliberately ignored or disrespected.

A democracy without democrats can mean only that old violent politics are played out under a different name. However, it would be a great disappointment if the process of creating new Iraq turned out to be playing a new game, with the same old and unpleasant rules. Despite deceiving appearances, ethnic and sectarian elections are exclusionary elections that have little to do with a genuine democratic process. These types of elections are usually devoid of any democratic meanings and work in isolation from democratic values and principles.

Before rushing to elections, there is a need for the rule of law, state monopoly of violence, and an end to the influence of all militias. Democracy also stipulates the separation of powers, a functioning party system, flourishing private economic initiatives, initiation of serious national reconciliation, and a departure from politics of victimization and revenge. Basham argues: "The White House is placing a very large political wager that the formation of democratic institutions in Iraq can stimulate a democratic political culture . . . On the contrary, the available evidence strongly suggests that the causal relationship between institutions and culture works the other way around. Political culture shapes democracy far more than democracy shapes political culture."[36]

The insistence of the Shiites of Iraq on rushing premature elections reflects a destructive and violent understanding of elections and democracy. In fact, the Shiites are not alone in this perception as they are only repeating the position of the many movements of political Islam in considering elections as a one-way ticket to power and nothing or very little beyond that. While democracy works for the benefit of the majority, if not the whole population, ethno-sectarian elections seem to be working mostly for the interest of a few political elites. It is unsurprising that the elected governments have failed to deliver to the very people who trusted and voted for their religious and ethnic leaders. Similar to former authoritarian regimes, sectarian and ethnic elections seriously suffer from a problem of legitimacy.

NOTES

1. International Crisis Group, "Iraq's Provincial Elections: The Stakes," *Middle East Report*, no. 82, January 27, 2009, 15, http://www.crisisgroup.org/library/documents/middle_east__north_africa/iraq_iran_gulf/82_iraqs_provincial_elections__the_stakes.pdf.

2. Reidar Visser, "A Litmus Test for Iraq," *Middle East Report Online*, MERIP, January 30, 2009, http://www.merip.org/mero/mero013009.html.

3. Liz Sly, "Iraq Sees Large Turnout for Kurdistan Election," *Los Angeles Times*, July 26, 2009.

4. Ibid.

5. Sandra Mackey, *The Reckoning: Iraq and the Legacy of Saddam Hussein* (New York: Norton, 2002), 308.

6. David McDowall, *A Modern History of the Kurds*, 3rd ed. (London: Tauris, 2004), 385.

7. Sly, "In Iraq, Kurdistan Election Campaign Heats Up," *Los Angeles Times*, July 23, 2009.

8. Sam Dagher, "As Kurdish Polls Open, Effort to Ease Parties' Grip," *New York Times*, July 25, 2009.

9. Antony Shadid, "Opposition Seeks Shift in Power as Iraqi Kurds Vote," *Washington Post*, July 26, 2009.

10. Ma'ad Fayadh, "Talabani before the End of His Presidency Term," *Asharq al-Awsat*, December 31, 2009.

11. Kenneth M. Pollack, "A Government for Baghdad," *The National Interest*, July 27, 2010.

12. Editorial, "Who Will Lead Iraq?" *Los Angeles Times*, March 30, 2010.

13. "Politicians and Electoral Lists Seduce Electorate Poor with Stoves and Blankets," *Asharq al-Awsat*, February 11, 2010.

14. Osama Mahdi, "Iraqi Elections Take a Dangerous Turn," *Elaph Electronic Newspaper*, March 3, 2010, http://www.elaph.com/Web/news/2010/3/539169.htm.

15. Journalistic Freedoms Observatory, *Metro Media*, no. 4, April 1, 2010, http://www.jfoiraq.org/Mettro_List.aspx.

16. Sabah al-Khafagi, "The Heat of Iraqi Elections reaches Two Printing Houses and Their Employees," *Elaph Electronic Newspaper*, March 3, 2010, http://www.elaph.com/Web/news/2010/3/539216.html.

17. "Clashes between Supports of Change and Security Forces in Sulaimaniya," *Asharq al-Awsat*, February 18, 2010.

18. "Experts and Parliamentarians: Electoral Expenses Are No Less Than $600 Million," *Asharq al-Awsat*, March 6, 2010.

19. Anthony Shadid, "Unity Elusive as Iraq Grasps Trappings of Democracy," *New York Times*, March 5, 2010.

20. Sunnis Arabs Votes Strongly for Secular Lists," *Asharq al-Awsat*, March 10, 2010.

21. Sly and Caesar Ahmed, "Basra Has a 'Good Feeling' about Vote," *Los Angeles Times*, March 8, 2010.

22. For further details on this see, for instance, the debate in the *Journal of Democracy*, vol. 15, no. 4 (2004) and vol. 14, no. 3 (2003).

23. Larry Diamond, "Building Democracy after Conflict: Lessons from Iraq," *Journal of Democracy* 16, no. 1 (January 2005): 18.

24. Andreas Wimmer, "Democracy and Ethno-Religious Conflict in Iraq," *Survival* 45, no. 4 (winter 2003–4).

25. International Crisis Group, "Iraq's Provincial Elections," 10.

26. Babak Rahimi, "Ayatollah Sistani and the Democratization of Post-Ba'athist Iraq," United States Institute of Peace, Special Report 187, June 2007, 10, http://usip.org/files/resources/sr187.pdf.

27. Ahmed H. al-Rahim, "The Sistani Factor," *Journal of Democracy* 16, no. 3 (July 2005): 50–51.

28. Arthur Chrenkoff, "After the War," *Wall Street Journal*, November 8, 2004.

29. International Crisis Group, "Iraq's Provincial Elections," 10.

30. Adeed Dawisha and Larry Diamond, "Iraq's Year of Voting Dangerously," *Journal of Democracy* 17, no. 2 (April 2006): 96.

31. Ernesto Londono, "In Iraq's North, Vote Tallies to Define Loyalties, Disputes," *Washington Post*, February 2, 2009.

32. Ian Fisher, "Iraqi Elections Face Crucial Test in Violent Mosul," *New York Times*, January 30, 2009.

33. Steven Lee Myers, "In Northern Iraq, a Vote Seems Likely to Split," *New York Times*, February 9, 2010.

34. Fisher, "Iraqi Elections Face."

35. Ibid.

36. Patrick Basham, "Can Iraq Be Democratic," *Policy Analysis* 505 (January 5, 2004): 8.

9

Confessionalism and Legitimacy

IDENTITY POLITICS AND LEGITIMACY

One of the most important issues relevant to legitimacy and democracy in new Iraq is the ethno-sectarian composition of the society. Iraq is blessed with ethnic and religious plurality. However, this plurality becomes problematic for any authoritarian regime that is grounded on the politics of exclusion, domination, and monopolization of power and wealth. A democratic system, in contrast, has to be inclusive of all communities sharing existence in the country. Actually, there is more than one option in ensuring inclusiveness. One is to build an inclusive system based on citizenship rights and equality. This system, which directly deals with individuals—the system that truly reflects democracy—has not yet been adopted in new Iraq. Instead, the country has opted for a system that is inclusive of all recognized communities.

According to this arrangement, it is assumed that individuals are included in the system through their respective communities. This system does not concern itself with the issue of ensuring that the inclusiveness of communities is also extended to individuals. Moreover, there is no effective mechanism of checks and accountability under this system. Two key questions consequently arise: Does the inclusion of the communities automatically translate into the inclusion of ordinary people belonging to their respective communities? Why has new Iraq opted for an indirect system of inclusion when there is another option that can ensure the direct inclusion of all citizens? These are crucial questions that touch the very essence of the democratic process being implemented in the country.

New Iraq has opted for a kind of democracy called consociational democracy, which is based on communalism and confessionalism.

Consociationalism involves a power-sharing system, *muhassasa*, between various confessional blocs. It is a model for conflict resolution in ethnically divided societies, which is grounded on quotas in government and bureaucracy, reciprocal veto rights, regional autonomy, and proportional representation. This political arrangement has been implemented in Lebanon. Thanks to this system, Lebanon has been presented as the only democracy in the Arab world for a long time. Perhaps, this made sense when Lebanon was surrounded by many authoritarian regimes. However, with the carefully controlled experiment in elections and democracy, this statement seems to be less credible today.

Dominated by authoritarianism, the Arabs seem to take pride in any nominal democracy, regardless of the nature of such democracy. In truth, Lebanese democracy is totally exaggerated, and consociationalism has been discredited by its very failure in Lebanon. When democracy means peaceful conflict resolution, it is unfathomable how a democracy can lead to 15 years of civil war and 200,000 deaths; or how a democracy fails to ensure the rule of law or allows various militias to operate and dominate the political system, to the extent that one militia succeeded in taking the whole country to war against the will of the nation, as was the case of the Hizb Allah-Israel war in 2008; or how a democracy fails to ensure a dignified life for its citizens to a level that prompted most of the population to emigrate.

Cammett argues: "Lebanon's power-sharing system is founded on pacts among elites, who forge pre- and post-electoral compromises, thereby ensuring the stability of the overall system, with little opportunity for meaningful input on the part of the citizenry."[1] Dawisha adds: "The confessional system guaranteed the political rights of each of Lebanon's diverse communities in the expectation that, by alleviating intercommunal suspicion and mistrust, the various groups would remain committed to the larger entity of Lebanon. What happened instead was an entrenchment of community-based attitudes and loyalties so great that the country ended up losing a quarter of its lifespan to a catastrophic civil war."[2] Analogy with present-day Iraq is striking.

The Lebanese experience is exactly happening in Iraq. With the insistence on applying political sectarianism and communalism, the country witnessed the worst sectarian violence in its history from 2005 to early 2008. Such insistence has led to exasperating ethnic conflicts between different communities, particularly between the Arabs and the Kurds. Not only did new Iraq not learn from the Lebanese experience, which was an obvious failure and a dangerous option to pursue, but it has also failed to learn from the experience of the north of the country in the aftermath of 1991. The two dominant Kurdish parties have applied a kind of power-sharing arrangement to divide the spoils of the new situation of quasi independence from the central government in Baghdad. However, this political or rather tribal solution of power sharing did not prevent parties from intense fighting from 1994 to 1997. The power-sharing arrangement benefited only a few elites from dominant parties, while the majority of the Kurdish population continues to suffer and to be marginalized. The Lebanese and Kurdish experiences clearly show the failure of consociationalism as a route to democracy, and it should have therefore been excluded from options available to new Iraq.

The apparent failure of the above-mentioned two experiences would leave the country with only one option to follow, and that is democracy pure and simple: the option of the democracy of the political majority and the opposition with constitutional, legal guarantees for minorities, and equal opportunities and rights to all citizens. Byman and Pollack argue that the most compelling reason to invest in building democracy in post-Saddam Iraq is that the alternatives are far worse. One of these alternatives is the creation of an oligarchy that incorporates the country's leading communities. However, whether or not these groups truly represent the interests and aspirations of the Iraqi people is absent from the discussion. "Attempts at a consociational oligarchy will only foster the potential for instability down the road."[3] This consociational oligarchy seems to reflect a junction of local authoritarianism and identity politics where the ethnic and sectarian elites pretend to represent community interests, while they actually strive to establish or consolidate their own interests. In so doing, they tend to reinforce an authoritarian order in society and the political process.

Internal political development since regime change in 2003 and constant conflicts arising from different ethnic and sectarian interests among the newly dominant elites clearly show that the country is moving in the direction of reestablishing authoritarian order with new faces. In fact, convenient use of the rhetoric of democracy and holding pointless elections by the new elites are mostly due to American intervention in enforcing certain visions and realities on the ground. Nonetheless, the hasty transfer of authority to the Iraqis, the withdrawal of the American military forces, and the increasing American disinterest and retreat from the whole process of building a new Iraq and establishing democracy in the Middle East would surely give the Iraqi elites a much needed respite from external pressures regarding the adoption of democratic system in the country. This could explain the increasing debacle of domestic politics and the increasing authoritarian essence of the current system. However, respite from external pressures does not prevent the native elites from developing a devotion to a democratic system, rhetorically at least, when they realize that formally adhering to and supporting this political game of democracy would serve their narrow interests best.

Within identity politics, a power-sharing arrangement clearly appears to be *a process of de-nationalizing*, or rather *a process of fragmentizing* a highly centralized authoritarian system for the immediate benefits of *multiple players* in contrast to the single player of the old regime. However, transforming a one-man rule into an oligarchy rule does not necessarily reflect democratic change, despite deceptive appearances. This is particularly true when the interests of the majority of the population continue to be economically and politically marginalized. Identity politics and power-sharing arrangements are more about the inclusion of various ethnic and sectarian elites in the political order and the power, wealth, and the material benefits associated with being part of that order than the asseveration of the best interests of ordinary citizens. It is unsurprising that Munson has called the elites who are presently ruling Iraq "opportunistic politicians."[4]

Although power sharing is presented as a form of democracy, its practical application makes it the very antithesis of democracy. By incorporating everyone in the system, there is practically no one left to form the opposition. Absence of an opposition is decidedly detrimental to the democratic process, particularly by weakening the accountability of the government. In this regard, it is important to stress that the success of any potentially effective opposition will primarily depend on whether or not there is a truly democratic government in power. Moreover, it has been argued that the system of power sharing creates its own checks and balances by including many politicians representing different interests. This, however, can make more sense in theory than in reality. A power-sharing system fails to provide accountability in practical terms *when all parties* are involved in corruption, lucrative privileges, mutual concessions, and inefficiency. In this case, the checks and balances become a policy of silence by all parties involved. While power sharing has a sense of legitimacy because it represents, in theory, all the communities, it negates legitimacy by producing an incompetent government that cannot deliver on its promises.

Power sharing is not based on institutions, but on personalities, sects, and ethnicities. There is a huge difference between political parties that represent the interests of their members and ethno-sectarian parties that represent the interests of sects or ethnicities, or more precisely the interests and positions of the dominant leaders of these communities. It is predictable, therefore, that the power-sharing system in Iraq has not yet produced a law that supervises and regulates party politics. The absence of such a law tends to put the democratic process on an unsteady footing. It is true that the power-sharing system often leads to negotiations and compromises, but middle grounds are not always fair, ethical, democratic, or legitimate, particularly when these solutions reflect a negotiation between ethnic and sectarian demands, which are often maximalist and unrealistic demands.

Power sharing makes elections meaningless because the electoral results will have little impact on the outcome of the government where all are included, whether winners or losers. Elections are insincere if they are grounded on ethno-sectarian grounds. Obviously, a national census will do the trick, without going through the pain of holding elections. A national census offers a measure of the demographic strength of each community. Elections, on the other hand, test the strength and viability of political parties and programs. When elections are not centered on contending political programs, they become an exercise in uselessness and waste.

Power sharing is an accommodation of elitist claims and interests, whereas the real challenge from a democratic point of view is to accommodate, reflect, and respond to the interests of the majority directly. Given that the interests of the ethnic and sectarian leaders are always represented, the power-sharing system appears to be working on the same authoritarian premise that when one captures power, then one is in power forever. Indeed, power sharing is a long-term political arrangement where the interests of sectarian and ethnic elites are at heart, with little or no accountability. In this sense, power sharing is the politicization of the ethno-sectarian plurality of the country. In the aftermath of 2003, Iraq has witnessed the institutionalization of politics of sectarianism and identity politics. Dawisha argues: "What happened in the post-2003 period was that ethnosectarian identities were reified into fixed political cleavages. Particularistic identities were fused into the concept of parties, so that national issues were now viewed from an ethnosectarian perspective, and subnational concerns would generally define national policy."[5]

Identity politics deals with various communities that share existence in one country as totally separate entities with nothing or very little in common. In identity politics, community interests are presented as incompatible, nonreconcilable, and irrevocable. Any convergence of these interests is strictly confined to the interests of the leaders of these communities in monopolizing wealth and power at the expense of ordinary citizens. With their common elitist interests, these leaders ensure the division and separation of communities by playing out a violent and destructive identity politics to the maximum. Thus when these communities are brought together in domestic politics, which is dominated by ethnic and sectarian perceptions, they are brought together as entirely different and detached groups. Democracy, on the other hand, is about diffusing primordial differences by creating new political constellations and alignments. With these, one can say that confessionalism is an inappropriate political arrangement as far as establishing democracy is concerned.

REPRESENTATION AND LEGITIMACY

In the rush to put an Iraqi face on the American enterprise of regime change, the U.S. administration established the IGC in July 2003 to provide advice and leadership to the country. This body consisted of 25 members representing major ethno-sectarian communities in the country: 13 Shiites, 5 Sunnis, 5 Kurds, 1 Turkman, and 1 Christian. Three of its members were women. However, it took the council more than two weeks to agree on a presidency, which was the first order of business. After a failure to agree on a single president followed by another failed attempt to agree on a three-member presidency, they finally agreed on a nine-member presidency rotating on a monthly basis. Still, they continued to disagree on who would be the first president. Finally, they agreed that the rotation would occur in alphabetical order. This clearly shows to what extent power sharing is an elitist political arrangement and to what extent Iraqi political culture is obsessed with the issue of leadership, *za'im*. This obsession with control is actually one of the most serious problems in Iraqi politics and involves all political parties and personalities regardless of political orientation.

The American administration promoted this council as the most representative body in Iraqi history. Yet many would argue differently. Dodge states that the primordialization of Iraqi society was one of the most destructive discursive mistakes made by the U.S. administration: "It was clear from the way that the IGC had been selected that the primordialism of the Iraqi exiles had come to dominate the way US officials running the occupation perceived the Iraqi population. This was in stark contrast to the reception the IGC got from Iraqi society."[6] The Iraqis question the ability of this rather enforced arrangement to serve the interests of all Iraqis and national interests. The thesis of the primordialization of Iraqi society is based on the assumption that Iraqi society is deeply divided along ethnic and sectarian lines, resulting in eternal animosity between the communities sharing their land. Obviously, this kind of perception can lead only to exasperating ethnic and sectarian division and polarization that can escalate in armed conflict and tense relations between these communities. This has been demonstrated in the violence that dominated Iraq in the aftermath of regime change.

Identity politics and the accompanying ethno-sectarian violence and tensions have led to the advancement of yet another thesis on the "artificiality" of the Iraqi State. This thesis claims that because the Iraqi state is unnaturally created, the division of Iraq is a "natural" solution to the problems of the country. This thesis was in wide circulation during the sectarian conflict in the country in 2005–8. Motivated by their self-interests, the Iraqi opposition, dominated by the Islamist Shiites and nationalist Kurds, have put forward, if not enforced this thesis on the new political discourse in the aftermath of the regime change. It is obvious that a divided Iraq is the only vision of an Iraqi society that can help these politicians preserve their interests and make claims to representation and legitimacy. This self-centered elitist vision uses Iraq's ethno-sectarian pluralism to its advantage. Political sectarianism becomes a deliberate process of the commercialization of the ethno-sectarian profile of the Iraqi society to serve the entrenched interests of leading politicians. It becomes imperative for these elites, therefore, to politicize the ethno-sectarian reality in Iraq. Unfortunately, this politicization of societal plurality comes at the expense of meeting the interests of the majority of Iraqis and establishing a veritable democratic process in the country.

Primordialization and power sharing are failures, regardless of where they are tried, be it in Lebanon, in the Kurdish enclave, or in new Iraq. The only explanation for the insistence on an arrangement that has a proven record of failure is the narrow interests of the leaders of various communities who are desirous of monopolizing access to wealth and power. This enforced vision of an Iraqi society and the benefits that come with it make these leaders unsuitable agents for establishing democracy in the country, no matter how loud their claims as representatives of their respective communities may be. Dodge points out that the bizarre nature of the arrangement of IGC and the "sectarian mathematic" that comes with it "certainly had the advantage of allowing its formerly exiled allies to pose as the representatives of Iraqi communalism, but its long-term ramifications may well be to leave a series of unrepresentative politicians at the head of a new Iraqi state, increasingly reliant on attempts at sectarian mobilisation as the only possible way to rally any support to their cause."[7]

As an assembly for the collection of narrowly defined sectarian, ethnic, partisan, and personal interests, the IGC suffered from lack of vision of Iraq as a nation, political paralysis, intense political disagreements, and high absenteeism. Unfortunately for the newly initiated democratic process and in a replica of the IGC, the new parliament eventually came to embody these very same problems. The electoral system that has been adopted in Iraq, the list proportional representation, fits very well the objectives and the rationales of the power-sharing arrangement of ruling by the new dominant political elites. This system considers Iraq as a single election zone, and people vote for closed lists decided by the leadership of the contestant political parties. Elections that are mainly focusing on primordial identity and the accompanying electoral system ensure that a weak and easily manipulated parliament emerges from these elections.

Power sharing is favorable to the ruling elites but not necessarily to the electorate. It places ethno-sectarian elites in total control over the electorate because people do not vote for individual candidates; they instead vote for closed lists that are decided, controlled, and manipulated by party leaders. This system also puts party leaders into an almost unchallengeable position of control over candidates on their lists, who feel they owe their loyalty to party leaders for selecting them to run on the list. In this sense, any bond between the legislators and the electorate is lost. Given this situation, the emerging parliament does not appear to be a genuine representation of the people. Rather than acting as a real, legitimate, and representative democratic institution, the Iraqi parliament is proving itself as a hollow institution, which is controlled from the outside by very few dominant political elites. Makiya emphasizes: "While that Parliament, as it is designed in the Constitution, looks like a democratic institution, it doesn't work like one. Rather, it is an artificially constructed collection of ethnic and sectarian voting blocs. If the experience of the interim government is any guide, the few people who control those blocs are the ones who will wield real power, and they will do so largely through handpicked committees and backroom wheeling and dealing."[8]

The double control of few party leaders over the electorate and also over their candidates severely affects the legitimacy of the national assembly. Ethnic and sectarian elections that are devoid of seriously competing political programs suffer from a problem of legitimacy.

Despite this, the ethno-sectarian focus of these elections might still offer a sense of legitimacy for legislators as representatives of sectarian and ethnic communities, regardless of how the interests of these communities are defined by the ruling politicians. It is no wonder that the parliament, dominated by the Shiite, Kurdish, and Sunni blocs, is working along ethno-sectarian lines. In addition, the perceived sense of legitimacy that is derived from being representatives of various communities compels legislators to adopt extremist and often uncompromising stands when discussing and deciding on ethno-sectarian issues. In fact, with the rise of identity politics, these ethno-sectarian issues have dominated the political process and parliamentary politics. The entire democratic process has been reduced to arguing about various ethno-sectarian issues, and sectarian politics has come to dominate all aspects of the democratic process. This situation tends to affect negatively the functionality and the longed transformation of the parliament into a truly democratic institution.

Nevertheless, the parliament has also witnessed a rare moment of breaking away from this pattern of conducting parliamentary politics toward the direction of establishing a genuinely independent and viable institution. During the debate over the issue of Kirkuk, in relation to the provincial election law in July 2008, an independent bloc, the so-called July 22 Gathering, emerged. It was the first time that members of the parliament voted according to their own convictions and not necessarily according to the visions or the decisions of their party leaders, who otherwise play a decisive role in how they vote. This parliamentary vote, which was facilitated by a secret-ballot system, led to the fury of big parties, particularly Kurdish parties, who angrily condemned this action as a coup against Kurdish interests. This event that could have revitalized the democratic essence of the parliament, away from ethno-sectarian politics and from the domination of few politicians, and this event that could have offered a new sense of legitimacy to the parliament remains, regrettably, isolated.

Thus the legislative assembly suffers from a problem of the real representation of the population, leading to a problem of accountability and delivery. An unrepresentative parliament has no obligation to serve the electorate. Indeed, the miserable records of the Iraqi parliament in reflecting and responding to the concerns and interests of the Iraqis do not come as a shocking surprise. Absenteeism, political disagreements, backroom deals, and mutual concessions between political parties that have little to do with the needs of the majority of the Iraqis have dominated the work of the assembly. The only successful, straightforward, and well-attended sessions of this parliament are when the specific and lucrative demands and interests of the legislators themselves are on the agenda.

In an interesting case, unanimity in parliament was secured not simply because of the immediate self-interests and concerns of the legislators. The case came when the assembly included on its agenda the trip to Israel of Mithal al-Alusi, one of the legislators. He participated in a conference on counterterrorism in September 2008. This session witnessed a stern condemnation of the trip and angry attacks on al-Alusi. The Iraqi parliament voted to strip him of his legal immunity as a member of parliament, and ban him from traveling outside the country or attending succeeding parliamentary sessions. The parliament also decided to prosecute him on charges of establishing contacts with an enemy state, according to a 1969 law that was promulgated by the deposed dictator. The unanimous condemnation of this action by the wide political spectrum is noteworthy and paradoxical. Unanimity in a controversial issue, such as this, can happen only in authoritarian politics. This incidence reflects a case where a democratic institution not only fails to respect and guarantee the freedom of expression and opinion of one of its members but punishes that member as well. It highlights the fragility not only of parliamentary life but of the entire Iraqi experiment in democracy.

However, while the IGC reflected the ethnic and sectarian balance of Iraqi society, the cabinet formed by this council should have been based on meritocracy rather than on sectarianism, ethnicity, or primordial loyalty. If the intention was to serve the interests of the Iraqis, there was then a need for an efficient government of technocrats to emerge from the transfer of sovereignty to the Iraqis on June 28, 2004. In fact, that was the vision of the UN envoy to Iraq, Lakhdar Brahimi, who planned for a technocratic government and called for those appointed to disavow party politics. Yet his plan was very unpopular with the political elites who dominated the IGC. Indeed, the emerging interim government was the very antithesis of the Brahimi plan.[9]

As a result of transferring sovereignty to the Iraqis, the interim government was created on June 28, 2004, to replace American authority in Iraq, the CPA. This cabinet was a caretaker government to prepare for the Iraqi national assembly elections on January 30, 2005, but lasted until the formation of the next government on May 3, 2005. However, due to pressures to accommodate all the contestant ethno-sectarian communities and personalities, intense political maneuverings caused a prolonged delay in the formation of cabinets. This is particularly true regarding the distribution of the five so-called "sovereign ministries": foreign affairs, oil, interior, defense, and national security. Thus it took the transitional government of Ibrahim al-Ja'fari (May 2005–May 2006), which followed the January 2005 elections, approximately four months to be formed. The first permanent government of Nuri al-Maliki (May 2006–December 2010), which followed the December 2005 elections, needed five months. The second Maliki government, which followed the March 2010 elections, took more than nine months to come into existence, and it was still only a partial cabinet.

Pressures to accommodate all political leaders have resulted in the outcome of exceedingly inflated governments. The interim government consisted of 30 ministers in addition to the prime minister, Ayad Allawi, and two deputies. The cabinet, which included 6 female members, was distributed among 16 Shiite, 9 Sunnis, 6 Kurds, 1 Turkman, and 1 Christian. A more or less similar pattern repeated itself in the subsequent governments. The transitional government of Ja'afari consisted of 35 cabinet members. The first government of Maliki consisted of 40 cabinet members, increasing to an extraordinary high record of 45 in the second Maliki cabinet in December 2010. Apart from the issue of efficiency, the big size of the governments makes them very costly for the Iraqi budget. Governments of this size are also highly susceptible to rampant corruption. These costs would make the power-sharing system of ruling a very expensive arrangement from a financial and economic point of view.

Thus the adoption of the power-sharing system implies that everyone, winners or losers, will be incorporated into the emerging government, thereby causing a considerable delay in the formation of governments. It also results in the formation of inefficient governments with an extremely weak capacity to serve the electorate. At the expense of meritocracy, which is the most crucial condition in deciding the ability of any government to deliver, loyalty to political leaders has become the only criterion for selecting cabinet members. The resulting government is unaccountable and unanswerable to the people, the parliament, and even to the prime minister. Those in cabinet positions are answerable only to their party leaders. Power sharing and national unity governments are ingredients for political paralysis and the failure to deliver electoral pledges.

There is a dismal record of the ruling elites and governments with respect to delivering on promises regarding security, rule of law, equality, basic services, a functioning economy, lower unemployment rates, and better educational and health services. The failure of the governing elites is even compounded considering that the stakes are very high in Iraq due to years of extensive militarization, wars, sanctions, and destruction. Dodge discusses how the formation of government becomes carving out fiefdoms for personal and factional benefits: "The record of the three Iraqi governments that have held power since the handover of sovereignty in June 2004 is very poor. One of the key reasons for this is that constitutionally real political power is vested in the political parties, not in the office of prime minister or president. Electoral success is rewarded by dividing up the spoils of government-cabinet portfolios and the jobs and resources they bring with them."[10] Indeed, incompetent governments that are centered on the interests of the few ruling elites would surely make the claim of representing the interests of ethno-sectarian communities no more than illusionary, if not very deceptive in its legitimacy.

NOTES

1. Melani Cammett, "Democracy, Lebanese-Style," Middle East Research and Information Project, August 18, 2009, http://www.merip.org/mero/mero081809.html.

2. Adeed Dawisha, "The Prospects for Democracy in Iraq: Challenges and Opportunities," *Third World Quarterly* 26, no. 4–5 (2005): 727.

3. Daniel Byman and Kenneth M. Pollack, "Democracy in Iraq?" *The Washington Quarterly* 26, no. 3 (2003): 120–21.

4. Peter J. Munson. *Iraq in Transition: The Legacy of Dictatorship and the Prospect for Democracy* (Dulles, VA: Potomac Books, 2008), 2.

5. Adeed Dawisha, "The Unraveling of Iraq: Ethnosectarian Preferences and State Performance in Historical Perspective," *Middle East Journal* 62, no. 2 (Spring 2008): 227.

6. Toby Dodge, "Iraqi Transitions: From Regime Change to State Collapse," *Third World Quarterly* 26, no. 4–5 (2005): 715.

7. Ibid., 719.

8. Kanan Makiya, "Present at the Disintegration," *New York Times*, December 11, 2005.

9. Dodge, "Iraqi Transitions," 717–18; on the Lakhdar Brahimi plan for Iraq, see 716–18.

10. Toby Dodge, "State Collapse and the Rise of Identity Politics," in *Iraq: Preventing a New Generation of Conflict*, ed. Markus E. Bouillon, David M. Malone, and Ben Rowswell (Boulder, CO: Rienner, 2007), 35.

10

Externalization of Legitimacy

ELECTIONS, DELIVERY, AND LEGITIMACY

Regime change in 2003 was followed by ethnic and sectarian elections, leading to the governance of the parties of political Shiism in alliance with the Kurdish ethnic parties. Despite the externally implemented regime change and the high hopes for democracy in Iraq, the country has followed a familiar Middle Eastern pattern where holding free elections tends to benefit political Islam. This outcome is a natural culmination of a long political development that has led to the dominance of authoritarian politics since independence. Religion provides the Islamists a kind of relative immunity from the repression of the authoritarian state. Meanwhile state repression largely weakens secular political parties, to the advantage of the Islamists. It is this structural advantage, however, that puts Islamist parties in a better position to capitalize on any exploration in democracy and elections in the region. This is reinforced by the deep economic and political crisis associated with the authoritarian regimes in power.

Moreover, this outcome is also related to the type of secularism implemented by authoritarian rulers, which is different from Western secularism, which emphasizes democracy, civil liberties, and separation of religion and politics. In contrast, what has been implemented by these regimes is an *authoritarian secularism* that is based on despotism and state domination over the entire society, including religion. This kind of secularism, which is associated with repression and lack of freedom, works for the benefit of the politicized religious movements. Possessing all these advantages, the Islamists became the natural winners in the recently held elections in the Middle East. Consequently, the region has witnessed the rise of many Islamists parties to power.

However, the rise of political Islam to power has triggered a heated academic debate on the compatibility, or the lack of it, of Islam and democracy. With the exception of the Islamists of Turkey, so far at least, the experience of the Islamists in power shows dismal records. These depressing records seem to confirm a widely held contention that the relationship between the Islamist parties and democracy is merely a one-way ticket to power. The question is whether the experience of political Islam, or rather political Shiism, in power in Iraq confirms the mainstream pattern of the Islamist ruling parties in the region. This question, however, has severe implications for legitimacy and democracy in Iraq.

One of the most important aspects for any political regime is the issue of legitimacy. Similar to other authoritarian rules, the former regime that came to power through a military coup suffered from a grim deficiency of legitimacy. The only exception is the first decade of its rule where a certain level of legitimacy was achieved through implementing some economic and social reforms that benefited a large section of the population, particularly the middle class. This was done despite severe political repression during the same decade. However, the next couple of decades, which were associated with extensive militarization, wars, and sanctions, did in fact wipe out the early achievement.

Thus authoritarian regimes that come to power via military takeover or other unconstitutional methods lack any sense of real legitimacy. By contrast, in terms of legitimacy, holding elections, irrespective of the nature and outcome, seems to offer a sort of alternative to authoritarian politics. The new dominating Iraqi political elites are fully aware of this simple reality, particularly when they present themselves as a replacement for the previous dictatorial regime. These elites, therefore, made sure to inject the mechanism of elections rather early, prematurely, and forcefully into the political process.

That people cast their votes for their representatives offers a certain level of credibility and legitimacy to the ruling regime. The mechanism of elections is an integral part of the democratic process. Still, despite the significance of elections to democracy, elections alone are an insufficient condition to attain legitimacy; otherwise, holding an election becomes an aim in itself or an end result rather than an instrument for achieving democracy and progress. People do not go through the trouble of voting just to put politicians in positions of power. Rather, they elect politicians who serve their interests. While elections are important, they make little sense if not accompanied by the ability to deliver on electoral pledges. The failure of delivery, in this sense, will always be punished by diverting legitimacy to those who appear to be, or give the impression that they are, more deliverable. In this respect, legitimacy that derives from the electoral process is only temporal and conditional, and there are dire consequences for any failure to comprehend or ignore this simple political reality. Yet it is this simple fact that the new ruling elites in Iraq appear to be neglecting.

The enthusiasm of the religious Shiite parties about holding elections, thanks to the demographic makeup of Iraq, is unmatched by a similar enthusiasm about delivering on electoral pledges that should naturally follow any election. The demographic majority of the Shiite makes it convenient for the Shiite parties in power to stress the legitimacy associated with holding an election. It is, however, an entirely different story when it comes to the legitimacy that is associated with serving the electorate, the legitimacy that derives from performance while in power. Yet meeting the expectations of the electorate stipulates entirely new economic and political structures that may conflict with the entrenched interests of the sectarian and ethnic elites. The poor record of these parties in power in delivering to the electorate and providing decent services and living standards is a clear indication of this reality.

Admittedly, there is a heavy legacy of solemn problems that can put any government in a difficult position, a situation worsened by an unstable security situation. Yet political development depends on which direction the new elites take; that is, if their policies are a continuation of the old politics or if they intend to establish a premise for new politics. This is indeed a crucial issue for the new order in Iraq. However, the answer seems to be blurred by the adoption of the mechanism of elections and the accompanying formal political institutions such as parliament. In other words, the key questions are whether elections and parliament become mechanisms for a true democratic process rather than becoming a continuation of the old violent politics under different names and whether democracy can be built without true democrats. The poor records of delivery seem to indicate clearly that the new elites are deriving a high level of satisfaction and legitimacy from the electoral process without any serious considerations of the issue of serving the people who elected them.

However, the game of reducing a complex democratic process to only a mechanism of election is surely convenient for the governing elites because it provides them with positions of power, wealth, and prestige without being accountable to the electorate. Nevertheless, where there are winners there are losers, and in this situation, the majority of the Iraqis feel they have been cheated out in this process. Subjecting the majority of the population to a losing situation is one of the striking features and basic contradictions of introducing certain democratic practices in an otherwise dominant authoritarian politics in the Middle East. This shows the resilience of authoritarianism in this region and how the intermarriage of authoritarian politics and democratic mechanisms is in fact detrimental to the interests of the majority of the population and to a genuine democratic process.

It is an irony and a paradox that the government that is the most representative of Iraqi society in a demographic sense is at the same time the least efficient. This reality tends to confuse the issue of legitimacy by making it a rather contradictory, if not bizarre. Those who rule are considered the most representative of Iraqi society, yet they are at the same time the least effective in serving the people. Thus despite claims of representation of communities, the ruling elites appear to be as illegitimate as the former regime. A legitimate political process can be ensured only by a serious commitment to delivering on electoral promises. "No delivery, no office" is a crucial logic and essence of any democratic process. However, thanks to politics of identity and ethno-sectarian politics, a power-sharing political arrangement contravenes this commonsense logic by allowing the possibility of public office without delivery or accountability.

It is understandable that dominant and self-serving politicians stress and profit from ethno-sectarian division and conflict. Yet the failure of these elites to respect and honor their pledges in improving services and living standards provides the majority of Iraqis across ethnic and sectarian lines with a common ground that can transcend their differences. Dissatisfaction with the miserable records of the ruling elites could lead to a new division in Iraqi society—a polarization between the ruling elites who dominate power and wealth and elevate primordial differences on the one hand, and the majority of the Iraqis who find themselves in a losing situation because of the actions of their rulers, regardless of their primordial affiliations. However, realizing that this divergence supersedes any other ethnic or sectarian polarization is a first, yet crucial, step in building a new experience of political awareness in the country.

The obvious failure of various governments in improving miserable living conditions for the majority of Iraqis would make holding elections in the country a very questionable issue. In the debate on the timing of elections in Iraq, it has been argued that the government of Ayad Allawi in 2004 suffered from deficient legitimacy because it had not been elected. Though elections are indubitably a source of legitimacy, the relationship between elections and legitimacy is not that simple. Elections can give only a first injection of legitimacy that nonetheless remains temporal and deficient if not cemented with a more solid and durable level of legitimacy when delivering on promises and serving the electorate. A far more important level of legitimacy derives from appreciating and acting on the wishes, aspirations, and interests of the population.

Thus an elected government that fails to honor its promises to the electorate does not necessarily represent a more legitimate government. Judging by the performance of the Iraqi governments since regime change, one can argue in one sense that the elected governments of Ja'fari and Maliki do not imply a higher level of legitimacy than the unelected government of Allawi. By improving security and promising an anticorruption campaign and better services, the first government of Maliki started to gain more legitimacy at the end of 2008 and beginning of 2009. Yet this gained legitimacy was somewhat lost when these promises remained unfulfilled and empty rhetoric.

Awareness about the strong linkages between elections and service is clearly reflected in the faded enthusiasm of the Iraqi electorate regarding the purpose of participating in the elections. A resident from Basra says: "I won't participate in the upcoming elections. What happened in the past is the best proof. We challenged the enemies and the security situation, yet regrettably, those we voted for didn't give us the simplest things, and that is services."[1] Another resident from Falluja mentions: "I did not vote because I could not find a qualified candidate that I can trust-all those candidates came for their personal benefits."[2] Another citizen concurs: "I don't trust any one of the candidates. I consider them as a group of thieves coming to get financial benefits for themselves and their political parties as Iraq is going to witness a campaign of reconstruction."[3] These frustrated comments clearly indicate that the nature of the elections held in Iraq and the elitist power-sharing political arrangement within the context of identity politics fail to provide the expected legitimacy that is associated with establishing democratic political system.

EXTERNALIZING LEGITIMACY

An unstable legitimacy derived from an ethno-sectarian electoral process accompanied by the inability to deliver to people make the search for alternative sources of legitimacy almost inevitable. Since legitimacy cannot be achieved intrinsically or democratically, the only option is to manufacture another pattern of legitimacy based on externality and conflict with the Other or the outside world. This seems to be the case of the new Iraq, but it is also a continuation of the politics of the old regime. To compensate for the lack of credibility, authoritarian regimes usually tend to invent other sources of legitimacy. If legitimacy cannot be passed down naturally by the very same dynamic and genuine political process, then the invention of external sources of legitimacy—external in the sense of external to the political process—becomes the recourse. In this sense, authoritarian politics seeks extra political sources of legitimacy such as religion, sectarianism, nationalism, animosity with the Other, whether local or foreign entities, and fabricated conflict with, for the most part, invented enemies.

A lucid picture of this policy is the way theocratic and authoritarian regimes in the Middle East manipulate the Palestinian problem or the conflict with the West in domestic politics. Iraqi history fits this picture extraordinarily well, particularly in recent decades. The deposed rule of Saddam Hussein is a prime example of a regime that lacked internal credibility yet at the same time used confrontation with the outside world as a compensating mechanism. Unfortunately, the regime change in 2003 did not result in an unambiguous interruption with the old policies, which sought externally derived sources of legitimacy. What make things even worse is that the absence of the rule of the law and the widespread corruption—the two issues that dominate the new experience in the country—are the very antitheses of legitimacy.

For Pan-Arab nationalism and militant Islamism, the nation-state and its borders are considered insignificant, a mere colonial creation that exists to divide and control the Arab or the Islamic nation. In this sense, interference in the internal affairs by the neighboring countries or even invasion by these countries becomes justified. The regime of Saddam Hussein in conceding territories to Iran in the Algiers agreement of 1975, the war with Iran, and the invasion of Kuwait are all clear illustration of these politics. Facing a grave legitimacy problem at home, Iran is also adopting a similar line of policies by interfering in the internal affairs of several countries in the region, including Iraq. It is no wonder that many people argue that it is Iran that emerged as the real winner of the 2003 Iraq War, led by the United States. Many of the dominant Shiite parties in Iraq are subscribing to a policy of exporting the Islamic revolution in Iran in the form of politicized Shiism. This politicization of sectarian Shiism, whose core identity is based on a perceived injustice against the Shiites by the majority Sunni Muslims, is a destructive and violent politics. Playing an active role in this vision of politicized Shiism might help to give the Iraqi Shiite politicians a perceived sense of legitimacy that can supersede a much desirable legitimacy derived from investing in a genuine democratic process that can serve the people of Iraq.

Thus failure to initiate a veritable democratic process that includes a built-in internal legitimacy based on delivery gives the new Shiite religious rulers of Iraq no choice but to emphasize externalized legitimacy, in much a similar way as the old regime. The most important aspect of this legitimacy is the Islamization of the Iraqi society. The religious ruling elites consider the Islamization of society a route to legitimacy. Islamization is related to religion and God, which are two "hard to dispute" sources of legitimacy. In the religious discourse of political Islam, religion firmly signifies legitimacy. As far as the religious parties are concerned, a great part of legitimacy is actually derived from the fact that the Islamists represent God on earth—and God, not people, is the ultimate source of legitimacy.

This perception tends to prevent religious parties from taking the issue of legitimacy in a more serious manner. It encourages religious parties to have a one-sided and deficient understanding of this crucial issue. For this reason, legitimacy is more a problem for the religious parties than for any other parties. For the majority of the Islamists, legitimacy is confined to holding elections, which is the only way to reach power in a democratic game. In fact, they perceive elections as merely an official confirmation of the legitimacy that these parties derive from religion.

Strong emphasis on religion and sectarianism tends to hamper the process of establishing a credible and legitimate politics in Iraq. The obsession with religion is well reflected in the national flag of Iraq. "Mighty is God," *allahu akbar*, was added to the Iraqi flag in the 1990s in a script that was modeled on Saddam Hussein's own handwriting. The new ruling elites who were adamant about wiping out all traces and legacies of Saddam failed to include this legacy in their effective campaign of eradication just because it was a religious writing. Ironically, this is the most visible legacy of Saddam as the national flag flutters every day and everywhere in the country. Obsession with religion and sectarianism is also reflected in the amount of attention that the ruling political elites and the government bestow on other aspects of Islamizing society such as the banning of alcohol, the veiling of women, and the extravagant celebrations of religious and sectarian festivities in the country.

The conservative drive to impose a ban on alcohol, bars, and nightclubs has started with a discussion in the parliament on the necessity and virtue of this ban, and it has intensified in 2010. Three provinces, so far, have initiated new policies to forbid and punish selling and consuming alcohol: Najaf, Basra, and Wasit. In the capital Baghdad, there is also an intense campaign to restrict access to alcohol. It started in the Green Zone, with Iraqi soldiers ordering restaurants to stop serving alcohol and confiscating bottles from politicians at checkpoints. Then, mysterious signs began to appear across the rest of Baghdad declaring alcohol is sinful. "Damned is he who sits at a table with alcohol," is one of the banners that appeared in Abu Nawas Street, the hub of nightlife on the banks of the Tigris River in downtown Baghdad.[4]

Finally, the crackdown came when soldiers and police officers descended on nightclubs, cabarets, bars, and liquor stores in the capital. The crackdown was headed by the Baghdad provincial council, which is controlled by the religious Da'wa Party. An owner of a nightclub on the Tigris River that was raided in the campaign and ordered to close comments: "Our new constitution guarantees all freedoms for all Iraqi people. But the political powers in control are Islamic, and they can't handle social freedoms such as alcohol because their minds are narrowed by religion."[5] It is noteworthy that incorporating sectarian militias into the state apparatus tends to enforce conservatism in society. The militia's vision of Islamizing society seems to be gradually adopted by the government.

Freed from repressive dictatorship, the Shiites have started to attach a greater significance to the observance of religious rituals. These rituals are particularly important in the month of *Muharram*, most particularly the religious observance of *Ashura*, the Shiite holy day of mourning to commemorate the death of Imam Hussein, grandson of the Prophet Muhammad, who was killed in 680 in a bid for power in the battle of Karbala in Iraq. The Shiites perceive the "martyrdom" of Hussein as a source of legitimacy for their distinction within the world of Islam. The Sunni-Shiite differences, which culminated in the death of Hussein, was in essence a struggle for power and a controversy over the meaning of legitimacy. The Shiites consider that a legitimate ruler should be a descendant of the family of the prophet, regardless of ability, whereas the Sunnis consider that any qualified Muslim could become a ruler regardless of family ties. This conflict reflects issues of nepotism, meritocracy, and ability to lead and deliver, which are core issues to the concept of legitimacy.

However, because of encouragements from the religious parties in power, the number of people participating in the religious rituals has become extraordinarily large. It is estimated that about 3 million people gathered in each of the ritual mournings in December 2009 and in 2010. Many of these people make the pilgrimage on foot, thus walking hundreds of kilometers to reach the holy city of Karbala. The rituals entail some of the excessive and violent expressions of mourning, such as flagellation or shedding one's own blood with cuts in the foreheads. Surely these are undesirable expressions in a supposedly nonviolent new Iraq. Furthermore, these rituals impose a great burden on the government. The Red Crescent needs to set up hundreds of tents to deal with pilgrims who have passed out from loss of blood and dehydration. Ten of thousands of security forces are mobilized and deployed to ensure the safety and security of the mourners, particularly when insecurity is still dominant.

The poor records in improving services and living standards for the people compel the Shiite sectarian parties and politicians in power to become more involved in sponsoring and supporting religious festivities. Although dominant politicians derive some feelings of satisfaction from attending to these religious activities, yet this is achieved at a risk that these gatherings could easily backfire when dejected living conditions continue to be the case. In fact, one of the most important reasons for the old regime to outlaw these rituals is the risk of turning these occasions into protest gatherings. Indeed, the latest occasions of sectarian ritual have witnessed manifestations of disillusionment about the government.

Criticism about financial corruption and the huge gulf between ordinary citizens and ruling politicians was heard during these rituals. An Iraqi citizen who participated in these religious rituals says: "We had believed that Maliki's government and most of the politicians were a part of us, and we used to support them. But finally, we discovered that they don't represent us, so we decided to protest against them for the first time on Ashura this year."[6] Another fellow continues: "After 35 years of repression we had anticipated a new government with a new style. People had ambitions to live in security and democracy, but those who came to power proved they were not worthy of the responsibilities and did not come to serve the people. I now have no desire to participate in the next elections." A third citizen expresses: "We know all these people now. They say one thing and then do another, so I am confused about whom to vote for." Yet another citizen concurs: "This government has not achieved anything: poor services, bad management and corruption everywhere doubled from before."[7]

Furthermore, exaggerated sectarian celebrations are incompatible with a tolerant, peaceful, and plural Iraq. Many people feel uncomfortable with rituals that involve large crowds, unmistakable sectarian chants, in addition to street closures and around-the-clock coverage of these celebrations on television and other media. This is even more so, considering the mobilization of various state resources for these activities, which gives the impression that the state is in the service of sectarian religious rituals rather than taking care of national interests for all citizens.

The identity politics associated with these activities helps to enforce politics of sectarianism, which is hardly the right premise for building a new experience in Iraq. It is quite possible that non-Shiites will perceive these rituals and the associated identity and sectarian politics as a threat. A Sunni citizen has this reaction: "It is part of their political dominance to show they are in control, and this is why they have pilgrims everywhere and are closing the streets. Definitely there are political motives behind this."[8] Indubitably, extensive celebration of these rituals is an expression of Shiite triumphalism in new Iraq. Although the ruling politicians use the mobilization of the Shiites in these rituals to ensure political allegiances for electoral purposes, sectarian politics is a risky and dangerous policy to pursue in new Iraq.

In the absence of internal democratic legitimacy, religious rituals seem to offer a sense of legitimacy for the new rulers. Apart from being risky, unstable, and questionable, this type of legitimacy is extremely negative, costly, and unproductive for both the people involved and the government. Considering that each ritual occasion takes a few days, the numerous religious festivities tend to cause the utmost paralysis in public life and governmental works. It is estimated that public holidays in Iraq, including weekends and all the many religious and sectarian rituals, could take up as much as six months in the year. This is without counting the fasting month of Ramadan, when the functioning of the public administration and of the economy is greatly reduced.

Indisputably, this is a huge burden on an already worn-out economy. Iraq needs to mobilize all its resources to recover from years of neglect, destruction, and isolation. Encouraging millions of people to take part in various sectarian rituals is in fact diverting the human resources available to society into unproductive purposes. With its devastated economy and huge need for reconstruction and development, Iraq cannot afford this dissipation. This waste not only concerns the government and the country but also extends to the people involved as well. Surely, there are better and more productive ways and purposes to use human energies that can result in raising the living standards for millions of Iraqi families.

The previous regime had a similar experience regarding the issue of legitimacy. Instead of religion, Pan-Arab nationalism and commitment to an Arab cause and the Palestinian problem, mostly rhetorical though, was regarded as a, if not the, source of legitimacy. This deceptive sense of legitimacy not only tended to discourage that regime from serving the interests of the people, but was even used to cause serious destruction and suffering by the population. The only difference between the old regime and the currently ruling religious parties is the adoption of the mechanism of holding elections, a new experience in the very recent history of Iraq. It is important to emphasize, however, that an election that is perceived as merely a vehicle to power will be empty of its necessary democratic content. In that case, the difference between the old and new Iraq becomes minimal.

Moreover, the two dominant Kurdish parties that are ruling in alliance with the Shiite parties use Kurdish nationalism as a source of legitimacy at the expense of taking care of the needs of the Kurdish population. This far-fetched nationalism is a Kurdish version of the same old nationalism that dominated the country for decades and contributed to the disaster of Iraq. Extreme nationalism tends to exacerbate conflict with central government and thus helps to destabilize the country. It also diverts attention from more urgent internal democratic reforms.

Whether using religion or nationalism to give the impression of legitimacy, whether adopting elections or a military coup to reach power, whether there are authoritarian or religious parties in power, there is a solemn problem of legitimacy in Middle Eastern politics. This problem of legitimacy is manifested in the miserable performance of the ruling parties in improving the living standards in these countries. The failure to deliver has plunged the region into a deep crisis on many fronts: political, economic, social, and intellectual. The fact that the Middle East is the only region in the world that is still stubbornly resisting democratic change is only one of the symptoms of this crisis.

Nevertheless, there seems to be hopes in the recent experience initiated by the ruling Islamists in Turkey. The Islamically rooted Justice and Development Party, AKP in Turkish, which is ruling the country since the November 2002 elections, is more successful than both the predecessor secular Turkish parties and the ruling parties of political Islam in the Middle East. The success of the Islamists of Turkey rests on at least two factors: moderate politics and the ascendancy of economics over identity politics. These factors have ensured a success in democracy and the economy for the benefit of the Turkish population. However, both of these factors are highly needed in a region that is still engulfed in extremism, violence, and economic failure. The region can benefit a great deal from studying the experience of Turkey.[9]

The Turkish experience can prove to be valuable for the Shiite religious parties and the Kurdish nationalist parties in Iraq. Both of these parties have accumulated rather depressing records of serving the people of Iraq. When external sources cannot provide credible legitimacy, as the case of the old regime in Iraq and the current theocratic regime in Iran clearly demonstrate, the search for internal sources of legitimacy should be inevitable. A different approach from externalized legitimacy that has proven records of failure would be a wise policy to follow by the new rulers of Iraq. If these rulers insist on building the new experience in Iraq within a religious framework, the experience of the ruling Islamists in Turkey that emphasizes moderation and primacy of economics would then appear to be an illuminating and helpful experience to consider. Moderate politics necessitates a departure from extremist positions in politics, de-Ba'thification, and narrow-minded sectarian and ethnic politics. It stipulates the creation of a more inclusive and transparent political process for the benefit of all citizens.

While economic interests define politics in a democratic system, the subordination of the economy to authoritarian politics is one of the main characteristics of authoritarianism. Marr urges Iraqis to step back from politics of identity, which is driving much of the current political process and producing much of the violence, and calls instead for the construction of a new consensus based on interests, not identity: "Leaders should be encouraged to concentrate on interests and goals, where all communities could gain by cooperating. Economic development, for example, not currently a focus of most leaders, needs to be raised to a higher priority. Oil legislation, which encourages a shared development of Iraq's main resources, as well as the equitable distribution of its revenues, is a prime example of how such mutual interests could be encouraged."[10] Basham adds: "In practice, the realization of Iraq's democratic potential will depend more on the introduction of a free-market economic system—and its long-term positive influence on Iraqi political culture—than on any UN-approved election."[11]

Prioritizing economic development and encouraging the private sector will unquestionably lead to the creation of an independent and self-sustaining middle class, a desirable development for strengthening democracy. Yet an economic policy that continues to be totally dependent on rentier economy and state involvement in the economy will only continue the same policies of old Iraq, which are associated with violence and authoritarianism.

However, a good economic performance stipulates the rule of law, which is also a prerequisite for legitimacy. In turn, the rule of law requires disbanding of all sorts of militias and ensuring security in the country. While security is a delicate and serious problem for new

Iraq, it can entail a double sense of risks. On the one hand, the government has often used the deterioration in security conditions as a pretext for the failure to improve services and economic activities. The other risk in relation to security, on the other hand, is that the government is exploiting the recently achieved relative improvement in security as a compensation for the continued miserable services and poor living standards. A purely militarist approach to security misses the important reality that an improved economy and services will positively influence security conditions.

Rule of law also requires equality before the law and that no one, regardless of position, should be above the law. It is unfathomable, in this respect, how an arrest warrant in place since 2003 has not been implemented until now in a new democratic Iraq. This is the case of the arrest warrant against Muqtada al-Sadr and 13 of his close followers for the murder of the Shiite religious leader, Abdul Majid al-Khoie. Not only was this warrant not implemented because of the intricacies of sectarian politics, but many leading politicians have also exploited this case to get electoral and deal-making concessions from the Sadrists. The politicization of a judicial case is contrary to the supremacy of the rule of law and to the legitimacy of the political process. It is always good to keep in mind that tyranny begins where law ends.

Thus there are two types of legitimacy. One is intrinsic, a natural part of a genuine democratic process. Democracy has a built-in legitimacy through a combination of intertwined election and delivery. The other type is the external legitimacy that often appears when intrinsic legitimacy is lacking or deficient. In this sense, external sources of legitimacy function as a compensatory, yet deceptive legitimacy. This legitimacy comes in many forms and can continue for many years, if not decades. By contrast, intrinsic democratic legitimacy is conditional on delivering on electoral pledges and is renewable every four years. Unlike external legitimacy, it is productive and works for national interests and for the benefit of people, and not just the ruling politicians. Because of the fact that the overthrow of the old dictatorial regime was done by an external military intervention, and legitimacy derived from holding elections remains deficient and insufficient, the new ruling elites in Iraq have few options but to invest in a genuine democratic process capable of serving the national interests of Iraq and the well-being of all Iraqis. In fact, the nature of legitimacy that these rulers adopt would determine the future of Iraq and the case of establishing inclusive and productive democracy.

NOTES

1. Kimi Yoshino, "Iraqis Skeptical about Politicians Ahead of Vote," *Los Angeles Times*, January 26, 2009.

2. Alissa J. Rubin, "Secular Parties and Premier Ahead in Iraq," *New York Times*, February 2, 2009.

3. Monte Morin, "Iraq Vote Turnout Fails to Meet Expectations," *Los Angeles Times*, February 2, 2009.

4. Ernesto Londono, "Crackdown on Alcohol Seen as Part of Conservative Moment in Iraq," *Washington Post*, January 4, 2010.

5. Liz Sly, "Baghdad Crackdown Corks Drinkers' Spirits," *Los Angeles Times*, January 24, 2010.

6. Qais Mizher, "Iraqi Shiites Protest Maliki Government," *New York Times*, December 28, 2010.

7. Saad Fakhrildeen and Ned Parker, "Iraqi Shiites Converge in Karbala for Holiday," *Los Angeles Times*, December 28, 2010.

8. Ibid.

9. For more details on the experience of the Islamists of Turkey and the implications for political Islam in the Middle East see, for instance, David Ghanim, "Turkish Democracy and Political Islam," *Middle East Policy* 16, no. 1 (Spring 2009): 75–84.

10. Phebe Marr, "Iraq's Identity Crisis," in *Iraq: Preventing a New Generation of Conflict*, ed. Markus E. Bouillon, David M. Malone, and Ben Rowswell (Boulder, CO: Rienner, 2007), 52.

11. Patrick Basham, "Can Iraq Be Democratic," *Policy Analysis* 505 (January 5, 2004): 8.

11

Federalism and Politics of Separatism

VICTORS' CONSTITUTION[1]

External military intervention in 2003 toppled the previous regime and opened the door for the emergence of new ruling elites in the country. Thanks to this intervention and to the demographic strength of the Shiites, political Shiism is now in power in Iraq, supported by the nationalist Kurds. The new Iraq has come to embody an alliance between Shiite sectarian politics and far-fetched Kurdish nationalism. The Shiites and Kurds were both victimized by the former regime, but they are now, while in power, unhesitant about initiating a new Iraq that is grounded on violent and destructive politics of victimization. They are adamant about "eternally" capturing the historical moment of their rise to power, by enshrining the triumphalism of Shiism and Kurdism into a constitution for the country. As a result, this constitution has mostly reflected the enforced visions and ambitions of the Shiites and the Kurds. It is hence unlikely to guarantee the future stability and prosperity of the country as a whole.

The constitution reflects the victimization of the past and the triumphalism of the present with no future perspective, except securing narrowly defined sectarian and ethnic interests. Those who have money and militia were successful in imposing their vision on Iraqi society, yet this will only lead to the continuation of violence and intolerance. This constitution was drafted under highly charged political atmosphere, sectarian divide, and ethnic animosity, which is hardly a proper condition for drafting a constitution that can be considered an anchor for the future. It is no wonder that this unnecessarily rushed

basic document emerged as highly controversial, embodying the
seeds of violent conflict, destabilization, and cessation.

Based on their earlier experience of victimization at the hands of the
old regime, the Shiites and the Kurds believe that they are entitled to
rule Iraq and to dictate its future. Thus a marriage of convenience
has been concluded, where the Kurds accept the rule of the numerical
majority of the Shiites and the various ways of Islamizing society,
while the Shiites accept that Kurdistan will continue to be separated
and shielded from the rest of Iraq in the name of ethnic federalism.
In the blunt words of O'Leary, a constitutional adviser to the Kurds,
"a federal bargain is the price of Shiite preeminence in Arab Iraq."[2]

It is a rather strange alliance considering the secularism of the
Kurds on the one hand and the religiousness of the Shiites on the
other. But nationalism and religion do often meet. An editorial in
the *New York Times* argues: "The Sunnis overwhelmingly favor a
strong central government. With them out of the negotiations, the
theocratically inclined Shiites and the separatist-minded Kurds found
it easy to cut a deal that favored their narrow interests at national
expense. The draft would reportedly allow the Kurds to reinforce their
autonomy under a weak federal government. The religious Shiites
pushed to enshrine Islam in the constitution and the legal system, all
the way up through the Supreme Court." The editorial continues:
"Months ago, the United States was assuring skeptics that the secular
Kurds would rein in the Shiite religious parties, while the majority
Shiites would limit Kurdish separatism. But instead of being counter-
weights, these two groups seem mainly to have reinforced each other.
Washington, desperate for any draft, encouraged their complicity."[3]

The politics of identity that is enforced on the new Iraq by the Kurdish
and Shiite politicians revolves around three concepts: consociation and
power sharing (*muhasasa*); ethnic federalism; and the sectarian and exclusionary constitution enforced on all Iraqis with the aim of weakening the
Iraqi state and Iraqi identity. This is the triangle of the new politics pursued by the Shiite-Kurdish alliance that has been ruling the country since
regime change. Yet identity politics and the Kurdish-Shiite alliance come
at the expense of national interests and of the inclusion of the Sunnis.

Though the Sunnis boycotted the constitutional elections of January 2005, they were added to the committee that was in charge of
drafting the constitution. But decisive negotiations, compromises, and
decisions were conducted by the leaders of the Shiite and Kurdish parties
away from the drafting committee. As a result, the Sunnis were marginalized, or in the strong words of Makiya, the constitution became a

punitive document, as if it was written to punish the Sunnis for the sins of the Ba'th.[4] Cordesman concurs: "It may well be more of a prelude to civil war than a step forward. Rather than an inclusive document, it is more a recipe for separation based on Shiite and Kurdish privilege."[5] Marr joins the discussion: "The resulting document reflected a bargain between the two winning tickets—the Shia coalition and the Kurds. Drawn up under pressure of time, the document had numerous gaps and inconsistencies and on balance gave considerable weight to the aims and desires of the two main Kurdish parties and the UIA [the Shiite electoral alliance]. Hence, the final document emphasized federalism and gave considerable powers to regions that could be formed under the constitution, leaving a weak central government."[6]

The constitution reflects a political compromise between the Shiites and the Kurds. The key question is: are all political compromises right, legitimate, or morally binding? This question is particularly valid considering the possible damage that such political compromise can cause for the country.

Apart from privileges of power and wealth, the ruling alliance rests on two pillars: religion and federalism. Religion is central to political Shiism and the vision of Iraq that the Shiites maintain. Enforcing the Islamization of society is vital for the Shiite politicians. The secular Kurds went along with this agenda in order to gain concessions from the Shiites regarding other issues. But the Kurds also make sure that this religious vision of the Shiites will not affect their region. Galbraith, who is the chief adviser to the Kurds during the constitution negotiations, states: "On Iraq's two most divisive issues—Kurdistan's status and the role of Islam in the state—there is a modus vivendi: Kurdistan is de facto independent, while the Shiites enforce Islamic law in their part of the country." He goes on: "Because Kurdistan is already functionally independent from the rest of Iraq, the Kurds have little incentive to block Shiite efforts to Islamicize Arab Iraq. In return, the Kurds expect Baghdad not to interfere in their affairs and to support Kurdish demands to control the oil-rich city of Kirkuk."[7] Elsewhere he says that religion, human rights, and gender are not among the exclusive powers of the federal government, and therefore regions are free to legislate as they see fit in these areas.[8]

It becomes obvious then that the Kurds consented to the Islamization agenda because they did not lose anything in that deal, being shielded from the effects of such a religious agenda. Yet one questions the morality of doing so, considering that this agenda is detrimental to the interests of minorities and women and is an agenda that is associated with violence and intolerance. On the danger of parceling out family law to the level of regions within a federal system, Nadje al-Ali and Pratt argue: "However, less attention was given to the impact of federalism on women's rights in the new Iraq. While federalism appeared to present a solution to the Kurdish question, guaranteeing autonomy and protection of Kurdish rights as an ethnic minority, it also presented the possibility of imposing different rights for women of different regions, thereby undermining universal citizenship for Iraqi women."[9]

Article 2 of the constitution declares that it is forbidden to enact laws that contradict the principles of Islam. This is perhaps, Zaid al-Ali argues, the most strongly worded provision in any Arabic constitution that would entail that all legislation contrary to Islam would be anticonstitutional and therefore liable to be revoked.[10] Marshall, on the other hand, argues that declaring Islam the principal inspiration for Iraq's laws could be dangerous; "Islam undefined" would then be "the constitution behind the constitution."[11]

The other pillar of the constitution is federalism. The issue of federalism was initially the vision of the Kurds but the Shiites subscribed to it eventually. The principal objective of federalism in this vision is to protect, if not expand, and institutionalize the semiautonomous status of the Kurdish region that has been in existence since 1991. The region is practically ruled by the two dominant parties: the KDP (led by Mas'ud Barzani) and the PUK (led by Jalal Talabani). Within politics of identity, federalism cannot take any form but ethnic and sectarian federalism. Therefore two powerful federations, a Kurdish one in the north and a Shiite one in the south, have been envisioned while drafting the constitution.

However, the bitter consequences of the violent escalation of sectarian politics, the wide popular resentment of the increasing Iranian influence in the country, and intense rivalries among various Shiite political factions have led to the downfall of the federation projects in the south. The project of initiating the federation of Basra, the economically vital province that produces most of the Iraq's oil and is the only port in the country, did not materialize due to the failure to collect the required 140,000 signatures. The other competing project of ISCI, that of establishing a big Shiite federation in the south comprising nine provinces, including Basra, was discredited by the results of the 2009 provincial election. These results signaled the importance of providing security, basic services, and economic prosperity rather than investing in disruptive projects under the influence of neighboring countries. Thus while the constitution allows any three provinces or more to form a federation, the Kurdish federation is the only one that functions.

The constitution provides for an extensive decentralization at the expense of an Iraqi identity and a unified functioning country. The paradox in the drive for extensive decentralization and weak central authority is that it is confined to the relation with the center only while the Kurdish region itself takes a wholly different orientation. The Kurdish regional constitution that was endorsed in June 2009 approves of a highly centralized system in the northern region, in addition to extensive and extraordinary power for the president of the region, including declaration of emergency and the right to dissolve all three sources of power. This regional constitution was hastily passed without the benefit of serious popular debate, not unlike the federal constitution. Still, opposition to the regional constitution exists. An opposition politician believed that "Kurdistan needed its own constitution but that the document in its current form planted the seeds of endless conflict with the central government and made the region's president an 'absolute' ruler. It turns all the other powers, including parliament, into cardboard figures."[12] Extensive decentralization has been arbitrarily decided, and ironically it does not appear to be valid everywhere.

The regional constitution also complicates the relation with the center as it explicitly declares the so-called disputed territories, including the oil-rich city of Kirkuk, as part of Kurdistan. An Arab politician comments: "This lays the foundation for a separate state—it is not a constitution for a region. It is a declaration of hostile intent and confrontation. Of course it will lead to escalation."[13]

The national constitution pronounces that it should be amended after four months from its approval. This clause made the Sunnis accept the deal despite serious hesitation and reservation. Yet a basic document that explicitly states that it will be revised after such a short period cannot but be a flawed and troubling document. In fact, the failure to settle several crucial issues and leaving the door open for earlier amendments would make this document more like an interim rather than permanent constitution, not unlike the previous constitutions of Iraq. The constitution gives the right of veto to two-thirds of any three Iraqi provinces to reject any modification, or even the entire constitution for that matter. This is designed to assure the Kurds that their perceived interests will not be compromised at any moment in the future. Yet by doing so, the constitution has given the Kurds a rather disproportionate power and say in all matters, even those affecting the entire country.

However, this veto means that in reality no alteration is possible if it comes in conflict with the entrenched ethnic and sectarian interests that have produced the constitution in the first place. Obviously, this will make the constitution a highly static and inflexible document. This is clearly demonstrated by the fact that no amendments have been made since 2005, despite the fact that a highly controversial document is in a serious need of alteration. Instead, several constitutional deadlocks were developed, jeopardizing peaceful coexistence in the country. These conflicting clauses in the same document are symbolic of the many fundamental contradictions that were allowed to exist in a rather rushed constitution in order to meet "sacred" deadlines. Prime Minister Maliki, who was a member of the drafting committee, admitted later on that "the constitution was written in an atmosphere where there were fears and concerns, but we went very far in concretization of these fears and aspirations. These fears were not objective and put many heavy obstacles to avoid repeating the past, but these obstacles jeopardized the present and the future."[14]

Considering the concerns of different communities living in the country is one thing, but the concretization of ethno-sectarian interests at the expense of national interests is quite another. The current constitution appears to concretize a short, yet dramatic, moment in Iraqi history rather than reflecting a rational and objective evaluation of past experience. It was drafted by a mentality of opposition politics rather than by a mentality of building a state. The constitution reflects the historical animosity toward the Iraqi state. Therefore the current constitution is oriented more toward the weakening, if not the very disintegration, of the Iraqi state rather than its consolidation and democratization. Haysom argues: "The constitution failed to underscore the importance of constitution making as nation building. The constitutional text has been deeply influenced by the drive for autonomy by the Kurdish community and, in the end, it accurately reflects the minimum demands of that community for reincorporation into the Iraqi state."[15]

It is noteworthy that the absence of the Sunni influence on the drafting of the constitution has resulted in the weakening of the Iraqi identity and nation-state. The important question in this regard is whether it is only the Sunni community that is interested in the Iraqi national identity and the preservation of the country as a whole. Why did the Shiite and Kurdish politicians who dominated the constitution-making process lack a nation-building perspective and focus, instead, on sectarian and ethnic gains? Does the securing of ethno-sectarian gains necessarily and always come at the expense of nation building? Or to reverse the question, does nation building necessarily exclude sectarian and ethnic rights? This was indeed the previous experience of Iraqi nationalism. Yet it is unfathomable to enforce a solution that advances sectarian interests at the expense of Iraqi identity, and not a nation-building process that is sensitive to the interests of various communities and is based on principles of citizenship and human rights.

Thus the current constitution contributes to what one might call the *ethno-sectarianization of national identity*, where this national identity cedes to transcend the sect or the ethnicity, and where this identity becomes meaningless beyond the borders of a sect or an ethnicity. It is remarkable that the constitution is making these borders even narrower than they really are. It states that Iraq is a multiethnic country while the Arab people in this country are part of the Arab nation. It is notable that this document manifests a difficulty in recognizing the right of more than 80 percent of the population to their perceived identity. This is so, even considering that the constitution fails to simultaneously advance or strengthen Iraqi national identity.

Failure to appreciate or recognize the Arab nationalist side of the identity will leave the majority Arabs with only Islam as a marker of their identity. Yet the Muslims in Iraq are divided into two opposing sects, hence exasperating sectarian conflict. Whether one agrees with it or not, Arab identity is what unites the Shiites and the Sunnis, and it is perhaps the glue that helps them to drive away from sectarian divide. Thus even though a world defined by religion and nationality is a narrow world, it has been made even narrower by discouraging one aspect of it.

Makiya emphasizes that federalism does not have to entail the dissipation of power: "A decentralized federal system that devolves power to the regions is not the same as a dysfunctional one in which power at the federal level has been eviscerated. The former preserves power while distributing it; the latter destroys it. At the moment Iraqis have a dysfunctional and powerless state. The Constitution does not fix this; it makes it worse."[16] Horowitz concurs: "The product of a Kurdish agenda to which Shiites signed on, the constitution creates an exceedingly weak central government and extraordinary powerful regions. The Iraqi state created by this constitution is probably the weakest federation in the world."[17]

The problem with the Iraqi application of federalism is that while it has been suggested that this is the best guarantee to prevent the return of authoritarianism, it has virtually worked for the immediate benefit of authoritarian parties and personalities, whether nationalist or sectarian. Zubaida argues: "The new Iraqi constitution divides that wealth between regions, transparently to the advantage of communally based regional governments with undefined powers. It is not so much orderly and defined decentralisation, but more the setting up of regional mini-states with the potential for new authoritarian regimes."[18] This risk of developing regional authoritarianism has provoked Haysom to recommend the reintroduction into the constitution of a chapter requiring at least the satisfaction of the basic principle of a regional accountable government.[19]

Makiya also warns that the logical conclusion of this constitution is the breakup of Iraq: "Profound tensions and contradictions have been enshrined in the Constitution of the new Iraq, and they threaten the very existence of the state. All signs suggest that this Constitution, if it is not radically amended, will further weaken the already failing central Iraqi state. It is disunity, diminished sovereignty and years of future discord that lie in store for Iraq if the Constitution is not overhauled."[20] Indeed, a reconsideration of the entire constitution appears to be inevitable. While the majority has voted for the constitution in a referendum, in one sense that does not necessarily make it legitimate. A true legitimacy comes when the document serves as a guarantee for the unity of the country and a provider for common identity and destiny. A legitimate charter helps to find constructive solutions to chronic problems, not a document that exasperates disputes and conflicts.

The Shiite-Kurdish alliance proved to be a serious obstacle to real progress in Iraq and a contributing factor to political paralysis since regime change in 2003, very much like the previous domination of the Ba'th Party in Iraqi politics. This alliance was successful in enforcing their version of the constitution on the Iraqi society. It is a victors' constitution, and the winners always seem to take it all. Yet by doing so, a new chapter in Iraqi misery was also born.

FEDERALISM OR DEMOCRACY

The Middle Eastern pattern of development is biased in favor of the cities at the expense of the countryside and is also biased in favor of the capital city at the expense of all the other cities. The highly centralized rule from the capital city is associated with many of the problems in the history of Iraq and cannot, therefore, be an optimal model for building a new democratic experience in the country. However, the key question is whether federalism is the proper, or the only, option to achieve the desirable objective of decentralization; and if so, what type of federalism to adopt, for what purposes, and at the expense of what interests.

The Kurds were instrumental in introducing, if not imposing the concept of federalism upon the political discourse in the new Iraq.

Their long sufferings at the hands of a highly centralized and authoritarian state and their experience of quasi independence since 1991 are no doubt the background to the Kurdish demands for autonomy and federalism. However, the Kurds also insist on adopting ethnic federalism and discarding the other option of territorial administrative federalism. Thus whereas the Kurds are strong players in the debate on the necessity of federalism for Iraq, their insistence on grounding this federalism on an ethnic-sectarian basis tends to complicate the whole issue of the introduction of federalism into Iraqi politics. It is no wonder that federalism became a vague and controversial concept in addition to being a source of disagreement and conflict in the new politics in Iraq.

On ethno-sectarian federalism, Dawisha argues: "A federalism entangled with communal divisions could all too easily promote evils ranging from ethnic cleansing to civil war and secession. The Kurds are responsible for the shift from territorial to ethnic federalism." [21] Instead of an ethno-sectarian federal solution, Dawisha suggests that it is far more propitious to divide Iraq administratively. "Such an arrangement would still serve the interests of the various communities, but could do so while shifting political and social attitudes away from blatant ethnic and sectarian concerns to more secular and political priorities that would spring from the inevitable competitions over resources."[22]

Dawisha continues: "The federal system in Iraq has to be territorially, not ethnically, based. Otherwise, in the long term, a sociopolitical environment may be created in which citizens' commitment to the 'general good' is gradually transferred to the 'good' of the narrower community. This is a recipe for civil breakdown, even for state collapse."[23] Thus Dawisha is in favor of a decentralized federal system on the basis of territory, not ethnicity or sect, "where local governments have responsibility for all citizens in their areas, not just for ethnic or sectarian co-nationals, is the best alternative for sustainable democracy in Iraq. Of all the Iraqi groups the Kurds are likely to be the most resistant to the above prescription."[24]

The debate on territorial versus ethnic federalism is strongly linked to the issue of democracy. Federalism and democracy are two related processes that are supposed to work in harmony. It would be interesting to examine whether the Iraq experiment with federalism confirms or denies this assumption. It is remarkable to note that the important term "federalism" was imposed on the Iraqi political process from above without the benefit of serious popular debate. Furthermore, the Kurds maintain that the age of one nation dominating another nation is over and that at present both the Arabs and the Kurds should decide the fate of Iraq.

Certainly, the domination of one nation is associated with misery as the history of Iraq surely confirms. The question is, however, why, in a mosaic society like Iraq, the domination of one nation is being replaced by the domination of two nations. Is this arrangement fair to the other ethnicities and religious minorities? Somer argues: "Ethnicity-based federations institutionalize-and indirectly promote-ethnic divisions, and create minorities within minorities."[25] Ethnicity-based federalism can very well lead to the oppression of other minorities, as for instance the earlier discussed report of the HRW about the oppression of minorities in Iraqi Kurdistan clearly shows.

Imposing ethnic federalism is strongly linked to the politics of victimization played by the Kurds, who no doubt had a history of suffering in the past. Nonetheless, they appear to be exploiting this suffering to promote an undemocratic or divisive vision for Iraq. In the politics of victimization, the aspiration is to find a niche in an authoritarian system of oppression rather than ensuring justice for everyone. If this is not the case, how can we explain the insistence of the Kurds that they share with the Arabs in deciding the fate of the country at the expense of all the other minorities sharing existence in this land? Is this not discrimination against these minorities by a minority that knows from experience the meaning and the cost of discrimination and suffering? Iraqi history shows that there is no monopoly over victimization and suffering. All Iraqis were, and still are, victimized; and at the same time all Iraqis have played a role, one way or the other, in this victimization.

Therefore all Iraqis, including smaller minorities, should decide the fate of the country, making decisions in the interests of the whole population. From a democratic perspective, this makes more sense than the contention that the two largest ethnic groups have the right to dictate things in the country. Turning Iraq from a country ruled by one ethnicity to a country ruled by two ethnicities does not necessarily make the country more democratic. Both unitary and bipolar systems of rule lack democratic content and inclusiveness in a pluralistic society such as the Iraqi one. Some people might question the fairness of according the Kurds, who represent only 17 percent of the population, an equal footing in ruling the country with the Arab majority, who represent more than 80 percent of the population. In this respect, it is easy for the third ethnicity, the Turkmen, to question the legitimacy of this bipolar arrangement and possibly even demand a tripartite solution. If that is the case, then all the other minorities would appear to be entitled to a similar arrangement.

Thus in the troubled history of Iraq, there is no end to the claims of victimization, sufferings, entitlements, and aspirations. Therefore the real question is not to prevent a previous victim from becoming a vic-timizer in the new experience. Rather, the question is how to find a political solution that can accommodate all these claims and aspirations while orienting them to the future of the nation-state where everyone belongs and has ownership. That is why the issue of federalism is much more complex than the simple and misleading perception that one par-ticular ethnicity tries to impose on a whole society.

Ethnic federalism is strongly related to the issues of confessionalism power-sharing arrangements, discussed earlier. Both concepts are driven by the same logic, the same vision, and the same entrenched interests of the political elites that come to dominate the experience of new Iraq. The failure to deliver democracy and to serve the interests of the majority of the population is a common ground between power sharing and ethnic federalism. Both of these two systems need serious reconsideration and rigorous scrutiny. The alternative is to build a democratic system and federalism based on individual citizens, as opposed to confessional blocs. The interests of different commun-ities are served as individual citizens entitled to all the rights and ben-efits of a citizen, regardless of any differences. Equality among all citizens would ensure equality among all communities, big or small.

The past experience of dealing with a central authoritarian and bru-tal state is reflected in the new agenda of federalizing Iraq. Federalism also reflects concerns about the danger of reoccurrence of similar expe-riences in the future. These concerns are no doubt legitimate and should be addressed. However, preventing these experiences from happening again depends on what means to employ. The Kurds, and to some extent the Shiites too, took the route of weakening the Iraqi state as a guarantee against the emergence of a new dictator in the center. While the concerns of the Kurds are legitimate, the question remains whether their remedy of weakening the central state is legiti-mate too, and whether this remedy is the only option available.

In struggling for their rights, legitimate or perceived, the Kurds have always worked for the objective of weakening the state. The only differ-ence is that before it was done by military conflict, while now this is done peacefully, democratically, federatively, and constitutionally. This, however, does not change the violent nature of this objective. Violent action and reaction are played together in a vicious cycle of violence. This is a clear illustration of an old politics played out in the new Iraq under new and different names. Rather than being a sign of democracy, weakening the state is a dangerous policy since it carries with it serious risks of fragmentation and sectarianism. While the rationale is to prevent or to block the way for any leader to turn the state into a dictatorship, by doing so, the state itself becomes so weak that can turn into an ungovernable and ineffective entity. Having an incapacitated state is a counterproductive policy that can easily backfire.

However, there is a fundamental problem with the logic behind the objective of ensuring a weak state at the center. It is grounded on the erroneous assumption that a strong state is forever an authoritarian state and that a weak state is eternally a democratic state. While there are perhaps historical experiences to justify the contention that a strong state is violent state, this is not necessarily an unceasingly valid contention. A strong state does not need to be violent. On the contrary, violence is the attribute of a weak state. Indeed, the Iraqi state has always been weak, despite claims to the contrary, and that is why it has invariably been violent.

One of the most serious dilemmas for the national state is that it is no match for a strong pluralistic and complex society. Therefore, the state resorts to violence to compensate for the asymmetry in the relationship between a weak state and a strong society. Thus an authoritarian and domineering state is perceived by those who rule as a way to redress the imbalance with society. It is arguably only democracy that can create a strong and peaceful state that can match a strong and complex society. A democratic state is surely an equivalent to a pluralistic society. This, however, is contrary to the second part of the fallacy of the rationale for a weak state at the center, which says a democratic state is a weak state, an assertion that makes sense only in sectarian politics. The experiences of democracy indicate that a democratic state has to be strong, effective, and capable.

Thus weakening the central government is not a viable option in a new democratic Iraq. A weak central state is an essential condition for the dominance of sectarian and ethnic politics, which are violent and authoritarian politics. It is this identity politics that prevents the new rulers of the country from appreciating and investing in a second option of preventing the state from degenerating into dictatorship, the option of building and consolidating a democratic state. It is the option of creating a powerful democratic national government with constitutional guarantees to block any tendency toward excessive centralization, unitary politics, or dictatorial orientation. While the Kurds and the Shiites have experienced the wrath of an authoritarian state, they do not have any experiences with a strong democratic state. They should, therefore, not only give this option a fair chance but also effectively contribute toward that outcome. After all, they are an integral part of the central authority and well represented in it. The fears of the Kurds regarding the central state are not only one-sided and exaggerated but also destructive and unhelpful. A strong but democratic central government is in the interests of everyone in Iraq.

Whether or not the concerns and the aspirations of the Kurds are accommodated, decentralization should be on the agenda in a truly new and democratic Iraq anyway. Devolution is a necessary and desirable objective as it decreases the overload on the central government, hence increasing its efficiency and capacity to deliver. It is also an important instrument of ensuring inclusiveness and wider participation in the authority, hence providing a better reflection of wider political and economic interests. It is significant to emphasize in this respect that to ensure these desirable outcomes, there is a need for a real transfer of power to local governments and councils that should particularly include budgetary and decision-making capacities. However, when there are demands from society for a democratic central government, democracy should also become the working principle and mechanism within local authorities as well. This is a significant issue considering that the experience of new Iraq with the local councils is marked by corruption and inefficiency.

Thus devolution is a valid objective for any geographical region, regardless of ethnic or sectarian profile or concentration. Administrative decentralization is part of any democratic experience. Whether or not it is called federalism, decentralization should be an inevitable working principle for governing new Iraq. However, when decentralization and democracy are strongly intertwined and work in harmony, is federalism still being considered indispensable for the new experience? In other words, if democracy can intrinsically ensure the desirable objective of achieving decentralization, why is federalism necessary? Can federalism strengthen democracy even further, and if so, does the experience of Iraq so far confirm this assumption?

Ethno-sectarian politics tends to confuse the relationship between federalism and democracy. This politics is based on the assumption that there is "no democracy without federalism." It is true that there is a link between democracy and federalism, but they are not essentially the same thing. Democracy necessarily entails decentralization, and respect for all citizens and their effective participation in political and economic life. Even without applying federalism, democracy is capable of achieving the objectives of administrative federalism through the built-in mechanisms and processes of decentralization. In other words, unlike democracy, federalism, particularly ethnic federalism, is not an absolute necessity in new Iraq. The Kurdish insistence on elevating ethnic federalism is not simply a question of naïveté but is rather a continuation of the old authoritarian politics of conflict between the central government and various regional powers. Ethnic federalism can function as an effective instrument for consolidating regional authoritarian interests and aspirations.

However, if the supposition of "no democracy without federalism" is inverted into a statement of "no federalism without democracy," an entirely new situation emerges. Ethno-sectarian politics underscores that the absence of federalism is authoritarianism. In reality, however, this is valid only if what is meant by federalism is administrative decentralization, which is an integral component of democracy and the reversal of authoritarianism. If federalism is perceived as ethnic federalism, similar to what the Kurds demand, then the statement is fallacious indeed; the absence of ethnic federalism is not authoritarianism but democracy, pure and simple. Ethnic identity politics is part of an authoritarian order and has little to do with democracy because it serves the interests of few ethnic and tribal leaders.

The essence of administrative federalism, or decentralization, is to prevent one sect, ethnicity, or group from monopolizing power and wealth. Its essence is the fair regional distribution of wealth and power aimed at providing the best services for all citizens. Thus decentralization is part of democracy because it ensures not just any kind of inclusiveness, but the type of inclusion and participation directly associated with serving public interests. Ethnic federalism, on the other hand, is basically oriented toward serving much narrower and elitist interests; hence, it hardly qualifies as an exercise of democracy.

Federalism can theoretically imply democracy, but it can also signify a negation of democracy. In fact, the very experience of Iraqi Kurdistan proves that ethnic federalism helps consolidate highly centralized autocratic and tribal politics. Hiltermann observes: "It is interesting to note that the Kurdish parties have made no corresponding push to take decentralization a step further and apply it within the Kurdistan region; their support of federalism strictly concerns the status of their region vis-à-vis the rest of Iraq."[26] The one-sided perception of the relationship between federalism and democracy is contradicting the officially declared and constitutionally enshrined politics that makes federalism a fundamental working principle in the new Iraqi experience.

For decades, the Kurds, joined by many other Iraqis, have raised the slogan of autonomy for Kurdistan and democracy for Iraq. Consequently, one expects that the Kurds really cherish and apply democracy in their internal regional affairs. Yet a scrutiny of the Kurdish experience, particularly after 1991, clearly indicates that their internal affairs are conducted with little reference to democratic values, despite formal rhetoric. Violence and animosity between different political factions, high levels of corruption, the marginalization of the majority of the Kurdish population, and the use of the national and regional wealth to serve the establishment and consolidation of tribal feudal fiefs are all indications of twisted and downgraded democracy.

Undeniably, federalism is essentially an experiment in democracy; yet it is highly questionable in the case of Iraq. It is true that applying federalism can help curb the excessive powers lodged in the central government, yet one crucial question remains: in the absence of real democracy, what will help check the powers of regional governments? When democracy fails to function in the proper sense, what will guarantee that regional powers under federalism will not be misused for the benefit of few families, personalities, or parties at the expense of the majority? In fact, the experience of Iraqi Kurdistan evidently shows that federalism can work, or rather can be used by the dominant elites to hinder the application of genuine democracy. Regional politics in Iraqi Kurdistan is a highly elitist and centralized experience accompanied by high levels of corruption and tight control over power and wealth. It then seems natural to question whether federalism, as claimed by identity and sectarian politics, is really in the interest of the majority of the Kurdish population.

Provided that democracy truly becomes a working principle for all levels of politics in Iraq, from the central government to the lowest administrative unit, one can argue that there is nothing to prevent local and provincial councils from serving the full political, economic, and cultural interests of the entire population. In this sense, every province in Iraq, from the north to the south, should enjoy real autonomy as part of the democratic process, away from violent and unconstructive ethnic and sectarian politics. It is in the interest of the Kurds, and of all Iraqis for that matter, to devote their energies to developing and democratizing local and provincial councils that can directly attend to public interests, away from tribal politics exercised under the cover of federalism that presently dominates the regional government, whether in Erbil or in Sulaimaniya. Incidentally, this will, perhaps, make the issue of Kirkuk and the rest of the so-called "disputed territories" less controversial.

One of the paradoxes of the drive to introduce federalism into Iraqi politics is that it disregards potential options of downsizing the state through a process of privatization. Encouraging and supporting the private sector is an effective way to ensure wider participation in wealth and power and to create new group interests outside the state. If federalism is intended as a policy to democratize Iraq by sharing power and wealth between the central state and the regions and provinces, so is privatization. A process of privatization would diminish the domination of the state over the economy, an objective that works in the interests of federalism and decentralization.

However, state domination over the economy continues to be the case in both the central government and the regional government in Kurdistan. To be sure, privatization is not an easy task to accomplish given the vested interests of the ruling elites, whether in Baghdad or in Erbil. The big benefits that accrue to these elites as a result of holding dominant positions within state domination over the economic resources accompanied by a wide window of opportunity for corruption and illegal profits make the continuation of the command economy imperative for these elites.

Thus there is a basic flaw in the insistence on federalism with the declared aim of ensuring democracy, when at the same time there is a determination to keep the economic structure of an authoritarian rule. If the aim of pursuing federalism is truly meant to ensure democracy for the country, one wonders why other options that can lead to the same outcome are not equally pursued with similar rigorous and enthusiasm. Naïveté or simple inattention to these options could not be the explanation to this vital issue for the experience in Iraq. A more plausible explanation could be found in the fact that ethnic federalism, as part of identity politics and as applied to Iraq, has nothing to do with democracy in the first place but is merely associated with establishing local authoritarianism for the benefit of a few political leaders.

Admittedly, the relationship between democracy, federalism, and the economy—including the oil factor—is complex. Significant oil revenues serve as the basis of the rentier economy and the social contract of coercion and rewards that has bound the rulers and the people of Iraq for decades. This social contract has developed into an entire system of benefits and patronage that works as a compensating mechanism for lack of democracy. This system became the basis of authoritarianism before 2003, but it continues to function in new Iraq. To be fair, a transition from a rentier economy to a more diversified economy is rather difficult, given Iraq's very high level of oil dependency. Unfortunately, unless it is debunked, this argument will forever trap the country within the curse of oil. If the real intention is to build genuine democracy, the process of creating a more diversified economy is unavoidable.

Notwithstanding rhetorical statements, the new rulers of Iraq have failed to develop a vision and concrete policies for pursuing a gradual and long-term process of ending the mono-economy character of the Iraqi economy. Even in Kurdistan, rentierism presently dominates the economic structure of the region, which is mostly based on the share of the region in the national budget that basically comes from exporting oil. Moreover, economic policies of prioritizing the development of local resources of oil and gas, which comes at the expense of developing other available resources, tend to strengthen the rentier character of economy of the Kurdish region. The unwavering insistence on the incorporation of the oil-rich Kirkuk into Kurdistan appears to be in harmony with the policy of consolidating the rentier and command economy of the region. The same system of patronage and cronyism that existed and still exists in Baghdad also functions in Kurdistan. This, however, is in stark conflict with the declared objective of building democracy through federalism.

Thus federalism in the sense of administrative decentralization, associated with a genuine democratic process, is a must for new Iraq. It would be naïve, however, to expect that the currently ruling political class is capable of delivering democracy or federalism. The entrenched interests of ruling elites compel them to cling to ethno-sectarian identity politics, which is detrimental to the establishment of democracy and decentralization. Within identity politics, federalism, and democracy for that matter, is reduced to mutual concessions aimed at serving and consolidating elitist interests.

Furthermore, Makiya argues against a purely utilitarian argument for federalism derived from the balance of power in the aftermath of regime change. According to this argument, the Kurds allow federalism not because they want it but because the regional situation does not allow them to secede and have a separate state in northern Iraq; and the Arabs concede federalism because the Kurds are today in a position to force it upon them. Makiya continues: "I do not think, however, that a project as big as restructuring the state of Iraq on a federal basis should be undertaken on the grounds of this kind of utilitarian calculus. No ordinary Iraqi citizen can be expected to opt for federalism on grounds of expediency."[27]

Federalism is important for the new Iraqi experience; hence, it becomes legitimate to raise the question of why the Kurds are allowed to dictate the definition of or how best to apply federalism. Indeed, federalism and democracy are too vital for new Iraq to be allowed to degenerate into a futile and destructive game of identity politics.

NOTES

1. The constitution and the resulting federalism have been discussed in the literature on Iraq. On the pros and cons of the constitution and federalism in Iraq see, for instance, *Iraq: Preventing a New Generation of Conflict*, ed. Markus E. Bouillon, David M. Malone, and Ben Rowswell (Boulder, CO: Rienner, 2007), particularly the contribution of David Cameron, Toby Dodge, Nicholas Haysom, Joost R. Hiltermann, John McGarry, Phebe Marr, and Brendan O'Leary. See also Faleh A. Jabar and Hisham Dawood, eds., *Naqd al-dustur* [A Critique to the Constitution] (Baghdad and Beirut: Publications of Iraq Institute for Strategic Studies, 2006).

2. Brendan O'Leary, "A Knitter's Nightmare: Iraq's Constitution Must Weave Together a Patchwork of Interests and Ideologies, Including the Kurds," *Los Angeles Times*, August 14, 2005.

3. Editorial, "Iraq's Unsettling Constitution," *New York Times*, August 23, 2005.

4. Kanan Makiya, "Present at the Disintegration," *New York Times*, December 11, 2005.

5. Quoted in Robin Wright, "Constitution Sparks Debate on Viability," *Washington Post*, August 25, 2005.

6. Phebe Marr, "Iraq's Identity Crisis," in *Iraq: Preventing*, ed. Bouillon, Malone, and Rowswell, 42–43.

7. Peter W. Galbraith, "Peril in Iraq's Constitution," *Los Angeles Times*, February 14, 2005.

8. Peter W. Galbraith, *The End of Iraq: How American Incompetence Created a War without End* (New York: Simon and Shuster, 2007), 200.

9. Nadje al-Ali and Nicola Pratt, *What Kind of Liberation? Women and the Occupation of Iraq* (Berkeley: University of California Press, 2009), 113.

10. Zaid al-Ali, "Iraq: A Constitution or an Epitaph?" *Open Democracy*, August 16, 2005, http://www.opendemocracy.net/conflict-iraq/constitution_2757.jsp.

11. Quoted in David Rohde, "A World of Ways to Say 'Islamic Law,' " *New York Times*, March 13, 2005.

12. Sam Dagher, "Kurds Defy Baghdad, Laying Claim to Land and Oil," *New York Times*, July 10, 2009.

13. Ibid.

14. Shatha al-Jubori, "A Conference in Baghdad Was Turned into a Theatre of Accusation between al-Maliki and His Deputy Barham Salih," *Asharq al-Awsat*, November 10, 2008.

15. Nicholas Haysom, "Forging an Inclusive and Enduring Social Contract," in *Iraq: Preventing*, ed. Bouillon, Malone, and Rowswell, 145.

16. Makiya, "Present at the Disintegration."

17. Donald L. Horowitz, "The Sunni Moment," *Wall Street Journal*, December 14, 2005.

18. Sami Zubaida, "Democracy, Iraq and the Middle East," *Open Democracy*, November 18, 2005, http://www.opendemocracy.net/democracy-opening/iraq_3042.jsp.

19. Haysom, "Forging an Inclusive," 146.

20. Makiya, "Present at the Disintegration."

21. Adeed Dawisha, "The New Iraq: Democratic Institutions and Performance," *Journal of Democracy* 16, no. 3 (July 2005): 41.

22. Adeed Dawisha, "Iraq: Setbacks, Advances, Prospects," *Journal of Democracy*, 15, no. 1 (January 2004): 16.

23. Adeed Dawisha, "The Prospects for Democracy in Iraq: Challenges and Opportunities," *Third World Quarterly* 26, no. 4–5 (June 2005): 727.

24. Ibid., 728.

25. Murat Somer, "Failure of the Discourse of Ethnicity: Turkey, Kurds, and the Emerging Iraq," *Security Dialogue* 36, no. 1 (March 2005): 123.

26. Joost R. Hiltermann, "To Protect or to Project? Iraqi Kurds and Their Future," *Middle East Report* 247 (summer 2008), http://www.merip.org/mer/mer247/hiltermann.html.

27. Kanan Makiya, "A Model for Post-Saddam Iraq," *Journal of Democracy* 14, no. 3 (2003): 7.

12

Nationalism and Territories

EXPANSIONISM AND TERRITORIES

One of the thorniest issues in Iraq in the aftermath of regime change in 2003 is what has been called the "disputed territories," particularly Kirkuk, an oil-rich city contested by the Arabs, the Kurds, and the Turkmen, but also containing various Christian communities. The dictatorial regime of Saddam Hussein started a process of Arabization of Kirkuk, forcing many of its Kurd and Turkmen residents to leave the city. It offered financial incentives to Arabs from the south to move into the city. In 1983, the regime issued a law denying the existence of a Turkmen nationality, hence forcing many to change their nationality to either Arab or Kurd. Aburish points out that Saddam began to Arabize the city as early as the 1970s, by encouraging Arabs to move there and by providing them with financial assistance for this purpose. However, he also reveals that Mustafa Barzani, the national leader of the Kurds at that time and father of the incumbent president of the Kurdish region, started doing the same thing and urged Kurds to live in Kirkuk.[1]

During the Iraq War, the two dominant Kurdish parties, the KDP and the PUK, and their militias were quick to occupy all the territories that the Kurds claim as theirs. They have occupied all governmental offices, spread their internal security forces, *asayish*, and imposed their authority on these territories, particularly Kirkuk. After enforcing new facts on the ground, Kurdish politicians moved to the next step of reflecting this newly enforced reality into the constitution. They believe that the charter will allow them to incorporate the disputed territories and Kirkuk in a "peaceful" way.

However, the constitution has proved to be a controversial, destabilizing, and divisive document, particularly the very same articles concerning federalism, disputed territories, and Kirkuk. While the interim constitution prevented Kirkuk, along with Baghdad, from joining a region, the permanent constitution dropped this provision, enabling its incorporation into the Kurdish region. Article 140 of the constitution provides that the government should work to implement a three-stage process (normalization, census, and popular referendum) to decide the fate of Kirkuk and the rest of the disputed territories by a date no later than December 31, 2007. Few of these steps have been implemented so far, and for strong reasons.

Apart from problems associated with the constitution itself and the version of federalism that have been imposed on the political process, there are other reasons that are specifically related to the city of Kirkuk itself. The step of the normalization that is stipulated in the constitution is meant to be the removal of the newly arrived Arabs, an outcome of the Arabization. However, many Arabs feel that Kirkuk became their city after living there for decades, and their children were born and raised in that city. Nonetheless, many Arabs have already left the city either in fear of Kurdish revenge or under various pressures on them to do so. Many took advantage of the financial incentives specifically allocated for encouraging the Arabs to leave the city.

Even worse, Kurdish politicians have a more expansive interpretation of the normalization that goes beyond the reversal of Arabization and aims toward the Kurdicization of the city. Leezenberg argues that the Kurds "have been trying to create facts on the ground by conducting media campaign and giving financial rewards to Kurdish families trying to return to their former dwellings (probably as much a sign of continuing KDP-PUK rivalry as of purely ethnic policies)."[2] In fact, the governor of Erbil confirmed that Kurdish authorities actually paid families $3,500 to return to Kirkuk.[3] Kurdish families that moved to Kirkuk admitted that each family received more than $6,000 from the PUK to help with costs. They have also been given plots of land by the Kurdish-controlled municipal council.[4]

The Arabs and Turkmen of Kirkuk have raised alarms that the influx of many Kurds into the city is far exceeding the original number of the Kurds deported by the old regime. They declare that under the pretext of normalization, many non-Kirkukis are among the new arrivals, an outcome facilitated by a generous financial stimulus. They also accuse the dominant Kurdish parties of using their de facto control of the city to pursue an aggressive policy of Kurdicizing the city. As a result of this policy, the total population in the province has jumped from 800,000 in 2003 to 1.3 million today.

The controversy over who are the original Kirkukis Kurds has serious ramifications for national and local elections. One of the tricky issues in the parliamentary debate on the electoral law was actually which voter registry to use for Kirkuk. The Arabs and Turkmen insisted on using the 2004 voter registry that was the basis for the January 2005 elections, which was created before the bulk of the Kurdish influx into Kirkuk. This registry contained 400,000 voters. Kurdish leaders, on the other hand, called for using the updated 2009 registry, which contains 900,000 voters, a stunning increase.[5] This is a spectacular boost indeed, considering that thousands of Arabs had already left the city even before the arrival of the Kurdish militias, and other Arabs left the city after 2003, taking advantage of the generous governmental financial rewards allocated for these purposes.

In the drive to find a solution to this conflict, all sides, however, agree to use the 1957 census, which is considered to be the last census untainted by demographic manipulation. Using this census, Batatu, who is an authority on the history of Iraq, underlines that Kirkuk, an oil center, lying 180 miles north of Baghdad, "had been Turkish through and through in the not too distant past. By degrees, Kurds moved into the city from the surrounding villages. With the growth of oil industry their migration intensified. By 1959, they had swollen to more than one-third of the population, and the Turkmen had declined to just over half, the Assyrians and Arabs accounting, in the main, for the rest of the total of 120,000."[6]

Batatu discussed the activities of the Communist Party in Kirkuk, which was active among workers in the oil fields. He indicates that it is striking that only 1 out of 5 members of the party in a position of responsibility, *mas'ul*, and 1 out of the 10 members of the local party committee of Kirkuk belonged to it by birth. Batatu continues: "[This] points not only to a strong movement of people into the province but also to eschewing of communism by its Turkoman middle classes. The Turkomans, it should be explained, had had close links with the bureaucracy of Ottoman times: this, added to their industriousness, materialized into an advantageous economic position."[7] This shows that the migration of the Kurds, and others, into the city was mainly induced by the 1927 discovery and development of oil activities, while the more affluent Turkmen, by contrast, were more established in the bureaucracy and other economic activities than oil.

McDowall, who is an authority on the history of the Kurds, stresses "that the Turkomans, the originally predominant element, and Kurds who had settled increasingly during the 1930s and 1940s, driven from

the land by landlord rapacity and drawn by the chance for employment in the burgeoning oil industry. By 1959 half the population of
150,000 were Turkoman, rather less than half were Kurds and the balance Arabs, Assyrians and Armenians."[8] He continues: "The 1947 census ... indicated that Kurds comprised only 25 per cent of the
population of Kirkuk town, and only 53 per cent of the province."[9]

Referring to the negotiations in the 1970s between the Kurds and
Saddam over the regional autonomy, McDowall calls attention to the following: "However, the chief sticking point was Kirkuk. Despite the relatively recent arrival of most of the Kurds in Kirkuk town and its oilfields,
the KDP felt passionately that it should be included in the autonomous
area. It also claimed fringe Kurdish areas down to Khaniqin, areas in
which oil was to be found."[10] He goes on: "When the government pro-
posed to apply the 1957 census to Kirkuk, Mulla Mustafa refused it, since
this was bound to show that the Turkomans, although outnumbered
in the governorate as a whole, were still predominant in Kirkuk town."[11]

Other writers have also stated similar facts. In referring to the massacre
of Kirkuk in 1959 that was discussed earlier, Farouk-Sluglett and Sluglett
bring to light this: "It was far more profoundly rooted in the deep-seated
antagonism between the original Turcoman population of the city and
the more recent Kurdish incomers."[12] Mackey adds: "During the 1950s,
the Kurds, like the Shia, migrated in great numbers to the cities. Most went
to Kirkuk or Sulaimaniyah. Some drifted to Baghdad."[13] Aburish concurs:
"Curiously, though both Arabs and Kurds claimed the city, the majority
of its inhabitants were neither Kurds nor Arabs but Turkomans."[14]

Despite these authoritative statements, the Kurds insist that Kirkuk
historically belongs to Kurdistan, thereby demanding its annexation to
the Kurdish region. Even with the recent arrival of the Kurds to the city,
after the production of oil in 1927 Kurdish politicians persist that the
claim about Kirkuk is a nonnegotiable issue in their dealings with the
central government. A Kurdish leader proclaims: "The 1957 census has
shown a majority of Kurds in Kirkuk and that majority should be the
sole criterion in determining its future."[15] The president of the Kurdish
region repeatedly declares: "I will never compromise on Kirkuk."[16]
In 2004, he was adamant: "The Kurds will never compromise on the
Kurdish identity of Kirkuk. They are prepared to fight to preserve the
identity of this heart of Kurdistan."[17] The president of Iraq, Talabani,
repeatedly affirmed that Kirkuk belongs to the Kurds and Kurdistan.

The uncompromising stand on Kirkuk is hardly a new development as this has been the case for decades. This hard-line position,
however, is causing major problems for both sides. Hiltermann

remarks: "Their stance, however, is the result of Kurdish leaders' own historically high expectations and their repeated attempts to realize their maximum ambition."[18] This is clearly reflected in what a Kurdish official admitted in an interview with Hiltermann in 2006: "We concentrated so much on Kirkuk, we would lose face if we now lowered our position. This is the problem."[19]

Notwithstanding official denial, Kirkuk is important to the Kurds because of the oil resources. Even Galbraith, a close partner with the Kurds, divulges: "In fact, there are no sacred sites particular to the Kurds in Kirkuk. But, Kirkuk sits atop Iraq's largest producing petroleum reservoir."[20] Some 460 schools in Kirkuk, out of a total of about 1,390, are funded by the regional Kurdish government, using its curriculum and books, and the teaching is conducted entirely in Kurdish. Kurdish textbooks identify Kirkuk as "the most rich oil-producing area in Kurdistan."[21]

Given that the Kurds form the majority outside the city of Kirkuk itself, one would have expected the Kurds to demand the incorporation of the countryside into their Kurdish region, which would have been more in line with historical facts. Yet their insistence on incorporating the city of Kirkuk is chiefly motivated by the oil industry, which appears to be important for the economic nationalism of the Kurdish region. The significance accorded to Kirkuk by the Kurds is in line with the economic vision and policy of using Kirkuk oil to build a rentier economic system similar to the one in Baghdad. When oil revenues function as an economic basis for authoritarian rule, this policy of insisting on the inclusion of Kirkuk with its oil resources seems to be a continuation of the destructive visions and policies of old Iraq.

However, Stansfield puts forward a "compromise" solution that would recognize the city of Kirkuk as part of a Kurdistan autonomous region, but distribute revenues from all of Iraq's oil fields, including that of Kirkuk, proportionally according to population. He adds: "A proposal along such lines would be difficult to argue against."[22] This is hardly new as the constitution proclaims that all the oil fields belong to all Iraqis. Thus it is in the interests of the Kurds to consider all the oil of Iraq, and not just that of Kirkuk, as theirs for the fact that they are equal partners in Iraq. This makes sense given that the Kirkuk oil fields are the oldest in production and therefore expected to be the first to diminish in economic value over time. Besides, recent explorations for oil and gas in the Kurdish region appear to be promising. The key question is, however, if all Iraqis could share the Kirkuk oil, as for the rest of the oil fields, why the city of Kirkuk will not have the same fate, by becoming an Iraqi city for all Iraqis. In fact, a multiethnic

Kirkuk where everyone lives peacefully with the other will, no doubt, be a shining example of a new, tolerant, and peaceful Iraq.

Nonetheless, instead of adopting this desirable vision of Kirkuk, the Kurds have stated the argument that Kirkuk is not a Kurdish but a Kurdistani city. In their view, this argument is a sort of compromise, because it recognizes the multiethnic nature of the city. They maintain that the roots of Kirkuk are geographically Kurdistani, even if the city is not exclusively Kurdish in terms of population structure. Stansfield and Ahmadzadeh elaborate more on this concept of Kurdistani as "an attachment to territory and acceptance of the concept by non-Kurds. 'Kurdistan Region' is a geographic construct to which people of any ethnicity or creed can subscribe." They add: "The term 'Kurdistani' is therefore being employed in the Kurdish region of Iraq as a means to construct a non-ethnic Kurdistani nationalism. Far from being a tool to engineer some form of civic nationalism among a wide range of peoples living in the Zagros mountains, the original 'Kurdistani' idea was distinctly ethnic in outlook and focused upon the promotion of a pan-Kurdish nationalist ideal, irrespective of international boundaries."[23]

However, the conceptualization of the term "Kurdistani" appears to be in harmony with a nationalist drive by the Kurds that aims to incorporate non-Kurds as well. The insistence on annexing Kirkuk and other "disputed territories" will no doubt create a problem of minorities in the expanding Kurdish region. Thus for the Kurds, the question is not only to nurture a dream of building a nation-state for the Kurds but also to build a state that has significant minorities. The policy of enforcing Kurdish nationality on other minorities in the northern region and the "disputed territories" (the Yazidis and Shabaks, for instance) and the recent encouragement of the Christians to move to Iraqi Kurdistan are apparent illustrations of the Kurdish drive to create a national entity that contains several minorities. In this respect, the existence of minorities appears to be a crucial marker, and a vital aspect of nationalism, whether Arab or Kurdish. However, in the absence of genuine democracy, the existence of minorities could possibly lead to yet another violent and extremist version of nationalism, as the history of Iraq has repeatedly demonstrated.

NATIONALISM AND EXTREMISM

One cannot understand the issue of Kirkuk and the rest of the so-called disputed territories outside the context of Kurdish nationalism. History shows that Kurdish nationalism is a frustrated nationalism. The Kurds are scattered in four countries: Iraq, Turkey, Iran, and Syria. Various differences among Kurds living across different countries, or even among those within a single country, are not trivial at all. It is important to stress that even the Arabs have experienced frustrated nationalism, in terms of their failure to achieve one nation-state for all Arabs.

Authoritarian regimes in Iraq have resulted in a conflict between Arab nationalism and Kurdish nationalism. Kurdish nationalism became deeper and deeper due to the brutality of the regime of Saddam and his ruthless campaigns against the Kurds. Naturally, violence breeds violence. Meanwhile, the challenge for the Kurds is to avoid falling into the trap of destructive victimization politics and instead try to steer Kurdish nationalism away from counterproductive extremism. This is, however, not an easy challenge, not only for Kurdish nationalism but for any nationalism for that matter.

Similar to any other nationalism, Kurdish nationalism has its own share of extremism. Some Kurds have rather expansive ideas about necessity for Arabs to leave the city of Kirkuk. One senior Kurdish official said: "The Arabization campaigns began in 1936, so Arabs who came after that should go."[24] After the discovery of oil, a mass migration of Kurds and Arabs to work in the oil fields of Kirkuk started, yet some Kurds believe that this right should be exclusive to the Kurds only. During the revolt of 1991 in the north, an eyewitness said: "While the Kurds were in control of Kirkuk, some Iraqis were not allowed to enter the city. They were told that this is Kurdistan. It was as if you now needed a visa to get in to your own country."[25]

Moreover, nationalism is forever associated with emotionalism, which is not always helpful. Mustafa Barzani once asserted that Kirkuk is the heart of Kurdistan, whereas Talabani claimed that Kirkuk is the Jerusalem of Kurdistan. According to an official explanation, because Kirkuk has a special place in Kurdish hearts the city should be annexed as the capital of the Kurdish region. This is a clear illustration of how nationalism feeds myths and how myths, in turn, feed and justify unrealistic nationalism. The analogy between Kirkuk and Jerusalem is an illustration of the irrationality of some nationalist demands that can prove futile, if not counterproductive, in the end. For instance, the inflexible position of Pan-Arabism regarding Jerusalem and the Palestinian question did in fact harm, rather than help, the Palestinians. The extreme demand for "all or nothing" resulted in the loss of everything in the end. In this regard, the experience of Arab nationalism should serve as a valuable lesson for nationalist Kurds.

However, this maximalist nationalism complicates the relations between the Kurds and the central government. Hiltermann states that now sitting in Baghdad, the Kurds "find themselves presented with an unprecedented opportunity to press forward with their bid for statehood. Their objective is to use the levers of state for a twofold purpose: to prevent a powerful central state from deploying its security forces against the Kurdish population, as happened so often during the past century, and to maximize Kurdistan's chances to secede. These twin goals are closely intertwined; jointly, they define the Kurdish past, present and future." He continues: "They hope thereby to build the foundations of an independent Kurdish state, an ambition that once and for all would allow them to trade in their barren mountain hideouts for a stable home in the fertile plains."[26]

Elsewhere, Hiltermann argues that if the Kurds want Kirkuk only because historically Kurds have lived there, and even have constituted a majority in the countryside, "then they run up against competing claims of the other communities that appear to have no less value. If the Kurds want Kirkuk in order to prevent a repeat of the atrocities of the past, then there are ways of providing the necessary protections for Kirkuki Kurds short of incorporating Kirkuk into Kurdistan. It is, however, because the Kurds desire independence that they feel they *must* annex Kirkuk."[27]

The long-term objective of the Kurds is to establish an independent state, and they declare this openly. Unquestionably, they have every right to do so. However, maintaining good relations with Baghdad is important for the Kurds, whether they have an independent state or as part of Iraq. Iraq will continue to be their neighbor, and a good relation with neighbors is important for the survival and security of any state. Moreover, regardless of the relation with Baghdad, secession has serious regional ramifications that could make it improbable for the time being. According to Wafiq al-Samar'ai, a former chief of Iraqi general military intelligence, Saddam once said to the Kurdish officials who came to Baghdad in 1991 for a talk: "Go and declare a Kurdish state, I will be the first to recognize it, if you will find someone else who is willing to recognize your state."[28]

Notwithstanding this sensitive regional situation, the Kurds on several occasions have threatened secession if relations with Baghdad are not in their best interest. Thus even when the regional situation continues to be detrimental to the construction of a Kurdish state, the Kurds insist they have decided to stay with Iraq as a voluntary concession from the Kurdish leadership. They use the "dream" of a Kurdish state, as presently unachievable as it is, as a bargaining chip to attain greater victories with the Iraqi state, for the benefit of obtaining generous concessions from Baghdad. This, however, is a dangerous and risky game that can easily backfire. Staying within Iraq is more a politics of pragmatism than a concession to the Iraqi state. Leezenberg argues: "While the Kurdish parties at times hint at the possibility of secession, this seems to be a negotiation tactic rather than a seriously contemplated option. The actual likelihood of secession of a single Kurdish region is relatively small, given the region's current division in two and the rivalries between the two Kurdish leaders in both the past and the present."[29] Obviously, adopting realistic claims and demands and pursuing constructive politics is in the interests of everyone.

It is true that the unfriendly regional situation makes the claim of a "voluntary" union of the Kurds with the rest of Iraq questionable, presently at least. Yet the Kurds are right to stress they belong to Iraq by their own choice, and not because of an imposed incorporation from a highly centralized and authoritarian government by brute force and intimidation as before. Not only is this perception of the Kurds important for them to believe they are equal partners; it is also important for all Iraqis. It expresses a desirable agency and active participation in contrast to the marginalization and passivity of the past.

However, this new perception and belonging to an inclusive and peaceful Iraq would also require from the Kurds a more constructive and positive approach to the Iraqi state. Identity politics associated with consociations, ethnic federalism, and the enforcement of a destabilizing constitution is hardly the appropriate policy to follow given the new situation for the Kurds in Iraq. It does not matter whether violence and animosity toward the Iraqi state was justified in the past; the policy of maintaining a weak and ineffective central state is an ill-designed policy that will surely fail to advance the real interests of the Kurdish population. Animosity toward the Iraqi state, whether in the past or now, is part of violent politics that keeps inventing enemies and always encourages conflicts with these enemies. Within this politics, exaggerated "historical" rights, inflexible demands, and "red lines" become unavoidable.

Barzani, who likened talk of a strongly unified Iraq to "bird dreams and wishes," warned: "If Article 140 is not implemented, then this will mean the demise of the Constitution and Iraq itself."[30] Yet history shows that demanding all or nothing is an extremist and counterproductive politics. A Kurdish journalist, on the other hand, recommends that the only hope left for the Kurds is to exploit the divisions among Iraq's other communities, namely the Shiites: "There are lots of opportunities for Kurds if they play it right."[31] Apart from the explicit and vulgar political opportunism involved in this statement, this kind of politics is an old Kurdish game that has more often backfired than not.

Exaggerated and inflexible demands were manifested in negotiations for the formation of a federal government following the 2010 elections. The Kurds presented 19 points for negotiations, but several of these points are maximalist to the extent that there is one point stating that the federal government should be considered dissolved if the Kurdish ministers withdraw from the cabinet. Demands like these not only complicate the already fragile political process but also are unhelpful and counterproductive. These demands may very well lead many Iraqis to show less understanding and support for legitimate Kurdish aspirations.

The Kurds argue that they have enjoyed autonomy since 1991, a de facto reality that they would like to institutionalize and legitimize through a system of regional federalism. This de facto situation is the result of previous brutalities against the Kurds and the foolish policies of the previous regime. However, if the old regime has not been toppled are Iraqis, for the sake of argument, supposed to accept the suppression of the Kurds as a de facto situation? The Iraqis have always condemned the brutality of Saddam toward the Kurds, and they are unhappy about the separatist policies of the ruling Kurdish elites. If the original brutality lacks legitimacy, then so do the resultant separatist policies.

Goldberg shares this anecdote: "In October, when I was last in the region, I called the office of a high official of the *peshmerga*, the Kurdish guerrilla army, but was told that he had 'gone to Iraq' for the week."[32] Thus perceiving Iraq and Kurdistan as two already existing separate countries seems to be a foregone conclusion in the separatist and extremist vision of some Kurds. Raphaeli brings to light that the oath of office taken by the regional prime minister and the ministers is almost completely separatist, in both word and intention. The oath reads: "I swear by God the Mighty that I will loyally defend the unity of the people and the land of Iraqi Kurdistan, that I will respect the law and I will serve the interest of the people."[33] Naturally, one wonders about the missing loyalty to Iraq and its constitution in this oath.

This and other ways of aloofness from Iraqi issues are hardly good gestures. Arabic has become much less important in the region. Those who were born after 1991 do not study Arabic at Kurdish schools. When Arabic is the official language and the language of more than 80 percent of the population in addition to being an influential language in business, politics, culture, and education, then there are serious questions about the integration of the Kurds into Iraq. Discouraging the learning of Arabic in the Kurdish region will distress the interaction with central government and federal bureaucracy. Separatist policies, even if they were pursued within a unified Iraq, are unconstructive, if not violent.

One can argue that there is no real justification for driving a separatist policy when there is presently an opportunity to build a democratic and inclusive Iraq for all the citizens of this country.

The military aspect in the relationship between the Kurds and the Iraqi central government is also a controversial issue. While the constitution forbids the existence of any independent militia outside the national army, the Kurds were successful in imposing their own interpretation that the Kurdish militia, the *peshmerga*, is a national force and a liberation movement in the service of all Kurds, rather than a militia army. In reality, however, each of the dominant parties has its own partisan militia, which functions under the direct control of the leadership of the respective party. These militias are the instruments to maintain political domination over particular regions. It is, therefore, unsurprising that the Kurds insist on keeping their militia as an independent force.

Nevertheless, a "compromise" was reached to officially name the Kurdish militias as "The National Guard of Iraqi Kurdistan." This compromise required the Kurdish leaders to surrender the nominal authority over the Guard to the national government but were granted the right to keep actual control in their hands. Since these militias are now nominally part of the Iraqi army, the deal expects central governmental financing for this force. Apparently, this deal favors the ruling Kurdish parties from every direction. It is important to stress, however, that the Kurdish militias are not the only private militia in the country since there are several Shiite militias. Many members of the Shiite militarized groups are allowed to join the Iraqi security forces, but their loyalty is questionable since they continue to be loyal to their respective political factions. New Iraq is working for the institutionalization of private militias in the country. The existence of individual militias is, nonetheless, a contravention to the rule of law and the monopolization of violence by the state.

However, it is difficult to know for sure the size of the Kurdish militias. It is estimated that the KDP has 60,000 and the PUK has 40,000; another estimate puts the figures at 55,000 (including 30,000 reserves) and 18,000 (not counting the reserves) respectively. Yet the minister of the *pershmerga* in the regional government declares that the number of the guards and the security forces in the Kurdish region is 200,000.[34] It is difficult to decide whether these official figures are real or imaginary.

Inflating the size of the Kurdish military forces could work for the benefit of the Kurds for several reasons. First, the central government is responsible for financing the Kurdish forces; therefore an inflated number means, in reality, a higher financial gain for Kurdish authorities.

Second, it is also functional for enhancing the position of the Kurds in relation to the central government, as a force to reckon with, especially when relations are tense and conflicting. Third, an inflated figure tends to project the power of the *peshmerga* in a better and more influential way, which is handy for intimidating the opposition and the population. However, the large size of the Kurdish forces does not seem to be effective in stopping the repeated bombardment of Kurdish villages by Iranian and Turkish artilleries, or the Turkish incursions into the region. Following a Middle Eastern military pattern, the army in this region appears to be mostly for internal security and the protection of the regime, rather than for the successful resolution of external conflicts.

Nonetheless, the president of Iraqi Kurdistan pronounced the intention to create a unified army for the region out of the existing militias, as one of "his old wishes." He even asked Americans to extend help to form, train, and arm the new special army for the region. The central government, on the other hand, rejected the move on the ground that the constitution does not allow the existence of a second army in Iraq. The federal government also invited Kurdish leaders, now that they are part of the Iraqi state, to strive to strengthen federal institutions that can provide security for everyone. Furthermore, the national Ministry of Defense has decided to close the two military academies in the region in January 2010 and turn them into schools for special fighting. In justifying its decision, the ministry states that there is an excess in the number of army officers and that the one military academy in Baghdad will suffice. The Kurds established these two academies in 1992, one in Qal'at Julan in Sulaimaniya, under the control of the PUK, and one in Zacho, under the control of KDP. The minister of the *peshmerga*, however, threatened that if Baghdad does not reverse its decision to close these academies, then "we are going to have another speech."[35]

The Kurds, who suffered earlier from the incursion of the Iraqi army into their cities and villages, demand that no Iraqi army should enter their autonomous region, unless with the approval of the regional parliament as is stipulated in the constitution. Their interpretation of the constitutional provision extends this prohibition to the "disputed territories" as well. These territories have been under the control of the *peshmerga* since 2003, and the Kurds refuse to evacuate them or allow the Iraqi army to settle there. An American report reveals that the area that falls outside the Kurdish region yet still under the control of the Kurdish militias reaches a figure of 500 kilometers, which were effectively taken from adjoining provinces.[36]

However, the arrival of Division 12 of the Iraqi army in Kirkuk has alarmed the Kurds whose militias have dominated the city since regime change in 2003. An incidence in Makhmur, a disputed town situated between Kirkuk and Mosul, could have developed into a serious conflict in June 2009. In a routine troop movement, the Iraqi army on its way to Mosul went through this town, only to be faced with Kurdish militia. Nevertheless, the army unit diverted its route to avoid a possible conflict, a decision that was taken after intense negotiations with the involvement of Americans.

The Kurds, however, considered this incident as more a provocation than misunderstanding. The then prime minister of the Kurdish government, Nechirvan Barzani, warned that the Iraqi army was biding its time until it became stronger. He insisted that Iraqi army commanders were still imbued with a "military-style mentality of being the Big Brother to impose their will." He continues: "Everything is frozen, nothing is moving. If the problems are not solved and we're not sitting down together [with the central government], then the risk of military confrontation will emerge." Asked whether the *peshmerga* had tanks, he replied, "Oh, yes. Yes, we do."[37]

While the Kurds insist that Baghdad should get their approval for any serious plan of arming and developing the Iraqi army, they enthusiastically work on developing and arming their own army without any considerations to the federal government in Baghdad. It became known by end of 2009 that consignments of armaments from Bulgaria had arrived in the Kurdish region. During the turbulent time of the Iraq War, the Kurds captured many sophisticated armaments, including tanks, and military equipment from the disintegrating Iraqi army in the north of the country. They did not return these military spoils to the central government, even when they became part of those who rule the country. However, a sophisticated level of militarization and highly inflexible and far-fetched nationalism is a dangerous combination, as the experience of the former regime has unmistakably demonstrated.

Apart from emotionality, which is hardly a ground for politics, nationalism is a strong contributing factor to the initiation and feeding of violence. If Arab nationalism is considered to have resulted in many disasters in the country and is therefore condemned, why should one expect Kurdish nationalism to function differently or even better? Iraqi Kurdistan has enjoyed extensive autonomy since 1991. Thus 19 years later, one expects the region to be a place of real political plurality and democracy, accompanied by economic prosperity for all the Kurds. Yet the reality is disappointingly far from this expectation. Even Halabja, a dear symbol of Kurdish agony and nationalism, suffers from neglect and lack of basic services. Hence, people wonder whether Kurdish nationalism is really in the interest of the Kurdish population, inasmuch as they question whether Arab nationalism really did benefit the Arabs.

Instead of focusing on serving the Kurdish people, Kurdish nationalism is driven either by internal conflicts and rivalries between two major parties or by nationalist territorial expansionism and the escalation of conflicts with the central government, not to mention recurrent secessionist threats. One may be tempted to ask: if the Kurdish leaders are ready to divide Kurdistan among themselves, will they mind partitioning and weakening the whole of Iraq for that matter? By its very nature, nationalism is an easy prey to conflicts with the Other. Perceptibly, to have nationalism that is devoid of external antagonism is a serious universal challenge. Both Arab and Kurdish nationalism demonstrate this case very well.

Arab nationalism that emphasizes Arab identity first, at the expense of all other non-Arabs (including the Kurds), has been discredited in Iraqi history. The brutality of campaigns against the Kurds in the name of Arab nationalism has fed a violent form of Kurdish nationalism. Both Arab and Kurdish nationalisms are products of the same violent process. Doubtless, however, both these versions of nationalism will continue to play vital roles in the years to come. The challenge in new Iraq is transforming nationalism from violence, intimidation, and animosity toward the Other into a peaceful, inclusive, productive, and viable force.

There is a need for what may be called *the Iraqification of nationalism*, an Iraqi nationalism that is neither Arab nor Kurdish, which is inclusive of all who share life in this country. There is a need for an Iraqi nationalism and Iraqi identity where race, religion, sect, and gender are overlooked, so that in the end all are Iraqis. There is also a need for the rationalization of nationalism in new Iraq, away from harmful emotionality and extremism. Besides, in a global and closely connected world, the demise of nationalism is expected. Meanwhile, there is a need to ground nationalism on national interests and pragmatism. In this sense, nationalism should be a productive force that is oriented toward the future, not toward the past. It should be a productive nationalism designed for economic success, benefiting all Iraqis.

NOTES

1. Said K. Aburish, *Saddam Hussein: The Politics of Revenge* (London: Bloomsbury, 2001), 87.

2. Michiel Leezenberg, "Iraqi Kurdistan: Contours of a Post-Civil War Society," *Third World Quarterly* 26, no. 4–5 (2005): 644.

3. Ibid., 646, fn. 27.

4. Liz Sly, "Kirkuk, Iraq's Simmering Melting Pot," *Los Angeles Times*, December 6, 2009.

5. International Crisis Group, "Iraq's Uncertain Future: Elections and Beyond," *Middle East Report* 94 (February 25, 2010): 21, http://www.crisisgroup.org/library/documents/middle_east__north_africa/iraq_iran_gulf/94_iraq_s_uncertain_f; ture__elections_and_beyond.pdf.

6. Hanna Batatu, *The Old Social Classes and the Revolutionary Movements of Iraq: A Study of Iraq's Old Landed and Commercial Classes and of Its Communists, Ba'thist and Free Officers* (London: Saqi, 2004 [1978]), 913.

7. Ibid., 649.

8. David McDowall, *A Modern History of the Kurds*, 3rd ed. (London: Tauris, 2004), 305.

9. Ibid., 314.

10. Ibid., 327.

11. McDowall, *A Modern History*, 329; Nader Entessar, "The Kurds in Post-Revolutionary Iran and Iraq," *Third World Quarterly* 6, no. 4 (October 1984):, 920.

12. Marion Farouk-Sluglett and Peter Sluglett, *Iraq Since 1958: From Revolution to Dictatorship* (London: Tauris, 2003), 71.

13. Sandra Mackey, *The Reckoning: Iraq and the Legacy of Saddam Hussein* (New York: Norton, 2002), 218.

14. Aburish, *Saddam Hussein*, 87.

15. Nimrod Raphaeli, "Iraqi Kurds at Crossroads," *Inquiry and Analysis* 168 (March 30, 2004), http://www.memri.org/report/en/0/0/0/0/0/0/1096.htm.

16. Sly, "Iraq Sees Large Turnout for Kurdistan Election," *Los Angeles Times*, July 26, 2009.

17. Adeed Dawisha, "The New Iraq: Democratic Institutions and Performance," *Journal of Democracy* 16, no. 3 (July 2005): 42.

18. Joost R. Hiltermann, "Kirkuk as a Peacebuilding Test Case," in *Iraq: Preventing a New Generation of Conflict*, ed. Markus E. Bouillon, David M. Malone, and Ben Rowswell (Boulder, CO: Rienner, 2007), 140, fn. 40.

19. Ibid.

20. Peter W. Galbraith, "Kurdistan in a Federal Iraq," in *The Future of Kurdistan in Iraq*, ed. Brendan O'Larry, John McGarry, and Khaled Salih (Philadelphia: University of Pennsylvania Press, 2005), 276.

21. Missy Ryan, "Iraq Polls Could Heighten Tensions over Kirkuk," *Reuters*, January 26, 2010, http://uk.reuters.com/article/idUKTRE60P2KE20100126.

22. Gareth Stansfield, "Governing Kurdistan: The Strengths of Division," in *The Future of Kurdistan*, ed. O'Larry, McGarry, and Salih, 210.

23. Gareth Stansfield and Hashem Ahmadzadeh, "Kurdish or Kurdista-
nis? Conceptualising Regionalism in the North of Iraq," in *An Iraq of Its
Regions: Cornerstones of a Federal Democracy?*, ed. Reidar Visser and Gareth
Stansfield (New York: Columbia University Press, 2008), 124.

24. Patrick Clawson, "Iraq for the Iraqis: How and When," *Middle East
Quarterly*, Spring 2004, http://www.meforum.org/article/601.

25. Kanan Makiya, *Cruelty and Silence: War, Tyranny, Uprising, and the Arab
World* (New York: Norton, 1993), 79.

26. Joost R. Hiltermann, "To Protect or to Project? Iraqi Kurds and Their
Future," *Middle East Report* 247 (summer 2008), http://www.merip.org/
mer/mer247/hiltermann.html.

27. Hiltermann, "Kirkuk as a Peacebuilding," 135, emphasis in the original.

28. Wafiq al-Samar'ai, "Iraqi Kurds Have the Right to Self-Destiny ...
But," *Asharq al-Awsat*, January 26, 2009.

29. Leezenberg, "Iraqi Kurdistan," 644.

30. Sam Dagher, "Election Victories Help Kurds in Iraq Push for More Sovereignty," *New York Times*, May 2, 2010.

31. Ibid.

32. Jeffrey Goldberg, "After Iraq," *The Atlantic Online*, January–February
2008, http://www.theatlantic.com/doc/print/20801/goldberg-mideast.

33. Nimrod Raphaeli, "Kurdistan—the Quest for Statehood," *Inquiry and
Analysis-Iraq* 298 (October 25, 2006), http://www.memri.org/report/en/0/
0/0/0/0/0/1791.htm.

34. Ma'ad Faiadh, "Barzani: We Have Decided to Form an Army for Kurdistan," *Asharq al-Awsat*, November 23, 2009.

35. Ibid.

36. Radio Sawa, "Fears of a War between the Kurds and Arabs," February 20, 2009, http://www.radiosawa.com/arabic_news.aspx?id=1825163&
cid=14.

37. Anthony Shadid, "Kurdish Leaders Warn of Strains with Maliki,"
Washington Post, July 17, 2009.

13

Armaments, Oil, and Corruption

ARMAMENTS AND CORRUPTION

International studies show that the armaments deal is one of the economic sectors prone to corruption, and the experience of Iraq confirms this reality. The Board of Supreme Audit investigated defense contracts that were signed beginning from the transfer of sovereignty on June 28, 2004, through February 28, 2005. The investigation uncovered a lack of transparency in the procurement of the Ministry of Defense and also widespread fraud and waste in contracts amounting to a total of $1.27 billion, nearly equal to the entire procurement budget of the ministry of $1.3 billion in that year. The scrutiny of the defense contracts revealed a persistent and disturbing pattern of corruption and deception. Multimillion-dollar contracts were awarded to favored weapons suppliers without a bidding process or the required approval from the prime minister's office. Officials kept little or no record of major purchases, sometimes noting lucrative deals in "undated and unnumbered" memos. Nearly all purchases contained a clause that required the contract's full value to be paid up front in cash, an unusual clause in international contracting of this magnitude. The money was paid at great speed out of the ministry's account with the central bank.

Instead of buying directly from a foreign company or government, the arms deals were made through middlemen who vanished after receiving the millions. The use of intermediaries was also helpful in hiding the huge kickbacks the senior officials at the defense ministry received from these contracts. The sole beneficiary on 43 of the 89 contracts investigated was a former currency-exchange operator, Nair Mohammad al-Jumaili, whose name does not even appear on the contracts. At least $759 million in Iraqi money was deposited into his personal account at a bank in Baghdad, according to the Board of Supreme Audit report. The report said that internal records incorrectly "indicated that the Ministry of Defense signed contracts with Poland, Arab countries, the United States and Europe, but we discovered that all contracts were signed and executed with Iraqi suppliers." An Iraqi official comments: "There are no real contracts, even. They just signed papers and took the money."[1]

The ringleader of this corruption scandal is Ziad Qattan, who is a dual Iraqi-Polish national. After spending 27 years in Europe, he returned to Iraq two days before the war in 2003. Despite the fact that he knew nothing about weapons procurement, he became the defense ministry's procurement chief since the transfer of sovereignty. As chief procurement officer with more than a billion-dollar budget, he turned to a recently established company, with no background in military procurement and with only $2,000 in paid-up capital, to provide the Iraqi army with equipment for its rapid-deployment forces.

The company, called *al-'Ayn al-Jariah*, the Flowing Spring, was established on September 1, 2004, with three shareholders: Abd el-Hamid Mirza, the secretary of the office of the then vice president; Zina Faatah, a Jordanian-based Iraqi and associate of Mish'al al-Sarraf, the senior adviser to the minister of defense; and the above-mentioned al-Jumaili, who operated the sham company. A warrant was issued for the arrest of Qattan, but he fled the country.[2] The arrest of the director general of finance at the Ministry of Defense, Sawsan Jassim, has led to the disclosure of the involvement of senior officials in this corruption case. Two of her colleagues at the ministry were murdered, however. The director general of planning, Issam al-Dujaili, was murdered while driving to work, and the inspector general of the ministry, Leila al-Mukhtar, was killed in the Green Zone in an obvious insider job.[3]

The then minister of defense, Hazem al-Sha'lan, also fled the country in 2005 and refused to return to face charges of $1 billion in fraud in connection with this case. For eight months, the ministry spent money without restraint. Contracts worth more than $5 million should have been reviewed by a cabinet committee, but Sha'lan asked for and received from the cabinet an exemption for the defense ministry. This scandal had even tarnished the reputation of the then interim prime minister, Ayad Allawi. An Iraqi official commented on these carefully planned dubious transactions: "It is possibly one of the largest thefts in history. Huge amounts of money have disappeared. In return we got nothing but scraps of metal."[4]

Most of the purchased armaments were overpriced, outdated, and unnecessary or unusable weapons. Military equipment purchased included 28-year-old Soviet-made helicopters that should have been scrapped after 25 years of service; armored cars that turned out to be so poorly made that even a bullet from an elderly AK-47 machine gun could penetrate their armor; other armored cars that leaked so much oil that they had to be abandoned; a shipment of the latest MP5 American machine guns, at a cost of $3,500 each, that consisted in reality of Egyptian copies worth only $200 a gun. A deal was struck to buy 7.62 mm machine-gun bullets for 16¢ each, although they should have cost between 4 and 6¢.[5]

In early January 2005, $300 million were taken out of Iraq's central bank, packed into boxes, and quietly put on a charter jet bound for Lebanon. The money was to be used to buy weapons according to officials from the Ministry of Defense. But exactly where the money went, to whom, and for precisely what remains a mystery. A prominent politician, Ahmad Chalabi, strongly criticized this mysterious action, saying that there was no legitimate reason why the Iraqi government should have used cash to pay for goods from abroad. The reply of the defense minister, Sha'lan, suggested that Chalabi had made the charges to further his own political ambitions, and he threatened to arrest him and hand him over to Interpol to face corruption chargers of his own.[6] In Jordan, Chalabi faces the charges of embezzling millions of dollars from the Petra Bank, which collapsed in the 1990s. But he has long maintained that these charges are baseless, part of a vendetta being carried out for his opposition to the regime of Saddam Hussein.

Dale Stoffel is an American contractor who had been active in the arms business since the mid-1990s. After the invasion of Iraq, he went to Baghdad to pursue business opportunities. He succeeded in 2004 concluding with the Ministry of Defense a multimillion-dollar contract for his company, Wye Oak Technology, to refurbish old military equipment. However, he was unsuccessful in getting the lump-sum $24.7 million payment from the ministry that he was seeking. Instead, the ministry cut three separate checks and sent them to a Lebanese intermediary for "processing." But when the businessman failed to send him the money, Stoffel suspected corruption in this deal. He alerted senior U.S. officials that his contract had fallen prey to corruption and self-dealing and that he suspected that the mysterious middleman's true role was to route payments back to Iraqi officials in the form of kickbacks. On December 8, he was summoned to the Taji military base north of Baghdad by the coalition military officials to discuss his concerns. Shortly after leaving the meeting, his car was ambushed and he was executed. His business associate, Joseph Wemple, was also killed. The killers tried to disguise this crime as a regular terrorist attack. Yet the timing and unusual details of the killing have raised strong suspicions that this attempt was merely a ruse to disguise a well-planned assassination.[7]

Lack of transparency in the arms deals continued even after the big scandal of the tainted arms purchases in 2004 and 2005. An $833 million arms deal was secretly negotiated with Serbia in September 2007 without competitive bidding. The deal sidestepped anticorruption safeguards, including the approval of senior uniformed Iraqi army officers and an Iraqi contract approval committee. Instead, the deal was negotiated by a delegation of 22 high-ranking Iraqi officials from the Ministry of Defense. At the urging of the new defense minister, abdul-Qadir al-Obeidi, the prime minister, Nuri al-Maliki, abolished the national contracts committee, a mandatory review agency for all government purchases exceeding $50 million. The defense minister was motivated to do the deal by the urge to expedite the Iraqi army's acquisition process. Nevertheless, in response to sharp criticism of this deal, Qadir froze some of the items thereby reducing the final contract price to $236 million; in turn, the deal was signed in March 2008. Even in this contract much of the purchased equipment turned out to be either substandard or inappropriate for military missions.[8]

Faced with persistent violence and terrorism, in 2009 the Ministry of Interior purchased from a British company a special hand-held device, ADE 651, which is supposed to detect car bombs and weapons, to be used at hundreds of security checkpoints. However, despite the omnipresent use of this device, deadly bombings have escalated. After widespread doubts and warnings by American military officials who never used the device, Britain finally banned the export of the apparatus and arrested the manufacturer for fraud. Even after Britain confirmed the scandal, officials at the Ministry of Interior continued to use the device and insisted on its effectiveness. The interior minister, Jawad al-Bolani, not only insists on the success of this device but he also declares that critics of the device are motivated by electoral politics against his ministry.[9] The minister is the head of one of the political lists that were competing in the 2010 election. Still, this gadget proved to be a very expensive hoax. Whereas the device costs only $250 apiece, the Ministry of Interior paid $60,000 each. As the ministry bought 800 pieces, the total cost of this suspicious transaction came to a figure of $48 million in wasted money. A British source gives even higher figures, £52 million.[10] A *New York Times* editorial comments: "The full history of war profiteering in Iraq may never be known, but it will be hard to top the magic wand known as ADE 651 as a symbol of corruption."[11]

Dubious and corrupt contracts of arms deals are not the only problem with the military sector. The security forces of Iraq, which totaled about a million members, are highly corrupt as well. The existence of thousands of phony names on the payroll is a serious problem that results in millions of wasted dollars in corruption. The security forces are infiltrated by recruits with criminal or terrorist records. The rank-and-file police officers have to pay bribes to be promoted. Cooperation with street crimes is also rife. Arrests by security forces to get ransom from the victims are pervasive. Likewise freeing convicted criminals in exchange for bribes is also common. It is true that security checks at the Ministry of Interior have led to the dismissal of 15,000 in 2008 and 60,000 in 2009, but these problems are still serious. A senior official from the ministry acknowledges the problem: "There's a need to reorganize and cleanse the security forces and armed forces from extremists and criminals. We need 10 years to reach the level of professionalism that we aspire for."[12]

It was revealed in March 2010 that there existed a secret prison in Baghdad under the direct control of Prime Minister Maliki, where 431 prisoners have been subjected to appalling conditions and torture. An inspection of the prison by the Ministry of Human Rights pointed out that some prisoners complained about the use of various methods of torture against them, and described guards extorting as much as $1,000 from prisoners who wanted to phone their families.[13] Sheikh Maher Sirhan was arrested on terrorism charges. He was held in a secret jail where he said that he underwent 16 days of beatings and torture, including the use of electric rods, to extract confessions. Then officers gave him the option of paying $50,000 to have his accusers drop their charges and free him from jail.[14] The many cases of ransoms and deals and the collusion between corrupt security forces and judges who issue warrants are so great that Iraq's Supreme Judiciary Council ordered an inquiry into the matter in June 2009. On the corruption and bribery in the security forces, one police officer elaborates: "A good cop was someone who took bribes only to release minor offenders and a bad cop was someone who accepted money to release a killer." Another police officer comments: "A country like this, with all the problems and misery—what do you expect people to do?"[15]

In one Wednesday afternoon in October 2009, two dark blue minibuses carrying 12 to 15 unmasked men parked a block away from a market in a neighborhood in Baghdad, where several jewelry stores are located. The men walked the rest of the way to the first store, shot the owner in the head with a gun equipped with a silencer, and robbed the place. They then looted two more jewelry stores, killing the owners. Along the way, they killed five other people, including a woman and her eight-month-old baby. Before leaving, they tossed hand grenades into the market and shot at cars parked nearby to ensure they were not followed. Since a checkpoint is located a few miles away, many residents stressed that soldiers there had allowed the assailants to pass unhindered. A local business whose store is near one of the jewelers said: "The policemen at the checkpoint know me, but they search me and search my car every time I leave and come back. It was an organized crime, and they were getting help from the police. They weren't even hiding their faces."[16] It is indeed difficult to imagine that a brazen, daylight crime that leads to the death of eight people can occur without the help of the security forces.

Bank robberies become common in Iraq where the rule of law is absent. One day in August 2009, nine members of the security forces entered the Zuwiya branch of the Rafidain Bank, tied up eight guards, and executed them point blank with silenced guns. Then they made off with two carloads of cash worth between $4.3 and 6.8 million, depending on sources. The gang of robbers did not have to worry about the police in this heavily guarded neighborhood in Baghdad. This area is under the security of one of the nation's most powerful men, the vice president Adel Abdul Mahdi. Investigations confirmed that five of the nine robbers were indeed in Mahdi's bodyguard battalion. The robbers took the money and went to a journal headquarters that belongs to Mahdi, who refused to give permission to the forces of the Interior Ministry, which succeeded in tracing the criminals, to enter the place and arrest the robbers.

At this juncture, there was a big risk of bloody conflict between the two opposing forces. Under pressure, Mahdi relented by striking a deal for the surrender of the robbers with the money and weapons in exchange for keeping quiet about the scandal. However, the four ringleaders of this gang, who have well-known ties with the Shiite political elites, managed to escape and flee the country toward Iran. The remaining five suspects were put on a two-day trial, where four were sentenced to death and one was acquitted. This brutal and organized crime reveals a high-level corruption in the country. Officials have been quick to discount the possibility that the vice president or his powerful political faction, the Islamic Supreme Council of Iraq, were involved. Ahmad Abdul Hussein, a journalist at the semiofficial newspaper, *al-Sabah*, received a threat to his life after he wrote an article on the case, and he went into hiding. He comments: "I am sure Adel Abdul Mahdi was not involved. But the Iraqi people have to think, do they want a leader who has bodyguards who rob banks and kill?"[17]

OIL AND CORRUPTION

International studies suggest that oil is one of the economic sectors most susceptible to corruption, and Iraq's oil is no exception. Because of the nationalization of the oil industry in 1972 and the shocking oil price increases since 1974, the government has accumulated huge financial revenues from the export of oil. Five percent of these revenues were set aside by the regime for the benefit of the ruling Ba'th Party and placed under the direct and personal control of Saddam Hussein. According to a former consultant at the oil ministry, this fund grew to $17.4 billion by 1990.[18] The imposition of stringent international economic sanctions against Iraq and the establishment of the UN oil-for-food program in 1996 provided the former regime with a wide window of opportunity for corruption.

This program became known as one of the biggest international corruption scandals in history, with the involvement of top-level UN officials and their immediate relatives. About 2,200 international companies were involved in allowing the regime to skim huge kickbacks in exchange for doing business with Iraq under sanctions. Illicit income from surcharges on oil sales and kickbacks on humanitarian purchases would represent between $268 million and $7.5 billion according to different estimates.[19] Even outside this program, smuggling of oil via neighboring countries generated huge illicit revenues for the regime, estimated at between $5.7 and $13.6 billion between 1997 and 2002.[20]

During the high insecurity time following the Iraq War in 2003, oil smuggling has reached an alarming level. Based on figures from the oil ministry, Iraq Revenue Watch, a New York-based agency that monitors Iraq's oil industry, estimates that 25 percent of Iraqi oil meant for domestic consumption is smuggled out of the country.[21] Ali Allawi, a former cabinet member, estimates that the total size of oil smuggling has reached $4 billion a year. The cost to the budget of Iraq's fuel imports ran to an annual level of $6 billion, of which about $200 million was probably skimmed off as commissions and kickbacks. The amount smuggled out of these fuel imports was nearly 30 percent, while domestic fuel products and crude oil were siphoned off a broad at a rate of probably another $2 billion.[22] Allawi concludes: "The theft and smuggling of fuel products involved thousands of people, and was a sophisticated and complex operation conducted by many groups inside and outside Iraq and by government departments."[23]

The domination of the Shiite militias over the oil-rich southern city of Basra has made it a center for lucrative oil trafficking that generated millions of dollars of illicit money to these militias. According to a calculation made by the oil ministry, a ton of diesel bought at the official subsidized price would cost the smuggler about $10, but sells at a smuggler's port in the south at $250; the net profit per truck of smuggled diesel, after payments for officials and the truck driver, was $8,400 per trip per truck.[24]

Baiji is Iraq's largest oil refinery, supplying eight provinces, and it became the center of oil trafficking during that time. Tankers were hijacked, drivers were bribed, papers were forged, and meters were manipulated, which resulted in diverting much of the oil produced to the black market where some of the earnings went to insurgents. In 2007, the U.S. Pentagon estimated that as much as 70 percent of the production of this refinery, or $2 billion in fuels like gasoline, kerosene, and diesel, disappeared annually into the black market. Iraqi security analysts estimated that al Qaeda in Mesopotamia received $50,000 to $100,000 per day from swindles related to the Baiji refinery.[25]

A former finance minister estimated that insurgents reap 40 to 50 percent of all oil-smuggling profits in the country. He admitted that the insurgency had infiltrated senior management positions at Baiji and routinely terrorized truck drivers there. A former oil minister expressed concerns that oil- and fuel-smuggling networks have grown into a dangerous mafia threatening the lives of those in charge of fighting corruption. Senior officials in the oil ministry complained that the "oil-smuggling mafia" not only siphons profits from the oil industry but also is said to control the allocation of administrative posts in the ministry.[26] A U.S. report admits that corruption in the oil ministry is a major problem and is partly to blame for lines of cars stretching for miles as Iraqis wait hours to fill up their tanks.[27]

As acts of economic sabotage, the insurgents often attacked the oil pipelines that link the Baiji refinery to the rich oil fields of Kirkuk and also the pipelines that link the refinery to Baghdad. These pipelines run through the Salahuddin province where the Jubouris tribe is powerful. To solve this problem, the former defense minister, Sha'lan, who is implicated in a serious corruption scandal, asked Mesha'n al-Jubouri, a member of parliament, to organize 17 battalions to be formed from the Jubouris tribe in order to protect the pipeline. Nonetheless, when attacks on the pipelines grew worse despite the formation of these battalions and the investment of millions of dollars, a government investigation revealed that Jubouri had created his own scandal of corruption.

According to these investigations, Jubouri stole money intended to hire and equip thousands of guards in 2004 and 2005, and there are even allegations of funneling some of that money to the insurgency. He included 200 to 300 imaginary names on the payrolls of the battalions and kept the fictitious soldiers' salaries for himself. The first month's salary of all the men in the battalions was not paid on the ground that the soldiers had not yet fully began their tasks. Through a company formed in the name of one of his sons, Jubouri also took charge of the money paid to feed the battalions, demanding a contract for about $102,000 to feed each battalion each month. However, only one-fifth of that amount actually went into feeding the oil protection tribal force. He also intervened in supplying weapons to the battalions, at one point directing soldiers to transport more than 200 Kalashnikov assault rifles in civilian vehicles. Insurgents attacked the vehicles, killed two of the soldiers, and took the guns. He even deployed some of the battalion troops to protect his homes, party headquarters, and relatives. The report of the investigation suggests that money embezzled in this affair amounts to millions of dollars. There are arrest warrants against Jubouri and his son, but they fled the country and are believed to be hiding in Syria.[28]

The International Advisory and Monitoring Board is a UN watchdog agency established by the Security Council to monitor Iraq's oil revenues. This agency oversees the financial records of the Development Fund for Iraq, the principal repository for Iraq's oil export receipts. Several audit reports commissioned by this agency revealed many irregularities and mismanagement in these revenues. These reports raise concerns about absence of metering equipment, lack of competitive bidding, missing contract information, unsupervised payment, and in some cases outright theft. They found that a system to track extraction, production, and sale of the oil lacks proper control, leading to mismanagement of funds. These audits noted large unreconciled differences regarding oil extraction, production, and reported export sales. The auditors note that investigators encountered difficulties in accessing information from the Iraqi ministries and were denied access to the accounting records of the KRG altogether.[29]

Lack of transparency and the secrecy surrounding oil contracts signed by the KRG and oil companies operating in the northern region is one of the serious issues that complicates the relationship between the regional government and the central government. The first oil company to win a contract in post-Saddam Iraq is DNO, a small Norwegian company that won a contract to explore and extract oil in the Kurdish northern region. The terms of the contract were kept secret even from the regional parliament in Kurdistan, and the deal was concluded without the knowledge or the approval of the oil ministry in Baghdad. It has been revealed that the deal is based on a production-sharing agreement, which is a policy not yet adopted, if not totally rejected, by the federal government.

However, the Oslo Stock Exchange released information in September 2009 suggesting nontransparent transactions in the dealings of DNO. The information disclosed that the KRG minister for natural resources, Ashti Hawrami, had been involved in nontransparent sales of DNO shares. The company accused the Norwegian bourse of breaching its confidentiality obligations, but the bourse replied that it was only following public disclosure laws, which stipulate the publication of all trade information. The bourse, however, fined the company after ruling that it failed to provide proper information to the stock exchange.[30]

Nevertheless, Kurdish politicians vigorously denied any insinuation of corruption in this deal, stating that they wanted to help the company only because its business is important for the Kurdish region. Hawrami lashed out at what he said was an "orchestrated" attempt to damage the KRG.[31] The regional government penalized the company by suspending its Kurdistan operations, and demanded compensatory measures to address reputation damage allegedly suffered by the KRG.[32] It even threatened that it "may consider termination of DNO's involvement in the Kurdistan region with or without compensation."[33] The dispute between the KRG and the Norwegian company was settled eventually. Still, the DNO affair has raised fresh concerns about business dealings in the Kurdish region, long plagued by allegations of official corruption. According to the Revenue Watch Institute, a U.S.-based organization that promotes responsible management of oil and gas resources, oil deals in Kurdistan "do not appear to us to meet the standards of transparency with regard to the terms or to who the actual contracting parties are."[34]

However, since new revelations have given this story a further twist, the scandal of the DNO is hardly over. Investigations conducted by Norway's most respected financial newspaper revealed that a third party was tasked to negotiate between the DNO and the KRG, which is related to the Tawke oil field in the Dohuk governorate. The interests of this third party were squeezed out when this deal was converted to a new contract in early 2008, and prompted a significant financial claim of approximately $500 million against DNO, which has yet to be settled. Of note, the "mystery stakeholder" involved in the claim was none other than Peter Galbraith, who allegedly held a 5 percent share in the oil deal within the Kurdish region.[35]

Galbraith, a former U.S. diplomat, with a Norwegian wife, and longtime advocate of Kurdish rights is the one who helped the Norwegian company to strike a deal with the KRG. He worked as an adviser to the Kurdish leaders during the constitutional negotiations in 2004–5. His advice was in harmony with the overambitious agenda of the Kurdish politicians, resulting in a divisive and highly controversial constitution that proved to be a factor for instability and conflict in new Iraq. The constitutional articles about natural resources that are biased in favor of the regional authority at the expense of the federal government seem to reflect a convergence of interests between what now appears to be the self-motivated business interests of Galbraith and the interests of the far-fetched Kurdish nationalism.

Galbraith reluctantly admitted his oil and financial interests in Iraqi Kurdistan, but he denied that these interests have anything to do with his advice to the Kurds regarding the Iraqi constitution. Still, his involvement in Iraqi oil came under severe criticism. Critics said he stood to gain financially from the political positions he was advocating, and that should have prompted him to make his business dealings public at the time.[36] Visser comments: "Galbraith, however, was always seen as 'Ambassador Galbraith,' the statesmanlike former diplomat whose outspoken ideas about post-2003 Iraq were always believed to be rooted in idealism and never in anything else. Instead, it now emerges, he wore several hats at the same time, and mixed his roles in ways that seem entirely incompatible with the capacity of an independent adviser on constitutional affairs."[37] A senior Kurdish government official states: "This guy was supposedly a friend of the Kurds, came to defend the Kurds, but for him to engage in business activities on the side like that, it is not nice, it is not proper."[38]

The many mysteries surrounding the activities of DNO are illustrations of how the KRG is running natural resources in the region. A former member of the politburo of the PUK indicates that no oil company operates in Kurdistan without paying commissions to party or regional-government officials.[39] However, the relationship between Kurdish politicians, oil, and corruption goes back to the 1990s when the Kurds played an instrumental role in the smuggling of Iraqi oil during the decade of international sanctions. Leezenberg states that while on the Iraqi government side, Saddam's son Uday was in control of this privatized smuggling; on the Kurdish side, Barzani's nephew Nechirwan, who was until recently the prime minister of the regional government, "appears to have steadily increased his control over the transit trade."[40]

There is, however, a strong tradition of cross-border smuggling in the north of Iraq. Smuggling has been the business of choice for the Kurds for a very long time. In fact, the control of the transit trade and smuggling was one of the crucial factors igniting the intra-Kurdish fighting for four years in the 1990s. This fighting stopped only when the UN program of oil for food allocated 13 percent of the receipts of this program to the Kurdish enclave, which meant in reality new corruption opportunities for the ruling Kurdish politicians.

It transpired in July 2010 that hundreds of millions of dollars in crude oil and refined products were smuggled from Iraqi Kurdistan to Iran, in contravention of international sanctions on Iran. The scale and organization of this operation is alarming. Hundreds of tankers, each with a capacity of at least 226 barrels, enter Iran every day. The operation is supported by an estimated 70 mini refineries, many of them unlicensed. Officials in the two ruling Kurdish parties and the KRG denied these accusations of smuggling. However, an electronic website run by the opposition Gorran posted an official document issued by the regional Ministry of Finance, which was acting upon instructions from the regional Ministry of Natural Resources, instructing customs officials to allow the fleet of tankers to cross the border with Iran without paying customs duties.[41]

A paper published by Gorran estimates that the revenues derived from this smuggling reach a level of $264 million a month, and these revenues do not reach the budget of the regional government.[42] A newspaper affiliated with the opposition Gorran, *Rozhnama*, published a story on July 20 claiming that the two ruling parties, KDP and PUK, have made millions of dollars from oil smuggling in Iraqi Kurdistan. In response, the KDP has filed a $1 billion defamation lawsuit, which is the biggest compensation request in the history of Iraqi journalism.[43]

A legislator from the Gorran opposition movement and member of the regional parliament's committee for industry, energy, and natural resources said: "I asked several questions to the regional minister of natural resources regarding the smuggling of oil and the revenues from these operations but I did not receive a single answer, and this in itself raises suspicions."[44] The questioned minister, Hawrami, enjoys a strong backing from the president of the Kurdish region, Barzani. The Kurdish legislator adds: "Kurdistan is like an island with no rule of law when it comes to oil." An oil specialist and founder of Iraqoilforum.com concurs: "They are running their own oil kingdom."[45]

NOTES

1. Hannah Allam, "Audit: Fraud Drained $1 Billion from Iraq's Defense Efforts," *Knight Ridder Newspapers*, August 11, 2005.

2. Ali A. Allawi, *The Occupation of Iraq: Winning the War, Losing the Peace* (New Haven, CT: Yale University Press, 2007), 365.

3. Ibid., 367–68.

4. Patrick Cockburn, "What Has Happened to Iraq's Missing $1bn?" *The Independent*, September 19, 2005.

5. Ibid.

6. Dexter Filkins, "Mystery in Iraq as $300 Million Is Taken Abroad," *New York Times*, January 22, 2005.

7. Ken Silverstein, T. Christian Miller, and Patrick J. McDonnell, "U.S. Contractor Slain in Iraq Had Alleged Graft," *Los Angeles Times*, January 20, 2005.

8. Solomon Moore, "Secret Iraqi Deal Shows Problems in Arms Orders," *New York Times*, April 13, 2008.

9. Radio Sawa, "Bolani: Talk on the Failure of Explosion Detectors Is Oriented against the Interior Minister," February 15, 2010, http://www.radiosawa.com/arabic_news.aspx?id=2169989.

10. "Fraud Probe Launched into £52m of Hand-Held Bomb Detectors Sold to Iraq That 'Do Not Work,' " *Daily Mail*, April 22, 2010, http://www.dailymail.co.uk/news/article-1267736/Fraud-probe-launched-52m-bomb-detectors-sold-Iraq-work.html.

11. Editorial, "Shock, Awe and Abracadabra," *New York Times*, February 1, 2010.

12. Nada Bakri, "In Iraq, Battling an Internal Bane," *Washington Post*, October 22, 2009.

13. Ned Parker, "Secret Prison Revealed in Baghdad," *Los Angeles Times*, April 19, 2010.

14. Parker, "Corruption Plays Key Role in Iraqi Justice," *Los Angeles Times*, June 29, 2009.

15. Robyn Dixon, "Culture of Corruption Haunts Iraqi Police Ranks," *Los Angeles Times*, May 8, 2003.

16. Bakri, "Eight Killed in Baghdad Jewel Heists," *Washington Post*, October 15, 2009.

17. Rod Nordland and Riyadh Mohammed, "In Bank Killings, High and Lows of Iraq Justice," *New York Times*, September 3, 2009; http://www.elaph.com/Web/Politics/2009/8/467461.htm.

18. Bilal A. Wahab, "How Iraqi Oil Smuggling Greases Violence," *Middle East Quarterly*, Fall 2006, http://www.meforum.org/article/1020.

19. Philippe Le Billon, "Corruption, Reconstruction and Oil Governance in Iraq," *Third World Quarterly* 26, no. 4–5 (2005): 693.

20. Ibid., 694.

21. Iraq Revenue Watch, "Oil Revenue Accountability in Iraq: Breaking the Resource Curse," Revenue Watch Briefing no. 5, February 2004, http://iraqrevenuewatch.org/reports/020304.shtml.

22. Allawi, *The Occupation of Iraq*, 360–61.

23. Ibid., 361.

24. Ibid., 359.

25. Richard A. Oppel Jr., "Iraq's Insurgency Is Running on Stolen Oil Profits," *New York Times*, March 16, 2008.

26. Robert F. Worth and James Glanz, "Oil Graft Fuels the Insurgency, Iraq and U.S. Say," *New York Times*, February 5, 2006.

27. Aram Roston and Lisa Myers, " 'Untouchable' Corruption in Iraqi Agencies," NBC News, July 30, 2007, http://www.msnbc.msn.com/id/20043428/.

28. Worth and Glanz, "Oil Graft Fuels"; Ellen Knichmeyer, "Graft Alleged in Iraq Oil Protection Effort," *Washington Post*, May 5, 2006.

29. Iraq Revenue Watch, "Audit Finds More Irregularities and Mismanagement of Iraq's Revenues," Review Watch Briefing no. 9, December 2004, http://www.iraqrevenuewatch.org/reports/120604.pdf; for more details on the various audit reports of the IAMB, see their website at http://www.iamb.info.

30. Sinan Salaheddin, "Iraq's Kurds Suspended Norwegian Oil Operations," ino.com, September 22, 2009, http://news.ino.com/headlines/?newsid=689658365687101.

31. Roula Khalaf, "Distrust Caps Kurdish Oil Exports," *Financial Times*, October 15, 2009.

32. Reider Visser, "Hassani Goes after Hawrami in the DNO Dispute," September 27, 2009, http://gulfanalysis.wordpress.com/2009/09/27/hassani-goes-after-hawrami-in-the-dno-dispute/.

33. Salaheddin, "Iraq's Kurds Suspended."

34. Khalaf, "Distrust Caps Kurdish."

35. Reidar Visser, "New DNO Revelations: While He Was Influencing the Shape of the Iraqi Constitution, Peter Galbraith Held Stakes in an Oilfield in Dahuk," October 10, 2009, http://historiae.org/galbraith.asp.

36. Roula Khalaf, Martin Sandbu, and Andrew Ward, "Galbraith Admits Kurdish Oil Interest," *Financial Times*, October 15, 2009.

37. Visser, "New DNO Revelations."

38. Sam Dagher, "Incremental Steps in Iraq to Let Kurdistan Oil Flow," *New York Times*, February 1, 2010.

39. Lennox Samuels, "The Myth of Kurdistan," *Newsweek*, March 23, 2009.

40. Michiel Leezenberg, "Iraqi Kurdistan: Contours of a Post-Civil War Society," *Third World Quarterly* 26, no. 4–5 (2005): 638.

41. Shirzad Shikhani, "Kurdish Opposition Publishes a Document on Allowing Oil Tanker to Cross the Borders without Paying Taxes,"*Asharq al-Awsat*, July 15, 2010.

42. Shikhani, "Regional Government of Kurdistan Calls for a Stop in Exporting Oil by Tankers," *Asharq al-Awsat*, July 21, 2010.

43. Journalistic Freedom Observatory, "Ruling Party Demands One Billion Dollars in Defamation Lawsuit," August 2, 2010, http://www.jfoiraq.org/newsdetails.aspx?back=1&id=719&page=.

44. Shikhani, "Gorran's Legislator Confirms Smuggling Oil from Kurdistan," *Asharq al-Awsat*, July 16, 2010.

45. Sam Dagher, "Smugglers in Iraq Blunt Sanctions against Tehran," *New York Times*, July 9, 2010.

14

Republic of Corruption

UNTOUCHABLE CORRUPTION

Relatively speaking, Iraq was not known as a country of corruption in earlier years. Despite the fact that a command economy naturally generates a high level of corruption, the deposed dictator minimized the problem. For example, as part of the omnipresent domination of the state over all aspects of society, the old regime monopolized corruption and restricted access to wealth and power, thereby limiting opportunities for corruption. Further, the dictator perceived any incidence of corruption as an act of challenging the regime, and utmost punishment was put in place. Specifically, in 1975 and 1976 the regime enacted Laws 8 and 52, which made receiving bribes and commissions punishable by death.[1] In addition, the economic prosperity of the 1970s helped minimize existing corruption.

However, extensive militarization, three devastating wars, and over a decade of stringent international economic sanctions changed the situation in Iraq for the worse. Deteriorating living standards resulting in the decimation of the middle class gradually led to widespread corruption. This corruption was also motivated by a decline in the capacity of the state during the 1990s. During this time the regime itself became highly corrupt and turned into a mafia-style rule where the president, his family, and his relatives engaged in high profiteering from oil smuggling and a flourishing black market. As such, corruption became uncontrollable in light of an increasingly narrowing social base of the regime. Aburish states: "Corruption was widespread, and Saddam would not and could not control it because that meant acting against his corrupt family, his primary source of support."[2]

Thus a legacy of pervasive corruption, though of recent creation, was inherited by the new regime in Iraq. However, for the new experience in the country to make real sense as the antithesis of the old experience, combating corruption should become the top priority. Sadly, reality took a different turn. Corruption became even more serious and the culture of corruption spiraled out of control. To be sure, corruption seems more prevalent during the transition from dictatorship. Whereas corruption was a social taboo in the past dictatorial regimes, cases of corruption are put under the limelight by free press and media in the new regime. Media attention to cases of graft tends to conflate levels of corruption, but this by no means precludes the seriousness of the problem.

According to Transparency International, Iraq was among the three most corrupted countries in the world during the period 2006–8. A slight improvement occurred in 2009 when Iraq became the fifth most corrupt country (out of 180 countries). The country rank for Iraq (176) came tied with the Sudan, but better than only Myanmar, Afghanistan, and Somalia. The corruption perception index for Iraq was only 1.5 (out of 10). This index remained the same during the year 2010, but the ranking of the country has dropped slightly, to 175, to become the fourth most corrupted country in the world. It is true that the index for the years 2009 and 2010 is a slight improvement from the index of 2008 (1.3), but this is still far behind the level of 2.2 and a country rank of 113 in 2003, the year of regime change.[3] While the Iraqi government acknowledges that a problem of corruption exists in Iraq, it nevertheless dismisses the figures of the international organization as sheer exaggerations.

Nonetheless, corruption, or the abuse of public roles or resources for private benefit, has grown in new Iraq like a fungus, touching almost every ministry and office. "We are seeing corruption everywhere in Iraq—in every ministry, in every governorate,"[4] is how the head of the antigraft agency described the situation in the country. A U.S. financial investigation from 2006 estimated that Iraqi government corruption could mount to $4 billion a year, equal to over 10 percent of the national income.[5] Petty corruption by lower-level government employees, who are looking out for their own survival in miserable living conditions, becomes widespread. Iraqis are expected to pay bribes for just about every government service. Even university students are purchasing pass or better grades at examinations.

Corruption also exists at the level of provincial and local councils. The outbreak of the cholera epidemic in 2008 was reportedly due to a failure to sterilize the local drinking water because Iraqi officials were bribed to buy chlorine from Iran that was long past its expiration date. The councilman involved in the chlorine contract, a member of the Babil city council, was released after a short arrest, thanks to his connections with the Islamic Supreme Council of Iraq, a powerful pro-Iran party.[6] In November 2009, a large-scale fraud in Baghdad city government occurred, where employees have stolen millions of dollars. Investigators found out that $20 million had been siphoned away by a gang cashing checks in the names of fake employees at a bank branch in city hall.[7]

The provincial council for Wasit has a different ingenuity. It issued a decision in October 2009 to appoint a *mahram* for every female member of the council. A mahram is a man who has a relationship that precludes marriage to his female relatives. The decision, which is officially motivated by reference to religion and tradition, states that the *mahrams* should get a monthly salary of 200,000 Iraqi dinars. Yet the same traditions that existed in the province before did not prevent women from going to job or school without accompanying male relatives. Though this decision has an unambiguous gender implication, it is a clear case of corruption because these mahrams are getting public money for unnecessary task.

In February 2010, two shipments of laptop computers arrived at Umm Qasr port in the south of Iraq. The 8,080 computers, worth $1.8 million, were a gift from the United States to the schoolchildren in Babil, modern-day Babylon. The American military has tracked them down and since April 2010 tried to clear them through customs but with no success. Instead, the computers have mysteriously disappeared from the port. Later investigations revealed that officials at the port auctioned off 4,200 of the laptops and sold them in August to a businessman from Basra for only $45,700. No officials could explain what happened to the rest of the computers. Iraqi officials said that investigation into this case has led to issuing arrest warrants for 10 customs employees, all low-level officials. Six were said to have been detained. Still, the suspects were not identified and no charges were made public. Reacting to this corruption case of stealing computers from Iraqi children, the head of the education committee in Babil's provincial council complained that government corruption was "bleeding the body of Iraq."[8]

Various ministries in the Iraqi government have become open empires of nepotism, corruption, and poor performance. It is no wonder that providing basic services to Iraqis is still an unachievable task even after almost eight years since regime change. Large-scale corruption by ministers and their relatives, particularly in lucrative international contracts, has reached an unprecedented level. Iraq Revenue Watch, an organization launched in May 2003 to monitor Iraq's oil industry and public finance, states that corruption had become an "open secret" within the Iraqi government, "that is the tragedy of Iraq: everyone runs their business like a private fiefdom."[9] Dawisha concurs: "Nor is it surprising that ministries become autonomous fiefdoms doing the bidding of ethnosectarian bosses and warlords, which they have done brazenly without trying to cover their tracks."[10]

The former minister of culture, As'ad al-Hashimi, was accused in 2007 of using his ministry as a torture house for opponents and a safe haven for religious extremists. He is accused of plotting a series of assassinations prior to and during his tenure in office. His death sentence became obsolete when he evaded arrest and fled the country.[11]

Lack of electricity is one of the strong factors causing a miserable living condition for ordinary Iraqis. The government has failed to provide a decent level of electricity services to its people, years after regime change. Part of the explanation is the high corruption at the Ministry of Electricity. In one case, $24.4 million was spent on an electricity project in Nineveh province in the north but an oversight agency found out that this project "existed only on paper."[12] Former electricity minister, Ayham al-Samarraie, is accused of overseeing more than $1 billion worth of improperly awarded contracts. He escaped from his Green Zone jail cell in December 2006 and fled to the United States where he also holds citizenship. Even in the United States his name has surfaced in connection with corruption trial of his old friend, Chicago real estate developer Tony Rezko. Federal prosecutors accused Rezko of bribing Samarraie to obtain an Iraqi electricity contract.[13]

A huge picture hanging at the front gate of the Ministry of Health removes any doubts about who runs the place. The photo is of the father and uncle of radical Shiite cleric Muqtada al-Sadr, whose the Mahdi Army militias control the ministry since 2005. By staffing the ministry with Sadrist loyalists, the then minister transformed the ministry into a fiefdom that belongs to his political faction and its militia. Under the influence of the Sadrist militias, Iraq's hospitals and clinics have been at the center of some of the country's worst sectarian violence. During the height of this violence in 2006, many Sunni patients avoided hospitals they knew were Shiite controlled, fearing they would be targeted by the Mahdi Army. Militia members frequently used ambulances to ferry around weapons instead of patients.[14]

The health ministry deputy, Hakim al-Zamili, played a leading role in transforming the ministry into a bastion of sectarian violence. He was arrested in early 2007 for allegedly funneling money to the militias, using the ministry's protection service as a private militia to kidnap and kill hundreds of Sunnis from 2005 to 2007, and using ambulances and hospitals to carry out the killings. He is the key suspect in the kidnapping and murder of his colleague, Ammar al-Saffar, who was also a deputy health minister and was gathering data on abuses at the ministry. Saffar vanished after telling associates that Zamili has threatened him. Zamili was freed after a two-day trial.[15]

Al-Sadr's control over Kimdia, the state-run company responsible for importing and distributing drugs and supplies to Iraqi hospitals, provided the Mahdi Army with a position of monopoly and a source of power for these militias. When one hospital challenged this monopoly by importing drugs on its own, the followers of al-Sadr planted a rumor that the drugs were infected with HIV, sending panic through the medical community.[16] The turmoil in the health sector and the deliberate targeting of professionals during the sectarian violence has forced most of the qualified doctors to leave the country.

Moreover, the militias' control over the health ministry provided them with an ample opportunity for profiteering and corruption. Medical supplies intended for the Ministry of Health were looted and sold by the Mahdi Army. Antigraft officials entered the ministry to conduct their investigations, but they were threatened with kidnapping so they stopped. The same threats against anticorruption officials have also occurred in the Ministry of Oil.[17] In June 2009, a fire started in the sixth and seventh floors of the Ministry of Health where documents and contracts of medicine imports are held. A significant part of these contracts were destroyed as a result of the fire, which also led to the destruction of six floors and the injury of 18 employees of the ministry. Many governmental offices, the Ministry of Oil for instance, witnessed similar incidences of fire, particularly when corruption investigations were ongoing.

In May 2007, at least 80 gunmen in police commando uniforms using a convoy of 19 land cruiser vehicles licensed to the Ministry of Interior stormed a heavily guarded Ministry of Finance complex just before noon, walked into the building, and kidnapped five Britons without firing a shot. The British were Peter Moore and his four bodyguards. Moore is a computer consultant working for an American company. He was employed to install a new computer tracking system that would have followed billions of dollars of oil and foreign aid money through the Ministry of Finance. The "Iraq Financial Management Information System" was nearly complete and about to go online at the time of the abduction. This system would have made it possible to reveal how the money of international aid to Iraqi institutions ends up in the hands of armed militias loyal to Iran.

The abduction was carried out by a splinter group of the Mahdi Army, called *Asa'ib al-Haq*, or the League of the Righteous. This group is linked to the Iranian Revolutionary Guards, which is accused of being behind the operation.[18] Investigations by the *Guardian* indicate that there is compelling evidence that this operation is connected to corruption within the Iraqi government. It reveals that there is strong evidence of collusion with Iraqi officials, particularly in the Ministries of Finance and Oil, in this operation, as the kidnapers knew which room they were heading to. At the time of the operation, a car carrying two Iraqi intelligence officers was parked just outside the building, and they were eyewitnesses to this kidnapping. Nevertheless, the following day, someone from the Ministry of Defense called the security intelligence and requested that they keep quiet and forget this subject forever, as if it did not happen at all.[19] Moore was held captive in Iran, but was released in December 2009 as part of a deal with the Iraqi government. The bodyguards, however, did not meet their families again; they were all killed.

The trade ministry oversees various imports including food staples, automobiles, and construction materials, and it also operates the food ration program. This program was established in the 1990s to distribute basic food to people during the years of international sanctions. It has survived regime change, and is accorded with an annual budget of $5–6 billion. For several years since 2005, the trade ministry faced serious accusations of corruption in the food ration program. When the ministry's inspector general raised some questions with the minister regarding allegations of corruption, he was reassigned to a post in China shortly thereafter. There was widespread public anger with people complaining that there were frequent shortages, only very few items out of the specified nine items were distributed, and most of the distributed food either was of poor quality or was expired and inedible. One merchant who is part of the network of agents for the distribution of this program admits: "People complain because the food they receive is not fit for human consumption."[20]

Corruption investigations have led to the allegation that the two brothers of the trade minister, who were employed by the minister himself as guards in the ministry, had skimmed millions of dollars in kickbacks on food imports. When antigraft officials went to the ministry to implement an arrest warrant on nine ministry officials, including the two brothers, the ministry's guards opened fire on the accompanying police force. The 15-minute gun battle allowed all the wanted employees but one, the ministry's spokesman, to escape out a back door. One of the brothers was eventually arrested in the south of the country carrying $150,000, $50,000 of which he offered to the arresting officers as a bribe to let him go free. The other brother is still at large.

The trade minister, Abdel Falah al-Sudani, who is from the ruling Shiite Da'wa Party, avoided facing the parliament to respond to corruption allegations. The legislators had been seeking to question him for more than a year, but the summons has never materialized. Yet when the legislators finally succeeded in summoning him in May 2009, he was uncooperative, denied the entire allegation against him, and refused to answer most of the questions put to him at the parliamentary session. Two big amounts, $18 million at the end of 2007 and $27 million at the start of 2008, were still unaccounted for.

He was forced to resign by the government when his case became an ugly embarrassment to the cabinet and the ruling party. A few days later, he was arrested when trying to flee the country to the United Arab Emirates. His plane was ordered back to Baghdad airport, and the minister was arrested on May 30, 2009. He was charged with embezzlement of public money, mismanagement of the trade ministry, employing his relatives including his two brothers, procuring substandard foodstuffs for the food ration program, and skimming millions out of the program. A member of the Iraqi parliament anticorruption committee estimates that the money skimmed from the program could amount to "hundreds of millions of dollars."[21] An Iraqi citizen cynically remarks: "It won't make a difference if they arrest him, because he's already smuggled all his money outside of Iraq."[22]

Under the pressure of this awkward scandal, Prime Minister Nuri al-Maliki pledged that the government will institute reforms and will search for the truth. He affirmed: "We will not remain silent over corruption after today. We will pursue those corrupt and bring them to justice."[23] Nonetheless, none of these promises were implemented. There were no reforms, no truth, and no justice in the aftermath of this outright scandal of corruption. The trade minister was not put on trial. Instead, he has threatened that in the event of a trial, he will disclose big secrets about corruption that could involve influential senior officials. There are reports that he was allowed to flee the country to the United Kingdom where he also holds citizenship.

Pernicious corruption takes many forms and modalities. The share of the annual budget that is allocated to the three presidential posts—the president, the prime minister, and the speaker of the parliament—reached a figure of $831 million in 2010 alone.[24] The president and his two deputies are each given $1 million a month as "social benefits." Much of this money ends up in the hands of supporters and cronies.

These practices are a continuation of the old policies of establishing and strengthening the authoritarian and rentier social contract and a system of patronage and favoritism. This kind of financial arrangement could easily become a source of high-level corruption, particularly when there is a weak and ineffective oversight institution. Moreover, hundreds of so-called advisers are working in the prime minister's and president's offices and in various Iraqi ministries. Although they receive lucrative salaries and benefits, they produce very little since their employment is done within a system of favoritism and patronage.

Furthermore, no closing financial statements for the annual national budgets have ever been made or published over recent years. Money is accorded, but no account on spending exists: how, where, and how much. Many ministers and legislators failed to submit their compulsory financial disclosure forms even after years in service. Some of the legislators, including some legislators from the Kurdish regional parliament, continued to receive social welfare and other social benefits for themselves and their families from their host countries of exile. Each legislator costs the Iraqi treasury $30,000 per month, including salary and security arrangement details for 30 bodyguards, not to mention a lifetime pension package of $7,200 per month that they can enjoy for serving just one term as legislators. At the end of 2009 and just two months before the end of their term, members of parliament unanimously voted for new benefits to convert into a grant the $60,000 loan each legislator had received to purchase a car. They also voted to give themselves and their families diplomatic passports valid for 10 years, and a piece of real estate.[25] These pieces of land are situated in one of the best locations in downtown Baghdad on the banks of the Tigris River. All former and current ministers secured similar grants of land.

In new Iraq, Kurdish politicians were able to secure the deal of allocating 17 percent of the annual Iraqi budget to their semi-independent northern region. This deal ensures that huge financial resources fall under the direct control of the two ruling parties in the northern region. In 2008, the Kurdish region received $6 billion, while in 2009 and 2010 the region's share reached an annual figure of about $9 billion. There are allegations that each of the two ruling parties takes as much as $35 million per month off the region's share of the national budget.[26] This means that almost a billion a year is directly appropriated by the two dominant parties. Officials deny these accusations but the annual budget of the Kurdish region remains an undisclosed mystery. Notwithstanding the huge revenues from Baghdad, popular grievances about corruption and poor services are rife. These complaints helped to give rise to the emergence of a viable political opposition for the first time in the region. The success of the opposition in the 2009 regional elections evidently shows to what extent discontent with official corruption is prevalent.

The power-sharing system that entails an equal division of governmental posts between the two leading Kurdish parties provides ample opportunities for corruption. These two parties run the region as if it was their own fiefdom. Most of the economic benefits go to companies owned or controlled by the clans of Barzani and Talabani. Businessmen have to pay bribes to party bureaucrats to win contracts. On this situation, the *Economist* writes: "Many Kurds have been disgusted by the extent to which people tied to the ruling clans, the Barzanis and the Talabanis, have lined their pockets. Despite regular elections since 1992, the two have acted in a quasi-feudal fashion, controlling a lion's share of business while also running security."[27] Rubin accentuates that corruption is rife in Kurdistan where few profitable businesses can operate without either silent partnership with or outright payment to the Barzani or Talabani families. "Barazani used the government budget as a family slush fund, for example donating hundreds of millions of dollars from public coffers to allow a relative to win a 2007 bid to operate an Iraq-wide cell phone company."[28]

Ordinary Kurdish citizens in the north of Iraq complain that corruption in the region is rife and jobs are few. They accuse the ruling parties of lack of accountability in the control they exert over almost all aspects of life, from appointments to lowly government jobs to multibillion-dollar deals.[29] A cell phone salesperson says: "We need change because there is corruption in the current government and there is cronyism."[30] Iraqi Kurdistan does not even benefit from the supervision and investigations of an antigraft commission as the rest of Iraq does. Stakes associated with the control of wealth and power makes Kurdish ruling politicians less interested in developing their own regional organization to combat extensive corruption. Meanwhile, monopolizing power and wealth by few tribal and authoritarian politicians plainly demonstrates that ethnic federalism can mostly function as a façade for chronic corruption.

Corruption in Kurdistan is an early experience in Iraq that points to the difficulty of escaping the trap of corruption in a time of political transition. On the contrary, corruption tends to increase because of political change as both the Kurdish and Iraqi experiences demonstrate.

COMBATING CORRUPTION AND POLITICS

The CPA issued Order 55 authorizing the establishment of the Commission on Public Integrity (CPI) on January 31, 2004, to enforce anticorruption laws and public service standards. The independent commission coordinates with two other pillars of antigraft institution: the Board of Supreme Audit was established by law in 1927, and inspectors general were appointed in every ministry as internal auditors. The head of CPI pointed out in 2007 that at least $8 billion allocated for reconstruction, military supplies, and food had disappeared.[31] Another antigraft official estimated that more than $13 billion meant for reconstruction projects in Iraq was wasted or stolen through elaborate fraud schemes; most of these projects were either not needed or never built, "ghost projects."[32]

According to CPI, corruption in the Iraqi government during the year 2010 exceeded $1 billion; 6,194 corruption charges were made in 2010, of which more than 2,500 were sent to judicial courts leading to guilty sentences against 709 officials, of which 75 officials were in the position of general director or above including 9 ministers. There are presently 1,437 officials serving prison sentences for corruption charges compared to only 148 condemned officials in 2007.[33] The CPI was also successful in sending 1,826 corruption cases to judicial courts during the period 2004–9, 889 in 2009 alone. The number of convicted persons during this period reached 692, 5 of which were former government ministers; 296 were convicted in 2009 alone.[34]

However, the activities of the CPI have been met with a stiff resistance from the government. Thirty-one of the investigators of the agency were assassinated. The head of the CPI, Radhi al-Radhi, who received repeated threats to his life, resigned and sought asylum in the United States. He too faces corruption charges, which he says are politically motivated because of his work to combat rampant graft in Iraqi government: "We have learned the hard way that the corrupt will stop at nothing. They are so corrupt that they will attack their accusers and their families with guns and meat hooks, as well as countercharges of corruption."[35]

Despite the official rhetoric of the government of al-Maliki on the need to conduct a campaign against corruption, similar to the campaign against terrorism and the militias, and the intention of making 2008 an antigraft year, corruption has been steadily increasing. The government itself proved to be the biggest obstacle in the fight against graft. The former head of the CPI underlines that the government lacks the political will or the capacity to root out corruption and accuses the government of deliberately thwarting corruption probes and protecting corrupt officials because of political pressure. He also stresses that the government works to undermine the independent status of the commission by trying to bring it under government control. In fact, the government invoked an old legal provision dating from 1971, Article 136B of the Criminal Procedures Code, to prevent the transmission of cases to the court "unless we received permission from the minister of the agency we were investigating; as for corrupt ministers, cases could not proceed without permission from the Prime Minister Maliki," according to Radhi.[36]

This old legislation was suspended by Paul Bremer when he established the integrity commission in 2004, but various Iraqi governments reinstated it. This law actually allows the prime minister to exempt cabinet ministers from prosecution and allows ministers to exempt their senior employees from antigraft actions. It encourages immunity from investigation and prosecution and offers a free pass for high-level corruption. About 3,000 suspected corruption cases went unprosecuted as a result of the reestablishment of this law. Moreover, there are allegations of favoritism and selective prosecution in the application of this legislation. Arbitrary application of this provision was unmistakable in an incident at the Ministry of Oil that implicated the Shiite minister and four other officials, three Shiites and one Sunni. The minister used this article to exempt the three Shiite officials from prosecution so that only the Sunni went to prison.[37] Apart from blatant corruption, the sectarian aspect of this case is quite evident.

It is a paradox that the new Iraqi regime, which is adamant about wiping out all legacies of the old regime and seems serious about eradicating all traces of Ba'thism, invoked this particular legislation from the era of Saddam Hussein. However, this paradox may make sense considering the new regime is turning the country into a republic of corruption. Specifically, the level of corruption in this country has become so widespread and pernicious that there is a need to initiate old legislation.

Corruption has reached an unprecedented and alarming level in new Iraq. An Iraqi citizen cautions: "With the current levels of corruption and embezzlement, I think that Iraq is heading to a total disaster."[38] Another citizen continues: "These seven years have made us go back a century because of corruption. We are not the first country invaded in a war, but we have a government that has accomplished nothing but corruption."[39] Zaid al-Ali concurs: "One thing is certain, however: the political class that is currently in control of Iraq, perhaps the most corrupt and incompetent that the country has ever seen."[40]

Indeed, the level of corruption and ineptitude that has characterized all governments ruling Iraq since regime change is totally astonishing.

Corruption and incompetence are strongly related. Incompetence is derived from placing the wrong people in governmental offices, a practice motivated by political loyalty rather than qualifications. Incompetence, which is a corrupt practice in itself, opens the door widely for corruption. Unqualified people cannot achieve goals or perform well, and the only thing left for them is to mismanage public office and funds for which they are responsible.

Indeed, the political system of power sharing tends to open a wide window for massive corruption because efficiency and capabilities are not regarded as serious considerations in the distribution of government offices. Power sharing tends to strengthen the personalization of governmental offices, which is corruption by itself. The personalization of offices leads to even more corruption because the public office is considered either a personal property or a "right" that belongs to the sect, ethnicity, or the party where the official belongs. This personalization comes at the expense of institutional changes and the establishment of a culture of institutions. A lack of a culture of institutions leads to deterioration in the functioning of the government, whether in the old or new Iraq, thereby exacerbating corruption.

However, the government always finds excuses to explain away its failure of combating graft. The insecurity and terrorism provide the government with a ready excuse for failing to focus on antigraft actions. An independent politician complains: "I don't see any difference between terrorists and corrupt people. Why are the authorities closing their eyes to corruption cases and focusing only on terrorism?"[41] The government adopts a rather narrow interpretation of how to solve the problem of terrorism and violence. It fails to see that violence and corruption are strongly intertwined. When Prime Minister Maliki fought the militias and stressed the slogan of the rule of law, his popularity increased, and this was reflected in his electoral success in the 2009 provincial elections. Yet when he failed to eventually match these slogans with a campaign to improve services and seriously combat corruption, his popularity plunged again. Providing basic services and fighting corruption are two imperatives for the rule of law. Rampant corruption is in fact a negation of the rule of law and a serious blow to the legitimacy of any government.

Sectarian and ethnic polarization since 2003 is implicated in the aggravation of corruption. The distribution of positions of responsibility in the administration is based on ethnic, sectarian, and partisan politics, rather than on qualifications and putting the right people in the right places. More seriously, this polarization functions as an obstacle in the fight against corruption. Any investigation on corruption is conveniently interpreted as an attack against the ethnicity, sect, or political party of the suspected individual. This situation thwarts any attempt at seriously dealing with problem. In fact, the government declared that the main reason for reinstating the Law of 136B is because it felt that "anti-corruption prosecutions were targeting on the basis of politics."[42] For more than three years (2006–8), the politicization of corruption and the general political paralysis, which came as a result of the adoption of power sharing, severely affected the work of the parliament, particularly in overseeing governmental actions. Despite widespread corruption, not a single government official was summoned before parliament during this period. The former speaker of parliament, a government ally, played a decisive role in this outcome.

However, the 2009 provincial elections had an impact on the political situation in the country with certain implications for corruption. The Shiite religious Fadhila Party who run the local government in Basra, where corruption was rife, lost the election. As a result, the legislators of the loser party became very outspoken against corruption in the parliament to punish the government and the Da'wa Party of the prime minister, who won the provincial election in Basra after fighting the militias that dominated and terrorized the city.

Moreover, the election of a new speaker in April 2009 opened the door for much questioning of ministers before the parliament, particularly the trade minister. Zaid al-Ali argues that this was considered as a declaration of war against the government, which soon retaliated by the assassination of a legislator, Harith al-Ubaidi, who is a close associate of the new speaker. With the election of the new speaker, al-Ali adds: "The floodgates were opened for the parliament to be used as a political weapon by the losers of the local elections against the winners. Therefore what many saw as a victory for parliamentary oversight and for government accountability was actually nothing more than a political vendetta, which will have no impact on the public wellbeing."[43] Thus the sudden reinvigoration of the oversight function of the parliament in its last year of mandate was mainly motivated by the results of the provincial elections, where the losers aimed to punish and embarrass the winners and made an attempt to regain popularity that was lost, ironically, because of high corruption.

Of all the issues covered in this work, corruption is the most difficult subject to research and write about. There are strong emotions involved in finding out how the wealth of the nation is misused for private gains when the country is submerged in destruction and poverty. The problem is not the absence of reports on corruption in new Iraq. On the contrary, the problem lies in the fact that there are plenty of reports, so many that the final analysis is very confusing. Everyone is talking about corruption, the government and the opposition alike, and each is accusing the other of corruption. This gives the impression that there is hardly anyone left who is uninvolved in this pervasive evil. There is an endless cycle of accusations and counteraccusations of graft.

This politicization of the oversight process or more precisely the politicization of the accusation of corruption tends to make reports on corruption highly unreliable. The highly charged and explicit debate on this issue seems to end up in a situation that supports rather than combats corruption. Although this situation is not necessarily created by top politicians and bureaucrats who are engaged in corruption, it helps their agenda of corruption very well. Under these circumstances, corruption becomes a ghost in the sense that one cannot be sure who is corrupt and who is not. Meanwhile, from another standpoint, the act of corruption itself is far from being a ghost; rather, it is real, alive, and ugly.

It is noteworthy that widespread corruption in Iraq coincides with the rise of political Islam. This raises the question of how representative of true Islam are the Islamist political parties. The ruling political Shiism in Iraq needs to combat seriously widespread corruption, in deeds not words. Unquestionably, the issue of corruption is a serious challenge for the new Iraqi experience. Corruption or the misallocation of public resources undermines economic growth, discourages foreign investment, and limits the resources available for infrastructure, employment, public services, and antipoverty programs. All of these are highly needed in a devastated country, such as Iraq.

Corruption is a continuation of the old social contract and state patronage that ensures loyalty and regime continuity through undemocratic means. It undermines the legitimacy and accountability of the government, and produces a wedge between the government and the people. Corruption contradicts the very basic principles of democracy by denying the rule of law and equal access to resources by all citizens of the country. A process that transforms the country from a republic of fear into a republic of corruption is hardly worth the name new Iraq. This process merely replaces one imposed suffering on the Iraqis with another. Unchecked corruption is an outright betrayal of the sufferings, aspirations, and dreams of the Iraqis, who certainly deserve a more honest political leadership and more decent standards of life.

NOTES

1. Said K. Aburish, *Saddam Hussein: The Politics of Revenge* (London: Bloomsbury, 2001), 109.

2. Ibid., 252.

3. Transparency International, "Corruption Perception Index," various years. http://www.transparency.org/policy_research/surveys_indices/cpi/2010/results; http://www.transparency.org/policy_research/surveys_indices/cpi/2009/cpi_2009_table.

4. Solomon Moore, "In Corruption, New Government of Iraq Faces a Tough Old Foe," *Los Angeles Times*, May 23, 2006.

5. BBC News, "Iraq Corruption 'Cost Billions,' " November 9, 2006, http://news.bbc.co.uk/go/pr/fr/-/2/hi/middle_east/6131290.stm.

6. Abbas Kadhim, "Iraq's Quest for Democracy amid Massive Corruption," *Arab Reform Bulletin*, March 3, 2010, http://www.carnegieendowment.org/arb/?fa=show&article=40278.

7. Reuters, "Iraq: Inquiry Begun on Municipal Fraud," *New York Times*, November 24, 2009.

8. Steven Lee Myers, "U.S. Gift for Iraqis Offers a Primer on Corruption," *New York Times*, September 25, 2010.

9. Dexter Filkins, "Mystery in Iraq as $300 Million Is Taken Abroad," *New York Times*, January 22, 2005.

10. Adeed Dawisha, "The Unraveling of Iraq: Ethnosectarian Preferences and State Performance in Historical Perspective," *Middle East Journal* 62, no. 2 (Spring 2008): 222.

11. Kadhim, "Iraq's Quest for Democracy."

12. Dana Hedgpeth, "$13 Billion in Iraq Aid Wasted or Stolen, Ex-Investigator Says," *Washington Post*, September 23, 2008.

13. CBS News, *60 Minutes*, "Iraq: State of Corruption," April 13, 2008, http://www.cbsnews.com/stories/2008/04/11/60minutes/main4009328.shtml.

14. Charles Levinson, "Sadrists' Grip on Iraqis' Health Care Takes Toll," *USA Today*, March 26, 2008, http://www.usatoday.com/news/world/iraq/2008-03-26-iraqnews_N.htm?csp=34.

15. Marc Santora and Michael R. Gordon, "Murky Candidacy Strokes Iraq's Sectarian Fears," *New York Times*, March 3, 2010.

16. Levinson, "Sadrists' Grip on Iraqis' Health."

17. CBS News, "Iraq: State of Corruption."

18. John Leland and Jack Healy, "Briton Kidnapped in 2007 Is Freed in Iraq," *New York Times*, December 31, 2009; "A Splinter of Briton's Kidnappers: Yes They Were Held in Iran," *Asharq al-Awsat*, January 1, 2010.

19. Meena Muhammed, Maggie O'Kane, and Guy Grandjean, "Iraqi Government Officials May Have Colluded in British Hostages' Kidnap," *The Guardian*, July 30, 2009; for a video link to the investigations by the *Guardian*:

http://www.guardian.co.uk/world/video/2009/jul/30/british-hostages-iraq
-govenment.

20. Timothy Williams and Abeer Mohammed, "Trade Official Quits as Iraq Continues Investigations," *New York Times*, May 25, 2009.

21. Liz Sly, "Ex-Trade Minister Arrested After Attempting to Flee Iraq," *Los Angeles Times*, May 31, 2009.

22. Nada Bakri, "Iraq's Ex-Trade Minister Is Detained in Graft Investigation," *Washington Post*, May 31, 2009.

23. Ibid.

24. Osama Mahdi, "The Three Iraqi Presidential Posts Get $831 million," *Elaph Electronic Newspaper*, January 26, 2010, http://www.elaph.com/Web/Economics/2010/1/527872.htm.

25. Kadhim, "Iraq's Quest for Democracy."

26. Lennox Samuels, "The Myth of Kurdistan," *Newsweek*, March 23, 2009.

27. "The Times They Are a-Changing," *The Economist*, July 28, 2009.

28. Michael Rubin, "Kurdish Leaders Are Drunk with Power," *Daily Star*, July 1, 2009, available at http://www.meforum.org/2172/kurdish-leaders
-drunk-with-power.

29. Antony Shadid, "Opposition Seeks Shift in Power as Iraqi Kurds Vote," *Washington Post*, July 26, 2009.

30. Sly, "Iraq Sees Large Turnout for Kurdistan Election," *Los Angeles Times*, July 26, 2009.

31. Nada Bakri, "Iraqi Leader Sees Fraud as a Top Worry," *Washington Post*, May 10, 2009.

32. Hedgpeth, "$13 Billion in Iraq."

33. Osama Mahdi, "Commission on Public Integrity: Condemning 9 Ministers and 66 General Directors," *Elaph Electronic Newspaper*, December 28, 2010, http://www.elaph.com/Web/news/2010/12/621122.html.

34. Commission on Public Integrity, "Annual Report for 2009," August 5, 2010, http://www.nazaha.iq/en_body.asp?field=news_en&id=189&page
_namper=e9.

35. Glenn Kessler, "Ex-Investigator Details Iraqi Corruption," *Washington Post*, October 5, 2007.

36. Ibid.

37. Aram Roston and Lisa Myers, " 'Untouchable' Corruption in Iraqi Agencies," NBC News, July 30, 2007, http://www.msnbc.msn.com/id/20043428/.

38. Robert H. Reid, "Ex-Iraqi Trade Minister Arrested for Graft," CBS News, May 30, 2009, http://www.cbsnews.com/stories/2009/05/30/iraq/main5050871.shtml

39. Riyadh Mohammed and John Leland, "In Heart of Iraq, a Plan to Revive the Pulse of a Central Artery," *New York Times*, December 30, 2009.

40. Zaid al-Ali, "Iraq: Face of Corruption, Mask of Politics," *Open Democracy*, July 2, 2009, http://www.opendemocracy.net/article/iraq-acts-on-corruption.

41. International Crisis Group, "Iraq's Provincial Elections: The Stakes," *Middle East Report* 82 (January 27, 2009): 9–10, http://www.crisisgroup.org/library/documents/middle_east__north_africa/iraq_iran_gulf/82_iraqs_provincial_elections__the_stakes.pdf.

42. Walter Pincus, "Shhh . . . There Is Corruption in Iraq," *Washington Post*, June 25, 2007.

43. Al-Ali, "Iraq: Face of Corruption."

Conclusion

Shortcuts are not always helpful, certainly not in the case of Iraq. A hasty war, leading to a hurried transfer of sovereignty, rushed empowerment of local autocratic elites, unproductive detachment, and speedy exit has made the American experiment in Iraq a pointless enterprise. When original reasons behind the war were proven false, democracy in Iraq remained the only "motive" capable of justifying the war. The U.S. administration, however, did not bother to ensure the realization of this vision, and opted instead to disengage prematurely and leave promptly. Even if the view about the wrong war in Iraq is granted, it is doubtful whether the new U.S. administration made things better by disengaging from Iraq and swiftly leaving the country. The entire endeavor has been allowed to degenerate into a situation where a wrong war was launched and the least costly remedy is departure. No one calls for a prolonged military presence, but responsible and serious commitment to the future of Iraq takes many forms. Regardless of what transpired earlier, Iraq—as a U.S. legacy—has already been created. The question is weather America wants a success story or a disastrous legacy in Iraq.

America's failed adventure in Iraq has serious repercussions for Iraq, the Middle East, and the United States itself. Although the decision to invade Iraq is associated with the Bush administration, the credibility of America is at stake. The failure to embrace democracy—or rather to accept an enforced democracy—leaves Iraq and the Middle East with revitalized authoritarianism, which is an unfortunate development for the citizens of the region who are paying much for being ruled by autocratic rulers. The reinforced authoritarian reality in the region, in turn, necessitates the elevation of security considerations in U.S. foreign policy in the area, a historically well-established yet unhelpful policy. The new supremacy of security considerations in the U.S. approach to the region is beneficial to the dominant authoritarian order but detrimental to the democratic prospects in this region.

The failure of Iraq to democratize appears to support the argument on the democratic deficit in the Arab world and the hopelessness of creating democracy in the region. This lends support to the Orientalist assumption that "what is good for us is not necessarily good for them." Democracy for us and dictatorship for them is accepted as a natural conclusion, and cultural relativism and essentializing differences become even more pronounced. After their long suffering and endurance, the Iraqis are left with the biggest disappointment as the nightmare of authoritarianism continues to dominate their lives, albeit with new players under different façades.

The case of Iraq will surely lead to the reconsideration of the policy of imposing democracy by external pressures or military intervention. Can we export democracy when the other side is not ready to import? Is it not true that imposing democracy externally reinforces passivity, which has been fed by decades of authoritarian depoliticization? How can we explain, otherwise, that 3 million Iraqis participate in one sectarian mourning ritual yet fail to initiate a single genuine demonstration against corruption and miserable services?

Moreover, it has been argued that the speedy exit of the Americans from Iraq will force the Iraqis to take their destiny in their hands and solve their problems. In reality, however, the gradual American distancing from Iraq did not improve things, and risks associated with the Iraqi experience have become even higher. The American retreat works to the advantage of ethno-sectarian autocratic politicians who are empowered, ironically, by the very American intervention. These politicians have shown an extraordinary level of selfishness at the expense of the interests of Iraqis who are supposed to be the real beneficiaries of this intervention. Notwithstanding the rhetoric of democracy in Iraq, the United States is back to the earlier policy of supporting dictators in the Middle East. As such, one of the significant lessons from this war, if there are lessons learned at all, is that the Iraqis should stop waiting for miracles and force themselves to confront their ugly and violent legacy, including the newly added legacy of U.S. intervention in their affairs.

The Iraq war and regime change in 2003 represent a real opportunity to forge a new experience that can delink Iraq from its ugly past and orient the country toward a prosperous future. Yet it appears to be the case that having an opportunity is one thing while seizing that opportunity to enforce desirable changes is something else. There is a gap between the mere existence of an opportunity and the actual exploitation of that opportunity for a desirable outcome. As this book shows, the development of Iraqi politics since 2003 indicates that the Iraqis have, disappointedly, failed to bridge that gap, at least until now. While there is still hope for the case of Iraq, the window of opportunity seems to be narrowing as time goes by. One of the main serious problems in the so-called new Iraq is that building the new political experience is entrusted to a political class that is the product of the old, violent Iraq. The Iraqi experience clearly shows that democracy cannot be built without the existence of an enlightened elite who truly believe in democratic values.

Instead, Iraq followed a rather familiar Middle Eastern pattern of using the mechanism of elections to project a façade of democracy. Dubious elections and illusionary democracy tend to strengthen, rather than dismantle, the authoritarian order that still stubbornly dominates the region. Illusionary democracy is manifested in the adoption of consociation and consensual power sharing, in total disregard of earlier failed experiences with this form of political arrangement, such as those of Lebanon and Iraqi Kurdistan. Power sharing is a continuation of the old authoritarian process of depoliticization that comes at the expense of developing real democratic politics. Engineering a new Iraq as a country of ethnic and sectarian communities rather than as a society of citizens contravenes the proclaimed objective of establishing democracy in Iraq, whether from the Americans or Iraqi elites. Confessionalism and identity politics tend to serve the narrow sectarian, ethnic, and personal interests of the dominant political elites. Yet this politics is detrimental to the interests of the majority of the Iraqis, as the new experience of Iraq would evidently demonstrate.

Another serious problem in the new Iraq is that the new experience is built on politics of victimization. This book questions and challenges the contention that victimization can lead to a tolerant and democratic Iraq. On the contrary, politicized victimhood can only feed a vicious and destructive cycle of violence and revenge. It is no wonder, then, that the list of new victims in Iraq is rather extensive, and the oppression of women and minorities is only part of this long list. Apart from

serving certain elitist interests, victimization politics becomes the
rationale that has motivated Iraqi politics since 2003.

This politics of victimization can explain the revengeful campaign
of uprooting the Ba'thists, deficient and flawed justice and trials, ethnic and separatist federalism, drafting of a highly controversial and
destabilizing constitution, and destructive identity politics that dominate Iraqi politics in the "new Iraq." Victimization politics is well illus-
trated in the fact that the new Iraq has become a republic of
corruption, in the sense that it is now the turn of the victims of the
old regime to "benefit" from the wealth of Iraq. This victimization
based "entitlement" is not confined to corruption only but extends to
the "legitimate" entitlement of ruling the country as well. This is,
rather, a deceptive legitimacy, as real legitimacy is strongly related to
the electoral delivery and respect of democratic values, both of which
the ruling and dominant elites are failing to provide.

There is a familiar saying in the Middle East: "Cairo writes, Beirut
prints, and Baghdad reads." No doubt, this saying conveys a positive
image about Iraqi passion for reading and portrays Iraq as a nation
of avid readers. The Iraqis often cite this saying and seem to take a
deserved pride in this reputation. Nevertheless, one still wonders
why all this reading did not help Iraq to progress, or at least to prevent
the country from degenerating into the current undesirable, if not miserable, situation. Why has the knowledge acquired through reading
not helped Iraq to find the best and the most constructive solutions
to its many problems? Why has this knowledge not been accumulated
into much needed wisdom that could have helped Iraq to develop into
a more peaceful and meaningful way?

Alternatively, perhaps the question should rather be what material
are the Iraqis reading, or possibly, even more importantly, what
material are the Iraqis not reading? Surely, what is, and what is not,
on the reading lists for the Iraqis depends on the level of liberty and
freedom that dominates the political life in Iraq. The authoritarian
politics that dominated the recent history of Iraq leaves little room
for intellectual freedom in the country. Yet intellectual creativity also
depends on a set of political, social, and cultural values that condition
the social existence, where many of these norms fail to be forward-
looking or tolerant. The new Iraq is supposed to challenge and recon-
sider many of these values and norms.

Despite the affirmative meaning of this saying, an alternative reading might imply a negative interpretation. Indisputably, reading is
good, but why should this be at the expense of doing other intellectual

activities too? Why does Baghdad not research, write, or publish? Why has the curiosity that is associated with reading not induced the Iraqis to be more involved in researching and writing? The Iraqis are missing a lot by not venturing into the highly creative activities of researching, writing, and publishing. Francis Bacon once said: "Reading makes a full man; conference a ready man; and writing an exact man." It is, perhaps, this exact man that seems to be missing in Iraq. The exactness of the writing process is an entirely different experience from reading or conversation. To be precise, to call things by their proper names is what the political process, whether old or new, needs in Iraq. Writing teaches people patience, tolerance, moderation, and clarity, all of which are great, yet missed out on, values that are helpful for the country.

As in the rest of the Middle East, research is neglected in Iraq. In preparing for my earlier book on gender and violence in the Middle East, I was bitterly shocked to discover how little research was conducted on gender in Iraq, even compared with other countries in the region. Despite the long history of violence and the strong impact of violence on the Iraqi society, there is little research in this area, and there is no research center in Iraq established to focus on the issue of violence. The same is true about gender, reconciliation, militarization, and oil, despite the importance of these issues to Iraq's future. Researching on these issues and writing about them is an important aspect of any new experience.

The lack of research and writing and the separation between politics and academia can perhaps explain the degeneration of Iraqi politics into rhetorical politics, instead of real politics. It also explains the poorness, if not the absence, of political programs being advanced by political parties, particularly when competing in elections. A serious and responsible political program needs well-established research centers and intellectual debates through research and writing, which are still lacking in Iraq, despite the seriousness of the challenges this country faces. The lack of research and knowledge about the country is perhaps one of the fundamental reasons behind the many problems and contradictions that characterize the American enterprise of regime change and the experience of building a new democratic Iraq. It has been argued that Americans do not understand the reality of Iraq. The question is whether the Iraqis themselves understand their reality, given the miserable intellectual atmosphere dominating Iraqi society.

The ugly and violent past of Iraq requires objective scrutinizing and learning real lessons that can help Iraq cut the road toward any

reoccurrence of its undesirable legacy. This entails a serious attention
to the centrality of violence in the country. This societal violence must
be placed into a broad economic, political, religious, gender, and cultural context. Likewise, the future of Iraq stipulates facing the challenges of globalization. It is in the interest of Iraq to depart from
recent Middle Eastern patterns of conflict with the outside world and
opt instead for constructive engagement with the international community based on mutual interests. A positive incorporation into the
international community could be a way out of the violent, futile,
and unproductive identity politics and conspiracy theories that dominate the Middle East. One can even argue that the success of Iraq in
facing the challenges of peaceful and fruitful integration with the
global and dynamic world will perhaps eventually turn the country
into a veritable new Iraq.

The totally uncompromising violent and ruthless character of the
previous regime, its strict control over knowledge and access to
knowledge, the overall lack of expression of opinion, wars and sanctions, and constant conflicts with the international community have
all contributed to the reality that the Iraqi society is less researched
and hence less understood. Yet we still wonder whether this is the
whole story and whether the Iraqis themselves are to blame. It is high
time to take the Iraqi passion for reading one step further, in the direction of establishing a society not only of fervent readers but also of
curious researchers and enthusiastic writers. This makes sense, considering the formidable challenges confronting Iraq at this juncture.

This book has perhaps succeeded, if there is any success at all, in
raising more questions than answers. These questions are only a small
part of the many open questions that await scrutiny and examination,
leading in turn to further questions and inquiries. In so doing, a cycle
of questioning and investigations is established. This possible creative
cycle is a good and desirable alternative to the old cycle of victimization and violence that destroyed and is still destroying Iraq. By establishing this new cycle of creativity, knowledge, and conscientiousness,
a new Iraq will soon genuinely make sense.

Selected Bibliography

Abdullah, Thabit A. J. *A Short History of Iraq*. Harlow, UK: Pearson, 2003.

Aburish, Said K. *Saddam Hussein: The Politics of Revenge*. London: Bloomsbury, 2001.

Albon, Mary. "Project on Injustice in Time of Transition." In *Transitional Justice: How Emerging Democracies Reckon with Former Regimes*. Vol. 1, *General Considerations*, edited by Neil J. Kritz. Washington, DC: Institute of Peace Press, 1995.

Ali, Nadje al, and Nicola Pratt. *What Kind of Liberation? Women and the Occupation of Iraq*. Berkeley: University of California Press, 2009.

Ali, Nadje al, and Nicola Pratt. "Women in Iraq: Beyond the Rhetoric." *Middle East Report* 239 (Summer 2006).

Ali, Zaid al. "Iraq: Face of Corruption, Mask of Politics." *Open Democracy* (July 2, 2007). http://www.opendemocracy.net/article/iraq-acts-on-corruption.

Ali, Zaid al. "Iraq: A Constitution or an Epitaph?" *Open Democracy* (August 16, 2005). http://opendemocracy.net/conflict-iraq/constitution_2757.jsp.

Allawi, Ali A. *The Occupation of Iraq: Winning the War, Losing the Peace*. New Haven, CT: Yale University Press, 2007.

Arendt, Hannah. *On Violence*. New York: Harcourt, Brace and World, 1969.

Arendt, Hannah. *The Human Condition*. Chicago: University of Chicago Press, 1998 [1958].

Atiyyah, Ghassan. "Wanted in Iraq: A Roadmap to Free Elections." *Open Democracy*, October 16, 2003. http://www.opendemocracy.net/conflict-iraqivoices/article_1541.jsp.

Basham, Patrick. "Can Iraq Be Democratic?" *Policy Analysis* 505 (January 5, 2004).

Batatu, Hanna. *The Old Social Classes and the Revolutionary Movements of Iraq: A Study of Iraq's Old Landed and Commercial Classes and of Its Communists, Ba'thists and Free Officers.* London: Saqi, 2004 [1978].

Bhutta, Nehdal. "Judging Dujail: The First Trial before the Iraqi High Tribunal." *Human Rights Watch* 18, no. 9 (November 2006). http://www.hrw.org/en/reports/2006/11/19/judging-dujail.

Billon, Philippe Le. "Corruption, Reconstruction and Oil Governance in Iraq." *Third World Quarterly* 26, no. 4–5 (June 2005).

Bouillon, Markus E., David M. Malone, and Ben Rowswell, eds. *Iraq: Preventing a New Generation of Conflict.* Boulder, CO: Rienner, 2007.

Brancati, Dawn. "Can Federalism Stabilize Iraq?" *The Washington Quarterly* 27, no. 2 (Spring 2004).

Brown, Nathan J. "The Final Draft of the Iraqi Constitution: Analysis and Commentary." Carnegie Endowment for International Peace, September 2005, http://www.carnegieendowment.org/files/FinalDraftofIraqiConstitution1.pdf.

Bruade, Joseph. *The New Iraq.* New York: Basic Books, 2003.

Bunton, Martin. "From Developmental Nationalism to the End of Nation-State in Iraq?" *Third World Quarterly* 29, no. 3 (2008).

Buruma, Ian. "The Joys and Perils of Victimhood." *The New York Review of Books* 46, no. 6 (April 8, 1999).

Byman, Daniel. "Constructing a Democratic Iraq: Challenges and Opportunities." *International Security* 28, no.1 (2003).

Byman, Daniel, and Kenneth M. Pollack. "Democracy in Iraq?" *The Washington Quarterly* 26, no. 3 (Summer 2003).

Cameron, David. "Making Federalism Work." In *Iraq: Preventing a New Generation of Conflict*, ed. Markus E. Bouillon, David M. Malone and Ben Rowswell. Boulder, CO: Rienner, 2007.

Cammett, Melani. "Democracy, Lebanese-Style." Middle East Research and Information Project, August 18, 2009, http://www.merip.org/mero/mero081809.html.

Clawson, Patrick. "Iraq for the Iraqis: How and When." *Middle East Quarterly* (Spring 2004).

Coleman, Isobel. "Women, Islam and the New Iraq." *Foreign Affairs* 85, no. 1 (January–February, 2006).

Davis, Eric. *Memories of State: Politics, History, and Collective Identity in Modern Iraq.* Berkeley: University of California Press, 2005.

Dawisha, Adeed. "Democratic Attitudes and Practices in Iraq, 1921–1958." *Middle East Journal* 59, no.1 (Winter 2005).

Dawisha, Adeed. *Iraq: A Political History from Independence to Occupation.* Princeton, NJ: Princeton University Press, 2009.

Dawisha, Adeed. "Iraq: Setbacks, Advances, Prospects." *Journal of Democracy* 15, no. 1 (January 2004).

Dawisha, Adeed. "The New Iraq: Democratic Institutions and Performance." *Journal of Democracy* 16, no. 3 (July 2005).

Dawisha, Adeed. "The Prospects for Democracy in Iraq: Challenges and Opportunities." *Third World Quarterly* 26, no. 4–5 (2005).

Dawisha, Adeed. "The Unraveling of Iraq: Ethnosectarian Preferences and State Performance in Historical Perspective." *Middle East Journal* 62, no. 2 (Spring 2008).

Dawisha, Adeed, and Larry Diamond. "Iraq's Year of Voting Dangerously." *Journal of Democracy* 17, no. 2 (April 2006).

Diamond, Larry. "Building Democracy after Conflict: Lessons from Iraq." *Journal of Democracy* 16, no. 1 (January 2005).

Dodge, Toby. "Iraqi Transitions: From Regime Change to State Collapse." *Third World Quarterly* 26, no. 4–5 (2005).

Dodge, Toby. "State Collapse and the Rise of Identity Politics." In *Iraq: Preventing a New Generation of Conflict*, ed. Markus E. Bouillon, David M. Malone, and Ben Rowswell. Boulder, CO: Rienner, 2007.

Dodge, Toby, and Steven Simon, eds. *Iraq at the Crossroads: State and Society in the Shadow of Regime Change*. New York: Oxford University Press, 2003.

Dworkin, Anthony. "The Trial of Milosevic: Global Law or War." *Open Democracy*, February 13, 2002. http://www.opendemocracy.net/conflict-yugoslavia/article_203.jsp.

Dworkin, Anthony. "The Trials of Global Justice." *Open Democracy*, June 15, 2005, http//www.opendemocracy.net/globalization-institutions_governemnt/war_crimes_2604.jsp.

Elster, Jon. "On Doing What One Can: An Argument against Post-Communist Restitution and Retribution." In *Transitional Justice: How Emerging Democracies Reckon with Former Regimes*. Vol. 1, *General Considerations*, ed. Neil J. Kritz. Washington, DC: Institute of Peace Press, 1995.

Entessar, Nader. "The Kurds in Post-Revolutionary Iran and Iraq." *Third World Quarterly* 6, no. 4 (October 1984).

Farouk-Sluglett, Marion, and Peter Sluglett. *Iraq Since 1958: From Revolution to Dictatorship*. London: Tauris, 2003.

Feldman, Noah. *What We Owe Iraq: War and the Ethics of Nation Building*. Princeton, NJ: Princeton University Press, 2004.

Galbraith, Peter W. *The End of Iraq: How American Incompetence Created a War without End*. New York: Simon and Shuster, 2007.

Galbraith, Peter W. "Kurdistan in a Federal Iraq." In *The Future of Kurdistan in Iraq*, ed. Brendan O'Larry, John McGarry, and Khaled Salih. Philadelphia: University of Pennsylvania Press, 2005.

Gat, Moshe. *The Jewish Exodus from Iraq 1948–1951*. London: Frank Cass, 1997.

Ghanim, David. *Gender and Violence in the Middle East*. Westport, CT: Praeger, 2009.

Ghanim, David. "Turkish Democracy and Political Islam." *Middle East Policy* 16, no. 1 (winter 2009).

Goldberg, Jeffrey. "After Iraq." *Atlantic Monthly,* January–February 2008.

Haysom, Nicholas. "Forging an Inclusive and Enduring Social Contract." In *Iraq: Preventing a New Generation of Conflict*, ed. Markus E. Bouillon, David M. Malone, and Ben Rowswell. Boulder, CO: Rienner, 2007.

Hiltermann, Joost R. "Kirkuk as a Peacebuilding Test Case." In *Iraq: Preventing a New Generation of Conflict*, ed. Markus E. Bouillon, David M. Malone, and Ben Rowswell. Boulder, CO: Rienner, 2007.

Hiltermann, Joost R. "To Protect or to Project?" *Middle East Report* 247 (Summer 2008). http://www.merip.org/mer/mer247/hiltermann.html.

Hiro, Dilip. *Iraq: A Report from the Inside.* London: Granta Books, 2003.

Human Rights Watch. "On Vulnerable Ground: Violence against Minority Communities in Nineveh Province's Disputed Territories." November 10, 2009. http://www.hrw.org/sites/default/files/reports/iraq1109 webwcover.pdf.

Humphrey, Michael. *The Politics of Atrocity and Reconciliation: From Terror to Trauma.* London: Routledge, 2002.

Huyse, Luc. "Justice after Transition: On the Choices Successor Elites Make in Dealing with the Past." In *Transitional Justice: How Emerging Democracies Reckon with Former Regimes*. Vol. 1, *General Considerations*, ed. Neil J. Kritz. Washington, DC: Institute of Peace Press, 1995.

International Crisis Group. "Iraq's Provincial Elections: The Stakes." *Middle East Report* 82 (January 27, 2009). http://www.crisisgroup.org/library/ documents/middle_east_north_africa/iraq_iran_gulf/82_iraqs_provincial _elections_stakes.pdf.

Jabar, Faleh A. *The Shi'ite Movement in Iraq.* London: Saqi, 2003.

Jabar, Faleh A., and Hisham Dawood, eds. *Naqd al-Dustur* [A Critique to the Constitution]. Baghdad and Beirut: Iraq Institute for Strategic Studies, 2006.

Khayyat, Sana al. *Honour and Shame: Women in Modern Iraq.* London: Saqi, 1990.

Kiss, Elizabeth. "Moral Ambition within and beyond Political Constraints: Reflection on Restorative Justice." In *Truth v. Justice: The Morality of Truth Commissions*, ed. Robert I. Rotberg and Dennis Thompson. Princeton, NJ: Princeton University Press, 2000.

Kritz, Neil J., ed. *Transitional Justice: How Emerging Democracies Reckon with Former Regimes.* Vol. 1, *General Considerations*. Washington, DC: Institute of Peace Press, 1995.

Leezenberg, Michiel. "Iraqi Kurdistan: Contours of a Post-Civil War Society." *Third World Quarterly* 26, no. 4–5 (2005).

Luizard, Pierre-Jean. "The Nature of Confrontation between the State and *Mar-ja'ism*: Grand Ayatollah Muhsin al-Hakim and the Ba'th." In *Ayatollahs, Sufis and Ideologues: State, Religion and Social Movements in Iraq*, ed. Faleh Abdul-Jabar. London: Saqi, 2002.

Lukitz, Liora. *Iraq: The Search for National Identity.* London: Frank Cass, 1995.

Lukitz, Liora. "Nationalism in Post-Imperial Iraq: The Complexities of Collective Identity." *Critical Review* 21, no. 1 (2009).

Mackey, Sandra. *The Reckoning: Iraq and the Legacy of Saddam Hussein.* New York: Norton, 2002.

Maier, Charles S. "Overcoming the Past?" In *Politics and the Past: On Repairing Historical Injustices*, ed. John Torpey. Lanham, MD: Rowman and Littlefield, 2003.

Makiya, Kanan. *Cruelty and Silence: War, Tyranny, Uprising, and the Arab World.* New York: Norton, 1993.

Makiya, Kanan. "A Model for Post-Saddam Iraq." *Journal of Democracy* 14, no. 3 (2003).

Makiya, Kanan. *Republic of Fear: The Politics of Modern Iraq.* Berkeley: University of California Press, 1998 [1989].

Mani, Rama. *Beyond Retribution: Seeking Justice in the Shadow of War.* Cambridge: Polity, 2002.

Marr, Phebe. "Iraq's Identity Crisis." In *Iraq: Preventing a New Generation of Conflict*, ed. Markus E. Bouillon, David M. Malone, and Ben Rowswell. Boulder, CO: Rienner, 2007.

Marr, Phebe. *The Modern History of Iraq.* 2nd ed. Boulder, CO: Westview, 2004.

McDowall, David. *A Modern History of the Kurds.* 3rd ed. London: Tauris, 2004.

McGarry, John. "Liberal Consociation and Conflict Management." In *Iraq: Preventing a New Generation of Conflict*, eds. Markus E. Bouillon, David M. Malone, and Ben Rowswell. Boulder, CO: Rienner, 2007.

Miller, John, and Aaron Kenedi, eds. *Inside Iraq.* New York: Marlowe and Company, 2002.

Minow, Martha. "Breaking the Cycles of Hatred." In *Breaking the Cycles of Hatred: Memory, Law and Repair*, ed. Martha Minow. Princeton, NJ: Princeton University Press, 2002.

Minow, Martha. "The Hope of Healing: What Can Truth Commissions Do?" In *Truth v. Justice: The Morality of Truth Commissions*, ed. Robert I. Rotberg and Dennis Thompson. Princeton, NJ: Princeton University Press, 2000.

Munson, Peter J. *Iraq in Transition: The Legacy of Dictatorship and the Prospect for Democracy.* Dulles, VA: Potomac Books, 2008.

O'Larry, Brendan. "Federalizing National Resources." In *Iraq: Preventing a New Generation of Conflict*, ed. Markus E. Bouillon, David M. Malone, and Ben Rowswell. Boulder, CO: Rienner, 2007.

O'Larry, Brendan, John McGarry, and Khaled Salih, eds. *The Future of Kurdistan in Iraq.* Philadelphia: University of Pennsylvania Press, 2005.

Opgenhaffen, Veerle, and Hanny Megally. "Saddam's Trial: The Needs of Justice." *Open Democracy*, October 19, 2005. http://www.opendemocracy.net/globalization-institutions_governemnt/trial_saddam_2940.jsp.

Perito, Robert. "Establishing the Rule of Law in Iraq." United States Institute of Peace, Special Report 104, April 2003. http://www.usip.org/files/resources/sr104.pdf.

Posner, Eric. "The Politics of Saddam's Trial." *Open Democracy,* October 31, 2005. http://www.opendemocracy.net/globalization-institutions_government/saddam_trial_2977.jsp.

Rahimi, Babak. "Ayatollah Sistani and the Democratization of Post-Ba'athist Iraq." United States Institute of Peace, Special Report 187, June 2007. http://usip.org/files/resources/sr187.pdf.

Rotberg, Robert I., and Dennis Thompson, eds. *Truth v. Justice: The Morality of Truth Commissions.* Princeton, NJ: Princeton University Press, 2000.

Schwartz, Herman. "Lustration in Eastern Europe." In *Transitional Justice: How Emerging Democracies Reckon with Former Regimes.* Vol. 1, *General Considerations,* ed. Neil J. Kritz. Washington, DC: Institute of Peace Press, 1995.

Shriver, Donald W., Jr. "The Long Road to Reconciliation: Some Moral Stepping-Stones." In *After the Peace: Resistance and Reconciliation,* ed. Robert L. Rothstein. Boulder, CO: Rienner, 1999.

Simon, Reeva Spector. *Iraq between the Two World Wars: The Militarist Origins of Tyranny.* Updated edition. New York: Columbia University Press, 2004 [1986].

Simons, Geoff. *Iraq: From Sumer to Post-Saddam.* 3rd ed. Houndmills, UK: Palgrave Macmillan, 2004.

Sissons, Miranda. "Iraq's New 'Accountability and Justice Law'." International Center for Transitional Justice, January 22, 2008. http://www.ictj.org/images/content/7/6/764.pdf.

Sissons, Miranda, and Ari Bassin. "Was the Dujail Trial Fair?" *Journal of International Criminal Justice* 5 (2007).

Somer, Murat. "Failure of the Discourse of Ethnicity: Turkey, Kurds, and the Emerging Iraq." *Security Dialogue* 36, no. 1 (March 2005).

Stansfield, Gareth. "Governing Kurdistan: The Strengths of Division." In *The Future of Kurdistan in Iraq,* ed. Brendan O'Larry, John McGarry, and Khaled Salih. Philadelphia: University of Pennsylvania Press, 2005.

Stansfield, Gareth, and Hashem Ahmadzadeh. "Kurdish or Kurdistanis? Conceptualising Regionalism in the North of Iraq." In *An Iraq of Its Regions: Cornerstones of a Federal Democracy?,* ed. Reidar Visser and Gareth Stansfield. New York: Columbia University Press, 2008.

Teitel, Ruti G. *Transitional Justice.* New York: Oxford University Press, 2000.

Torpey, John, ed. *Politics and the Past: On Repairing Historical Injustices.* Lanham, MD: Rowman and Littlefield, 2003.

Tripp, Charles. *A History of Iraq.* 2nd ed. Cambridge: Cambridge University Press, 2002.

Visser, Reidar, and Gareth Stansfield, eds. *An Iraq of Its Regions: Cornerstones of a Federal Democracy?* New York: Columbia University Press, 2008.

Wahab, Bilal A. "How Iraqi Oil Smuggling Greases Violence." *Middle East Quarterly,* Fall 2006.

Wardi, Ali al. *Lamahat ijtima'iya min ta'rikh al-iraq al-hadith* [Social Aspects from Modern Iraqi History]. 6 vols. Baghdad: n.a., 1969–79.

Wimmer, Andreas. "Democracy and Ethno-Religious Conflict in Iraq." *Survival* 45. no. 4 (winter 2003–4).

Yapp, M. E. *The Near East since the First World War.* 2nd ed. Essex, UK: Longman, 1996.

Zakaria, Fareed. "Rise of Illiberal Democracy." *Foreign Affairs* 76, no. 6 (November–December 1997).

Zubaida, Sami. "Contested Nations: Iraq and the Assyrians." *Nations and Nationalism* 6, no. 3 (2000).

Zubaida, Sami. "Democracy, Iraq and the Middle East." *Open Democracy,* November 18, 2005. http://www.opendemocracy.net/democracy-opening/iraq_3042.jsp.

Index

Abbadi, Imad, 14
Abu Nawas Street, 154
Aburish, Said K., 65, 181, 184, 213
Academic research, 235, 236
Afghanistan, 42, 214
Ahrar, 122
Albon, Mary, 77
Algiers Agreement, 152
Ali, Nadje al., and Nicola Pratt, 5, 44, 164
Ali, Zaid al., 164, 223, 225
Allawi, Ali, 203
Allawi, Ayad, 72, 121, 123, 145, 150, 198
Alusi, Mithal al., 81, 144
American: adventure in Iraq, 7, 62, 67, 231; authority in Iraq, 107; occupation, 55, 80, 109
Amin, Rizgar, 98
Amnesty International, 108
Anfal, 100, 101
Apology, culture of, 179–81
Arab Journalists Union, 111
Arab Lawyers Union, 112
Arab world, the, 41, 43, 93, 96, 106, 108, 111–12
Arabization, 34, 181, 182, 187
Arabs, 35, 93, 96, 130, 135, 136, 169, 170, 177, 181, 182, 183, 184, 187, 194
Arendt, Hannah, 89, 92

Ashura, 154, 155
Associated Press, 58
Authoritarianism, 2, 3, 4, 24, 33, 36, 49, 60, 61, 64, 65, 66, 67, 77, 93, 109, 117, 120, 135, 136, 144, 147, 158, 176; authoritarian structure and culture, 4, 85; de-authoritarianization, 85–86; and democratic experimentation, 149–50; economic structure of, 176, 185; and elections, 125; and federalism, 167–68, 169, 171–72, 174, 176; legacy of, 102, 115; and legitimacy, 148, 151–52; local, 137; oligarchy of autocrats, 7, 137, 138; personalization of, 4, 62, 64; reestablishing, 6, 8, 13, 14, 16, 137, 138, 231–32; resilience of, 124, 150; and secularism, 147
Ayn al-Jariah al., 198

Babil (Babylon), 114; city council, 215
Bacon, Francis, 235
Baghdad, 1, 9, 14, 22, 23, 35, 37, 38, 39, 46, 48, 64, 73, 84, 85, 115, 118, 119, 121, 122, 123, 128, 137, 154, 163, 176, 177, 182, 183, 184, 185, 188, 192, 193, 198, 199, 202, 204, 206, 220, 234, 235; provincial council, 74, 154, 215
Baiji refinery, 204
Bandar, Awad al., 96, 98

Bank robberies, 202
Barzani, Mas'ud, 117, 119, 164, 184, 189, 192, 207, 208
Barzani, Mustafa, 38, 181, 184, 187
Barzani, Nechirvan, 193, 207
Barzanis clan, 221
Basham, Patrick, 16, 131, 158
Basra, 23, 36, 46–47, 84, 119, 151, 154, 164, 203, 215, 225; provincial council, 74; Shiite Republic of, 23
Batatu, Hanna, 39, 183
Ba'th Party, 23–24, 28, 53, 55–57, 61–65, 71, 72, 74, 75, 79, 80, 81, 84, 85, 92, 95, 123, 168, 203; admiration of, 75–76; membership, 62–68; and Sunnis, 28, 33, 83
Ba'th regime, 5, 53, 63, 101, 106
Ba'thification, 61–68
Ba'thism, 26, 58–59, 62, 68, 72, 75, 79, 85, 123
Ba'thists, 26, 28, 33, 54, 57, 58, 59, 60, 61, 62, 72, 73, 75, 77, 78, 79, 80, 81, 82, 84, 99, 101, 113, 130; killing of, 22, 23–24, 84; uprooting of, 5, 12, 46, 59, 75, 76, 82, 234
Bazaar, political, 13, 124
Bolani, Jawad al., 83, 122, 200
Brahimi, Lakhdar, 144
Bremer, Paul, 54, 64, 82, 85, 223
Britain, 68, 200, 219
Brown, Nathan J., 43, 44
Bulgaria, 193
Buruma, Ian, 29, 31, 60

"Cairo writes, Beirut prints, and Baghdad reads" saying, 234–35
Cammett, Melani, 136
Capital punishment, 108–10, 113, 115
Carpenter, Scott, 62, 66–67
Chalabi, Ahmad, 54, 73–74, 199
Chemical weapons, 100–101
China, 218
Cholera epidemic, 214
Christians, 34, 35, 36, 140, 145, 181, 186; Armenians, 184; Assyrians, 36–37, 183, 184
Clark, Ramsey, 96
Clientelism, 13

Coalition Provisional Authority (CPA), 53–54, 62, 67, 108, 144, 222
Commission on Public Integrity (CPI), 222, 223
Communist regimes, 60, 64
Communists, 75
Confessionalism, 14, 135, 140, 171, 233
Consociation, 4, 135–37, 162, 189, 233
Conspiracy theories, 19–20, 236
Constitution, 12, 13, 58, 72, 74, 83, 97, 108, 142, 154, 162, 185, 189, 190, 192, 207, 234; amendment, 119, 165–66, 168; Article 7, 58; Article 41, 43; Article 76, 122; Article 140, 182, 189; and de-Ba'thification, 58–59; disproportional power to Kurds, 165; drafting, 44, 45, 83, 117, 118, 162, 163, 166; and elections, 122; enshrining Islam, 43, 162, 164; and ethno-sectarian politics, 161, 166; and federalism, 165; and identity of the Arabs, 167; and Iraqi identity, 166; and Iraqi state, 167, 168; and legitimacy, 168; and Kirkuk, 181–82, 185; Kurdish regional constitution, 165; and nationbuilding, 166–67; punishing Sunnis, 162–63; referendum, 117, 168; and sectarianism, 167; and separatism, 162, 163; and Shiism and Kurdism, 161–62, 166; victor's constitution, 161–68; and women, 42–46, 48
Cordesman, Anthony, 163
Corruption, 4, 10, 15, 25, 66, 67, 74, 75, 78, 90, 91, 120, 121, 123, 124, 125, 128, 151, 152, 155, 173, 222; ADE651, 200; advisers, 220; annual national budgets, 220; anticorruption laws, 213; in armaments deals, 197–200; Article 136B, 223, 225; Board of Supreme Audit, 197, 198, 222; and command economy, 176, 213; and crime, 36, 201–2; and democracy, 226; in food ration program, 218; and incompetence, 13, 67, 78, 123, 138, 145, 146, 173, 224; in Kurdistan, 175, 120–21; and media, 214; in Ministry of Culture, 216; in Ministry

of Defense, 197–200, 218; in Ministry of Electricity, 216; in Ministry of Finance, 217–18; in Ministry of Health, 216–17; in Ministry of Interior, 200, 217; in Ministry of Oil, 24, 203, 204, 206, 217, 218, 223; in Ministry of Trade, 218–19; and nepotism, 13, 25, 67, 120, 154; and oil, 203–8; and oil corruption in Kurdistan, 205–8; oil-for-food program, 203; and parliament, 220, 225; and political Islam, 226; politicization of antigraft, 222–26; and power sharing, 224–25; in provincial councils, 118, 214–15; republic of, 4, 223, 226, 234; and sectarianism, 223; and security, 224; in security forces, 201–3; and social benefits, 219–20; stolen computers, 215; and victimization, 234
Crime, organized, 5, 36, 201–2
Cronyism, 4, 24, 120

Da'wa Party, 47, 72, 83, 95, 101, 107, 114, 118, 154, 219, 225
Dawisha, Adeed, 136, 139, 169, 216; and Larry Diamond, 128
Death of a dictator, 112, 114
De-Ba'thification, 26, 53–59, 60, 61, 62, 64, 66, 67–69, 75, 77, 80, 83; Accountability and Justice Act, 55–58; and American policies, 5, 53–54, 62, 66–67, 85; and constitution, 58–59, 83; and elections, 26, 58, 72–76, 123; The Movement People for, 74–75; politicization of, 71–76, 82–85; and reconciliation, 58–59, 80–82, 84; and revenge, 76–86; and sectarianism, 33, 58, 71–76, 82–84; Supreme National Commission for, 54–57, 71–72, 73–74, 81, 82–83, 84, 123
Democracy, 2, 28, 30, 43–45, 49, 77, 85, 90, 94, 95, 113, 129, 136, 137, 140, 148, 158; and absence of party politics law, 71, 139; and accountability, 135, 138, 139, 143, 149, 150; and authoritarian politics, 125, 149–50;

and confessionalism, 11, 130, 135–40; and elections, 14, 117, 124, 125–26, 128–31, 148, 233; façade of, 13, 137–38, 233; failure to deliver, 14, 140–41, 145, 149, 159, 171; and federalism, 169–77; illusionary, 14, 74, 124, 125, 142, 144, 233; imposing, 231–32; and inclusiveness, 29, 39, 59, 77, 135, 138, 158, 159, 173, 174, 194; and Iraq War, 3, 7, 231; and legitimacy, 151–52, 159; in the Middle East, 130; and opposition, 121, 138; and political Islam, 148; and violence, 130; without democrats, 125, 149. *See also* Iraqi politicians; legitimacy; power sharing
Demography, 13, 49, 128, 129, 149, 161; census, 13, 139; census of 1957, 183, 184
Demonstration, public, 15
Depoliticization, 114, 232, 233
Development Fund for Iraq, 205
Diamond, Larry, 126
Diasporas, 123
Disputed territories, 13, 34, 129, 165, 175, 181, 182, 192. *See also* Federalism; Kurdistan; Kurds
Diyyar Satellite Channel, 14
Dodge, Toby, 140, 141–42, 146
Dohuk, 37, 206
Drimmer, Jonathan, 99
Dujail trial, 77, 95–102, 105, 107–8, 114
Dujaili, Issam al., 198
Dulaimi, Khalil al., 97
Dulaimi, Naziha al., 41
Dworkin, Anthony, 90

Economist, the, 221
Economy, 28, 63, 67, 68, 125, 131, 145, 156–58
Elections, 11, 13, 27, 117–24, 125, 157, 158, 159; and authoritarianism, 125, 126, 127; and constitution, 122; and de-Ba'thification, 26, 58, 72–76, 123; December 2005, 117, 118, 145; and delivery, 14, 119, 121, 123–24, 148–49, 150; and democracy, 14, 117,

122–23, 124, 125–26, 128–29, 130–31,
148, 157, 233; faded enthusiasm,
123–24, 151, 155; and federalism,
118; and ethnic tensions, 129–30;
ethno-sectarian, 12, 13, 43, 117, 118,
123, 127, 128–31, 139, 142, 143, 147;
January 2005 constitutional, 43,
117–18, 126, 128, 144, 145, 162;
January 2009 provincial, 9, 117,
118–19, 128, 164, 224, 225;
July 2009 elections in Kurdistan, 68,
117, 119–21, 221; and Kirkuk, 183;
lack of political programs, 73, 123,
128, 129, 139, 142, 235; and
legitimacy, 131, 143, 146, 148–51,
153, 157, 159; March 2010, 13, 26, 72,
117, 121–24, 129, 130, 145, 190, 200;
May 1992 elections in Kurdistan,
120, 127; and political Shiism,
126–28, 129, 131; and power
sharing, 139; proportional representation, 136, 142; provincial election
law, 129, 143; rushing, 14, 126–28,
130, 131, 148
Electricity, 216
Elster, Jon, 85
Empathy, 112
Empowerment: Shiites and Kurds, 12,
106, 128
Erbil, 175, 176, 182
Ethnic tensions, 20, 129–30
Ethno-sectarian politics, 2, 12, 13, 20,
25, 33, 77, 85, 101, 128, 129–30,
140–41, 144, 150, 158, 232; and
constitution, 161; and corruption,
224–25; and ethno-sectarian parties,
138–39; and federalism, 173–74, 175
Europe, 31, 71; Eastern, 60, 64
Exclusionary politics, 12, 26, 59, 67, 74,
131, 135
Expression: freedom of, 14–15

Faatah, Zina, 198
Fadhila Party, 83, 122, 225
Faili Kurds, 33
Falluja, 151; Brigade, 80
Farouk-Sluglett, Marion, and Peter
Sluglett, 22, 184

Fatwa (religious edict), 36, 47, 127
Fear, 14, 46, 47, 62, 63, 79, 98, 226
Federalism, 11–12, 13, 25, 76, 164, 168,
169, 173, 175, 182; and
authoritarianism, 167–68, 171, 174,
176; and 1957 census, 183; and
corruption, 175, 176, 221;
decentralization, 12, 13, 165, 167,
168, 169, 173, 176, 177; and
democracy, 13, 168–77; ethnic, 12,
13, 162, 164, 169, 170, 171, 173–74,
176, 189; ethnic separatism, 2, 5, 129,
162, 165, 188, 190–91, 234; federal
government, 163, 167, 171, 187–89,
190, 191, 194; federation of Basra,
164; federation in the south, 118,
164; Kurdish federation, 165; Kurds
and, 169, 171, 174, 177; local
governments, 169, 173, 175; and
power sharing, 171; and
privatization, 175–76; regional
government, 175; sectarian, 164;
Shiites and, 118, 171, 177; territorial,
169, 173–74; and utilitarianism, 177;
weak federal government, 118, 162,
163, 169; and women, 164. *See also*
Disputed territories; Kurdistan; Kurds
Forgiveness, 81, 89

Galbraith, Peter, 163, 185, 206–7
Gandhi, Mahatma, 11
Gender, 10, 43, 47, 49, 86, 90, 163, 194,
215, 235, 236
Germany, 59–60, 61, 81, 90, 91–92
Globalization, 194, 236
Gnostic community, 35
Goldberg, Jeffrey, 190
Goldhagen, Daniel: *Hitler's Willing
Executioners*, 91–92
Gorran, 11, 119, 120–21, 122, 123, 208,
221; *Rozhnama*, 208
Government, 62, 78, 107, 110,
112, 113, 118, 123–24, 125, 128, 131,
144–46; formation, 13; and state, 60,
62, 68, 112
Green Zone, 154, 198, 216
Guardian, the, 15, 218; lawsuit
against, 36

Habubi, Yusuf al., 119
Hadba al., 130
Hakim, Abdul-Aziz al., 42
Hakim, Muhsin al., 41–42
Hakki, Zakia, 41
Halabja, 21–22, 25, 100–101, 193–94
Hammurabi, 114
Hashimi, As'ad al., 216
Hawrami, Ashti, 206, 208
Haysom, Nicholas, 166, 168
Hilterman, Joost R., 21–22, 26, 27, 78, 174, 184–85, 187–88
Hiro, Dilip, 62
History: learning from, 8, 10, 11, 16, 29, 136–37, 201, 235–36
Hitler, Adolf, 71, 91
Hogland, Jim, 115
Holocaust, 11
Homosexuality, 36, 74
Horowitz, Donald L., 167
Human resources, 61, 62
Human rights, 44, 49, 53, 54, 59, 78, 79, 80, 163, 167; culture, 11, 85, 94, 96, 113; Ministry of, 201
Human Rights Watch (HRW), 34, 46, 96, 99, 108, 170
Humphrey, Michael, 20, 26, 91, 93
Hussein, Ahmad Abdul, 202
Hussein, Imam, 23, 114, 127, 154
Hussein, Nidhal Nasser, 48
Hussein, Saddam, 1, 3, 4, 9, 11, 19, 21, 24, 28, 31, 34, 35, 38, 39, 49, 57, 60, 63, 64–65, 77, 79, 82, 91, 92, 93, 94, 95, 105, 107, 108, 120, 152, 153, 181, 184, 187, 188, 190, 203, 223; execution, 100, 101, 105–16; trials, 95–102
Husseini, Amin al., 37
Hyse, Luc, 82

Identity politics, 1, 3, 5, 12, 20, 29–30, 44, 45, 47, 69, 77, 128, 129, 130, 137, 138, 139–40, 141, 143, 150, 151, 156, 157, 158, 162, 164, 172, 174, 175, 176, 177, 189, 233, 234, 236; and legitimacy, 135–40. *See also* Iraqi politicians; power sharing
Independent High Electoral Commission, 122

International Center for Transitional Justice (ICTJ), 57, 63, 78, 97, 99, 109
International Covenant on Civil and Political Rights, 108
Iran, 2, 21–22, 63, 73, 74, 80, 105, 119, 129, 152, 158, 186, 192, 202, 208, 214, 215, 217, 218; guardian of the constitution, 74; involvement in Iraqi politics, 2, 76, 152, 164; revolutionary guards, 22, 218; winner of Iraq War, 1, 152
Iran-Iraq War, 1, 2, 3, 21–22, 63, 76, 152
Iraq: division of, 141; nation-state, 12, 25–26, 28, 30, 128, 166–67, 171; national flag, 153; U.S. legacy, 8, 231
Iraq Financial Management Information System, 217
Iraq War, 1, 2, 5, 13, 61, 120, 152, 181, 231; and legitimacy, 2, 3, 7; an opportunity, 6–7, 8, 9, 16, 233
Iraqi Accord Front, 118
Iraqi army, 4, 37, 54, 60, 62, 85, 191, 192, 193
Iraqi Communist Party, 38–39, 183
Iraqi Front for National Dialogue, 118
Iraqi Governing Council (IGC), 41, 42, 54, 95, 140–42, 144
Iraqi High Tribunal (IHT), 95, 105, 108, 109
Iraqi identity, 125, 165, 166, 167, 194
Iraqi National Alliance, 73, 121–22
Iraqi politicians, 2, 28, 54, 66, 69, 77, 78, 81, 94, 116, 124, 127, 131, 137, 138, 140, 141, 142, 146, 232; failure to deliver, 7, 124, 131, 140–41, 145–46, 149, 150, 155, 158, 159, 177, 232; mentality of opposition, 108; opportunistic politicians, 138; and rhetorical politics, 119, 138, 235; undemocratic elites, 3, 4, 24, 79, 141, 149, 233. *See also* Identity politics; power sharing
Iraqi Special Tribunal, 95
Iraqi state, 4, 5, 25, 54, 60, 61, 165, 166, 167, 168, 171, 172–73, 188, 189, 192, 194; "artificiality" of, 141; and society, 172; strong state versus weak state, 172

Iraqia (Iraqi National List), 72, 118, 121
Iraq's Supreme Judiciary Council, 201
Islam, 36, 38, 43–44, 45, 47, 48, 110;
    political, 1, 5, 35, 46–47, 71, 76, 101,
    119, 131, 147, 148, 152; and
    corruption, 226; and democracy,
    148; and legitimacy, 153
Islamic Supreme Council of Iraq
    (ISCI), 21, 42, 83, 118, 122, 164,
    202, 215
Islamic Union of Kurdistan, 118,
    120, 122
Islamist Party, 83
Islamization, 2, 35, 36, 38, 44, 45, 47, 48,
    153, 154, 162, 163; banning alcohol,
    153–54; and elections, 153; veiling
    women, 153
Israel, 37, 136, 144
Istrabadi, Feisal al., 83

Jabar, Faleh A., 22
Ja'fari, Ibrahim al., 154, 151
Jama'a al-Islamiyyia al., 122
Japan, 59, 61
Jassim, Sawsan, 198
Jews, 37–38, 115; prophet Ezekiel, 38;
    farhud (pogrom), 37
Jordan, 199
Journalists, killing of, 14; Journalists
    Union, 14; Journalistic Freedom
    Observatory, 14, 123
Jubouri, Mesh'an al., 204–5
Jubouristribe, 204
Juhi, Ra'id, 57
July 22 Gathering, 143
Jumaili, Nair Mohammad al., 197
Justice, 33, 73, 77, 89–95, 97, 108, 109,
    111, 112, 113, 114; accountability, 84,
    90, 91, 92, 93, 98, 100; amnesty, 91;
    complicity, 36, 65, 84–85, 92;
    culpability, 27, 89, 92; culture of
    impunity, 91, 97, 100; culture of
    responsibilitiesand rights, 91;
    deficient, 90, 102; distributive, 90;
    guilt, 27, 57, 77, 78, 92, 93, 97, 98, 99;
    and national healing, 89, 90;
    prosecutions, 89, 91, 92;
    punishment, 77, 85, 89, 90, 91, 94;

responsibility, 30, 57, 77, 78, 91,
    92–93, 98, 99; restorative, 89–90;
    retributive, 89, 92, sectarian
    application of, 113; and trials, 90–95,
    95–102

Kafir (apostate), 23
Karbala, 84, 119, 155; Battle of, 114,
    127, 154
Khaniqin, 184
Khoie, abdul-Majid al., 110, 159
Kifl al., 38
Kimidia, 217
Kirkuk, 23, 35, 38, 118, 128, 129, 143,
    163, 165, 175, 177, 181–86, 187, 188,
    193, 204
Kiss, Elizabeth, 89
Krauthammer, Charles, 110
Kurdicization, 182
Kurdish identity: enforcing, 34–35;
    Kurdistani identity, 186
Kurdish Institute for Elections, 119
Kurdish-Shiite alliance, 25, 33, 48,
    161–62, 168, 172
Kurdistan, 24, 48, 68, 117, 118, 119, 120,
    123, 141, 162, 163, 165, 170, 174, 175,
    184, 185, 187, 188, 190; Asayish
    security forces, 34, 35, 181;
    autocratic governance, 15, 120–21,
    165, 174, 175; corruption in, 11, 15,
    24, 120–21, 175, 205–8, 220–21; and
    democracy, 11, 174–75, 193–94; and
    elections, 11, 119–21, 127; and ethnic
    politics, 11, 182; expansionism, 34;
    intimidating journalists, 14–15;
    intra-Kurdish fighting, 11, 24, 120,
    137, 208; Jerusalem of, 187; minor-
    ities in, 186; nation-state, 186, 188;
    National Guard of Iraqi Kurdistan,
    191; peshmerga, 22, 23, 181, 190,
    191–93; power sharing, 11, 120, 137,
    233; regional constitution, 165;
    regional parliament, 118, 120, 121,
    205, 220; rentierism in, 177, 185;
    secession, 187–88, 194; separatist
    oath, 190; share of national budget,
    177, 220; unified army for, 192, 193.
    See also Federalism

Kurdistan Democratic Party (KDP), 14, 83, 117, 119, 120, 164, 181, 182, 184, 191, 192, 208

Kurdistani Alliance, 117, 118, 119, 122

Kurds, 12, 19, 20, 21–22, 25, 27, 28, 29, 33, 38–39, 48, 75, 77, 83, 97, 100, 101, 113, 128, 129, 136, 140, 141, 143, 145, 161, 162, 163, 168–69, 170, 171, 173, 174, 181, 182, 183, 184, 185, 186–87, 188, 189, 190, 192

Kuwait: invasion of, 1, 22, 61, 80, 105, 111, 120, 152

Lami, Ali al., 73

Lebanon: civil war, 11, 130, 135; confessionalism, 11, 136, 137, 141, 233; democracy, 130, 136; Hizb Allah, 136; reconciliation, 11

Leezenberg, Michiel, 24, 182, 189, 207

Legitimacy, 113, 127, 141, 143, 148, 152, 154, 157, 158, 159, 224; and authoritarianism, 148, 151–52; deceptive, 14, 146, 157, 159; deficiency in, 142, 150–51;and delivery, 140–41, 143, 150–51, 234; and democracy, 27–28, 151–53, 159; and elections, 128, 131, 148, 150–51; externalization of, 14, 151–59; and identity politics, 135–40; and martyrdom, 154; new Iraq as a source of, 10; and representation, 128, 141–42, 143, 146, 150; and Shiite rituals, 156; and victimization, 19–20, 27, 78, 234

Libya, 111

Looting, 5

Los Angeles Times, 123

Luizard, Pierre-Jean, 41–42

Lustration, 59–69, 77, 82

Machiavelli, Niccoló, 7

Mackey, Sandra, 22, 23, 184

Mahdi, Adel Abdul, 202

Mahram, 215

Maier, Charles S., 92

Majeed, Ali al. ("Chemical Ali"), 100

Makhmur, 193

Makiya, Kanan, 22, 23–24, 25, 28–29, 92, 101, 142, 162–63, 167, 168, 177

Maliki, Nuri al., 15, 55, 72, 74, 81, 107, 115, 118, 119, 121, 122–23, 145, 151, 155, 166, 200, 201, 219, 222, 224

Mandaeans, 35–36

Mandela, Nelson, 11

Mani, Rama, 92, 93

Marji'iyya, 107, 126, 128

Marr, Phebe, 24, 158, 163

Marshall, Paul, 164

Martyrdom, 31, 75, 112, 154

Mass graves, 90–91

McCarthyism, 74

McDowall, David, 38, 68, 183–84

McFaul, Michael, 16

McKiernan, Kevin, 100–101

Mecca, 106

Media, 14, 214; silencing, 14–15

Meritocracy, 39, 144, 145, 154

Mesopotamia, 114

Middle class, 148, 158, 183, 213

Middle East, the, 1, 2, 41, 43, 44, 48, 49, 80, 93, 108, 111, 112, 120, 147, 168, 192, 231, 232, 235, 236; authoritarianism in, 14, 147; crisis in, 157; democratic deficit, 6, 124–25, 130, 157, 232, 233; and democratic mechanism, 149–50; democratization of, 3, 147; elections in, 147, 149; incubator of violence and terrorism, 5; new, 5, 137; politics in, 10, 152, 157; reconciliation in, 11; social capital, 11

Militarization, 1, 36, 37, 75, 91, 115, 146, 148, 193, 213, 235

Militias, 4, 5, 12, 24, 25, 35, 36, 38, 42, 58, 80, 84, 113, 154, 158, 191, 203, 217, 222; Asa'ib al-Haq, 73, 218; Badr, 21; Mahdi Army, 110, 216, 217; Kurdish, 181, 191–93; Popular Resistance Force, 38; Shiite, 24, 25, 46–47, 112, 119, 191

Milosevic, Slobodan, 98

Mino, Martha, 92, 93

Minorities, 2, 5, 10, 12, 26, 31, 33–39, 40, 46, 83, 129, 137, 163, 170, 186, 233; in Kurdistan, 186

Mirza, abdel-Hamid, 198
Moore, Peter, 217–18
Mosul, 38, 80, 128, 129, 193
Muhammad, prophet, 23, 114, 154
Muharram, 154
Mukhtar, Leila al., 198
Mukhtar, Omar el., 111
Munson, Peter J., 5, 16, 138
Mustafa, Nosherwan, 120
Mutlaq, Salih al., 72
Myanmar, 214
Myths, 10, 16, 20, 28, 187

Najaf, 22–23, 42, 47, 84, 110, 154
Nasser, Gamal abdel, 112
Nation-state, 152
Nationalism, 10, 30, 36, 37, 59, 76, 79,
    157, 187, 193, 194; Arab, 79, 187, 193,
    194; and extremism, 76, 187–94;
    Iraqi, 167, 194; Kurdish, 48, 59, 76,
    79, 157, 161, 184–85, 186–94, 207;
    and legitimacy, 14, 152, 156–57; and
    myths, 187; Pan-Arabism, 80, 111,
    152, 156, 187
New Iraq, 2, 3, 6, 9, 10, 12, 19, 20, 21,
    27, 28, 29, 31, 33, 39, 41, 48, 49, 62, 64,
    68, 76, 78, 79, 82, 83, 86, 90, 94, 110,
    113, 114, 117, 135, 137, 141, 177; myth
    of, 16; source of legitimacy, 10
New York Times, 110–11, 115, 162, 200
Newsweek, 85
Nineveh province, 34, 216
Nuaimi, Najib al., 96, 97
Nuremberg trials, 90, 95

Obeidi, abdul-Qadir al., 72, 200
Oil, 176, 235; curse of, 176; DNO,
    205–6, 207; and insurgency, 204–5;
    International Advisory and
    Monitoring Board, 205; Iraq Oil
    Forum, 208; Iraq Revenue Watch,
    203, 215–16; and Kirkuk, 183–85,
    187; in Kurdistan, 177, 205–8;
    legislation, 158; and militias, 203–4;
    Ministry of, 203, 204, 206, 217, 218;
    nationalization, 203; oil-for-food
    Program, 24, 203, 208; production
    sharing agreement, 206; and

rentierism, 67, 176–77; Revenue
    Watch Institute, 206; smuggling, 24,
    203–4, 207–8; Tawke oil field, 206.
    See also Corruption; economy;
    Kirkuk; Kurdistan
O'Leary, Brendan, 162
Orientalism, 6, 232; neo-orientalism, 6
Oslo Stock Exchange, 206
Other, the, 6, 14, 59, 77, 78, 81, 106, 152
Othman, Sardesht, 14

Palestinian question, 111, 152,
    156, 187
Parliament, 4, 45, 46, 47, 55, 57, 58, 74,
    81, 95, 117, 121, 122, 125, 128, 129,
    142–44, 149, 153, 220, 225
Patriotic Union of Kurdistan (PUK),
    31, 68, 83, 117, 119, 120, 121, 164, 181,
    182, 191, 192, 207, 208
Patronage, 13, 34, 54, 68, 120, 176, 177
Perito, Robert, 92
Petra Bank, 199
Political culture, 24, 59, 67, 75, 77, 79,
    80, 81, 83, 84, 85–86, 90, 95, 114, 115,
    131, 140
Pollack, Kenneth M., 122; and Daniel
    Byman, 137
Populism, 113
Posner, Eric, 98
Power sharing (*muhasasa*), 4, 11, 13, 55,
    58, 136, 140, 141, 142, 145, 162, 221,
    233; and accountability, 138, 139,
    150; and authoritarianism, 138, 139;
    and compromises, 139; and
    corruption, 138, 145, 224; and
    delivery, 138, 145, 150; and
    democracy, 130, 138, 139; and
    elections, 139; and elitist interests,
    139; and federalism, 171; in
    Kurdistan, 137; and legitimacy, 138,
    150; and minorities, 39. *See also*
    Identity politics; Iraqi politicians
Primordialization, 130, 140–41, 144
Privatization, 158, 175–77; and
    federalism, 176
Prostitution, 74
Provincial councils, 74, 118, 128,
    214–15

Qaddafi, Ai'sha, 96
Qaeda al., 3; in Mesopotamia, 204
Qal'at Julan, 192
Qaraqosh, 35
Qassim, abdul-Karim, 42, 96, 106, 115
Qattan, Ziad, 198
Qur'an, 41, 45

Radhi, Radhi al., 222, 223
Rafidain Bank, 202
Rahman, Raouf abdel, 98
Ramadan, 106, 156
Ramadan, Taha Yassin, 96, 98
Raniya, 23–24
Raphaeli, Nimrod, 190
Rashed abdel-Rahman al., 74
Rashid, Ali, 37
Reconciliation, 5, 10, 26, 27, 55, 58–59,
    75, 80, 85, 89, 91, 92, 95, 131, 235;
    impediments, 11, 29–30, 81, 125, 126;
    in the Middle East, 11
Regime change, 1, 2, 3, 4, 7, 10, 19, 21,
    22, 26, 46, 60, 61, 69, 71, 75, 76, 81, 83,
    84, 117, 126, 137, 141, 147, 152, 168,
    181, 233
Religion, 10, 30, 100, 106, 125, 126, 147,
    152, 153, 154, 156, 163, 167, 194; and
    legitimacy, 14, 153, 157
Revenge politics, 2, 5, 12, 26, 27, 29, 33,
    58, 66, 67, 69, 75, 76, 80, 84, 85, 90, 95,
    101, 106, 110–16, 125, 131
Revolt of 1991, 22–24, 91, 120, 187
Rezko, Tony, 216
Rhetorics, 79, 235
Rich land/poor people paradox, 91
Rubin, Michael, 80, 81, 221
Rule of law, 5, 12, 25, 28, 84, 85, 90, 93,
    95, 112, 113, 119, 131, 145, 152, 159,
    191, 202, 224

Sabah al., 202
Sab'awi, Yunis al., 37
Sadr city, 84, 119
Sadr, Muhammad Baqir al., 110
Sadr, Muqtada al., 73, 110, 159,
    216, 217
Sadrists, 83
Saffar, Ammar al., 217

Salahuddin province, 204
Salim, Ali, 7
Samar'ai, Wafiq al., 188
Samarraie, Ayham al., 216
Samawa, 23
Sanctions, 1, 35, 48, 60, 61, 62, 146, 148,
    203, 213, 236
Sarraf, Mish'al al., 198
Schwartz, Herman, 64, 82
Secret prison in Baghdad, 201
Sectarian: vengeance, 102, 108, 108–10;
    violence, 67, 94, 110, 118, 127, 130,
    136, 141, 164, 216
Sectarianism, 2, 10, 12, 20, 41, 58, 59,
    106, 112, 142, 144, 152, 153, 155–56,
    167, 171, 172; and corruption, 48–49,
    223, 224–25; political, 12, 48, 49, 58,
    66, 73, 76, 101, 106, 112, 118, 119,
    127–28, 129, 130, 136, 141, 159
Secularism, 147; authoritarian, 147
Security, 15, 25, 94, 124, 145, 149, 151,
    158–59, 164
Self, the, 78
Serbia, 200
Services and Reform List, 119
Shabaks, 34–35, 186
Sha'lan, Hazem al., 198, 199, 204
Sham'un, Mar, 37
Sharf, Michael, 99, 101
Shari'a, 40, 41, 42, 46
Shiism, political, 30, 41–43, 76, 114,
    126–28, 147–48, 152–53, 161, 163;
    demographic majority, 43, 128, 149;
    and Iran, 2, 21, 129; martyrdom, 154;
    Shiite-Kurdish alliance, 25, 33, 48,
    161–62, 163, 168, 172; Shiite political
    elites, 106, 113, 126, 127, 153, 202;
    Shiite religious parties, 41, 44, 45, 47,
    48, 149, 152, 157; Shiite rituals,
    154–56, 232; Shiite-Sunni differ-
    ences, 154; Shiite triumphalism, 156;
    and victimization, 30
Shiites, 12, 19, 20, 21, 22–23, 25, 27, 28,
    29, 33, 39, 41, 48, 77, 81, 82, 83, 101,
    106, 107, 111, 112, 113, 118, 128, 131,
    140, 141, 145, 154, 156, 161, 162, 164,
    167, 189; *husainiyya*, 23
Shriver, Donald W., 114

Sidqi, Bakir, 37
Silence, 14, 36, 111
Simmel, 37
Simon, Reeva Spector, 37
Sirhan, Maher Sheikh, 201
Sissons, Miranda, 57, 63, 99; and Ari
    Bassin, 99, 101, 108
Sistani, Ayatollah al., 36, 47, 123,
    127–28
Social contract, 44, 62, 63, 67, 176,
    220, 226
Somalia, 214
Somer, Murat, 170
South America, 60
Sovereignty, 107; transfer of, 2, 54, 126,
    127, 137, 140, 144, 146, 231
Stansfield, Gareth, 185; and Hashem
    Ahmadzadeh, 186
State of Law, 119, 121
Stoffel, Dale, 199–200
Sudan, 214
Sudani, abdel-Falah al., 218–19
Sulaimaniya, 11, 23, 68, 119, 123, 175,
    184, 192
Sunnis, 28, 33, 48, 77, 83, 101, 106, 107,
    111, 113, 117, 118, 122, 128, 140, 145,
    152, 154, 162–63, 165, 167, 216, 217
Supreme Court, 162
Susskind, Yifat, 41, 42
Syria, 53, 186, 205

Talabani, Ala' al., 31
Talabani, Jalal al., 11, 31, 68, 117, 121,
    164, 184, 187
Talabanis clan, 221
Taliban, 42, 46
Tawafuq, 122
Terrorism, 1, 3, 5, 35, 110, 144; and
    corruption, 224
Tigris River, 154, 220
Tikriti, Barzan Ibrahim al., 96, 98, 105
Tikriti, Raghad Saddam al., 96
Tikriti, Uday Saddam al., 207
Tikritis clan, 65
Transparency International, 214
Tribalism, 64–65, 77, 125
Tripp, Charles, 22
Truth, 20, 91

Turkey, 148, 157–58, 186, 192; Justice
    and Development Party (AKP), 157
Turkmen, 35, 38–39, 140, 145, 170, 181,
    182, 183, 184

Ubaidi, Harith al., 225
Ulama, 41, 42
Ulum, Muhammad Bahr al., 41
Umm Qasr, 215
United Arab Emirates, 219
United Iraqi Alliance, 117, 118
United Nations, 1, 2, 3, 109, 122, 144,
    158, 203
United States, 5, 6, 46, 74, 97
Unity of Iraq, 122
U.S. administration, 140; Bush
    administration, 231; and
    democratizing Iraq, 3, 4, 5, 6, 231;
    detachment and hasty exit from
    Iraq, 7, 137, 231, 232; and
    empowering autocratic elites, 4, 7, 8,
    140, 231; and exclusionary politics,
    5, 6; and institutionalization of de-
    Ba'thification, 5, 53–54, 62, 66–67,
    85; and legacy of Iraq, 8; and
    Machiavelli, 7; Obama
    administration, 231; and partner-
    ship with Iraqi politicians, 2, 3–4, 7,
    140; policies in the Middle East, 6;
    and security considerations, 6, 232;
    and shortcut solutions, 7, 231; toler-
    ating violence, 5
U.S. army in Iraq, 8, 73, 105

Vetting, 78–79
Victimization, 5, 19–31, 33, 75, 90, 115;
    approach to history, 20; and
    corruption, 24, 234; cycle of, 24–27,
    30, 78, 171, 236; dichotomy, 30; and
    legitimacy, 19–20, 27, 234; mentality
    of, 29–30; monopoly of, 28–29, 113,
    170; own victimization, 20–22; and
    passivity, 31; politics of, 12, 19–20,
    26–31, 33, 125, 131, 161, 170, 187,
    233; and pride, 31; and revenge, 233,
    234; survivor, 30; trap of, 30–31;
    victim, 19–25, 29–31, 33, 34, 49, 56,
    64, 76, 78, 89, 91, 93, 98, 100, 109, 111;

victimhood, 13, 19, 25, 27, 29, 31, 48,
  115; victimizer, 24, 27, 30, 33, 78, 115;
  and violence, 21–24, 27, 29, 233
Violence, 5, 10, 21–24, 26, 30, 31, 33, 34,
  35, 37, 38, 45, 46, 48, 49, 53, 55, 60, 66,
  67, 68, 75, 80, 82, 84, 86, 90, 91, 93, 94,
  95, 102, 106, 107, 108, 111, 112–13,
  114, 123, 125, 129, 130, 141, 152, 158,
  161, 164, 171, 172, 187, 189, 193, 194,
  233, 235, 236
Visser, Reidar, 119, 207

Wa'ily, Sharwan al., 83
Wasit, 154; provincial council, 215
Weapons of mass destruction, 3
Wemple, Joseph, 199–200
West, the: conflict with, 1, 152, 236
Wimmer, Andreas, 11, 126
Women, 2, 5, 10, 12, 26, 36, 37, 40–49,
  121, 140, 145, 163, 164, 233; *abay'a*,
  46; child custody, 40–41; and
  constitution, 42–46, 48, 49; Decree
  137, 42–43; disempowerment of, 45;
  divorce, 40–41; and elections, 127;

emancipation of, 45–46; and
  federalism, 164; female quota, 45;
  gender equality, 45–46, 49; gender
  segregation, 47; inheritance, 40, 41,
  42; *khula'*, 40; Law of 188, 40–42, 43,
  48, 49; marriage, 40, 41, 48–49;
  nahwa, 40; and political Islam,
  46–47; and political Shiism, 21,
  41–43, 46; polygamy, 40, 41; right to
  vote, 49; and sectarianism, 41, 44,
  48–49; shame and honor, 47, 49; and
  Shiite-Kurdish alliance, 48; veiling,
  36, 46; violence against, 46–47
Women for Women International, 48
World War II, 59, 61
Wye Oak Technology, 199

Yazidis, 34, 186

Zacho, 192
Za'im (leadership), 140
Zainab (sister of Imam Hussein), 127
Zamili, Hakim al., 216–17
Zubaida, Sami, 38, 167–68

About the Author

DAVID GHANIM, PhD, is an independent scholar of Middle Eastern studies and gender studies. His published works include Praeger's *Gender and Violence in the Middle East* (2009). A native of Iraq, Ghanim holds his doctorate from the Corvinus University of Budapest in Hungary.